THE ETHICS OF NARRATIVE, VOLUME 2

THE ETHICS OF NARRATIVE, VOLUME 2

ESSAYS ON HISTORY, LITERATURE, AND THEORY, 2007–2017

HAYDEN WHITE

EDITED AND WITH AN INTRODUCTION
BY ROBERT DORAN

FOREWORD BY MIEKE BAL

CORNELL UNIVERSITY PRESS
Ithaca and London

First published 2023 by Cornell University Press

Librarians: A CIP catalog record for this book is available from the Library of Congress.

ISBN 978-1-5017-7358-7 (hardcover)
ISBN 978-1-5017-7359-4 (paperback)
ISBN 978-1-5017-7396-9 (epub)

Contents

FOREWORD

TURNING, TOWARD A TURN

MIEKE BAL

"If he read this, he would turn in his grave." That well-known phrase denotes a response to something shocking said or written about someone who is no longer alive. The deceased person would be very upset if they knew what was being written about them, their work, their legacy, their ideas. They would feel ignored, misunderstood, betrayed, by the banalities or polemics later scholars would utter about their work. The phrase came immediately but paradoxically to my mind, with a very different association, when I saw the project of the two-volume edition and publication of papers—unfinished or finished, unpublished, partially published, or published but difficult to find—from the final two decades of Hayden White's long career. It took me a few seconds to understand why that phrase "turning in his grave" came to me in that context. In White's spirit, I took it literally, and stuck a different meaning onto it. For White frequently appealed to literal, or etymological meanings in his quest for a better sense of history than the usual meanings that seem to contradict what we tend to make of a word or concept. A strong example is "identity" in the first volume, where the current quest for a European identity flounders under the weight of the original Latin meaning. That was a tautological "self-same," and the end result is a *choice* (a word used here for a purpose) for a process-oriented usage of the word, now meaning "identifying," rather than something fixed and fixating, in other words, rigid. In that third chapter of the first volume, he ends up with the verb, meaning identifying-*as*, rather than that even more drastic change, identifying-*with*, frequently used in affect-oriented readings.

That White stopped at identifying-as is not due to a rejection of affect but to his precision in word choice, always open to expansion but never over-the-top wide-ranging. The brilliant psychoanalytically inclined semiotician and film and photography theorist Kaja Silverman famously proposed, in what is for me her best book, *The Threshold of the Visible World* (1996), a distinction, derived from early psychoanalytic theory, between "idiopathic" and "heteropathic" identification. The former is appropriative: the reading identifier makes the (fictional) "other" self-same. Silverman qualifies it as "cannibalistic." The latter is bold and generous: the reading identifier goes out of the self to encounter the otherness of the other. In "Search for a European Identity," Hayden White is not on the track of sentimentalism, a wrongly but persistently assumed connotation of identification. That would be excessively and mistakenly assigning an emotion-oriented trait to all Europeans, and thereby neglecting the political aspect of "Europeanness." Instead, he does what scholars of Silverman's caliber also do: he goes along as far as he can with the reasoning he is critically examining, and when they must part ways, he says so with utmost clarity. (Silverman did that with Lacan: following his theorizing as far as she could, then halting when the companion became an opponent.) It is that refined precision in reasoning, articulating, and formulating that I deeply admire in White's work.

Yes, he would turn in his grave, but not for the negative reasons attached to the cliché. On the contrary, instead of being upset, he would open his face with a big smile, characteristic in my memory of him, expressing communication, satisfaction, happiness, the sense that all that hard work, to which he had devoted so much of his life, was not finished, let alone buried. I can see his face with that smile, and deeply sympathize with it.

What a wonderful, impressive, and generous gesture on the part of Robert Doran, to make the important work of Hayden White endure even more than his famous books already guarantee, and to display the great diversity of topics he has discussed and analyzed. I know how time-consuming and labor-intensive the work of editing is, and even more so in the case of the legacy of someone who is no longer alive, hence, cannot answer the inevitable questions and hesitations an editor has to face. There is no more effective way to bring this important thinker back to us, back to (at least intellectual) life; no greater favor the editor could have done for our intellectual community. That endeavor amply deserves a Whitean smile.

For it is obvious that in Euro-American thinking about history, in other words, historiography, White is a, conceivably *the*, key figure. He opened up both the older speculative and the newer empirically grounded procedures of acquiring knowledge about, or of, the past, and by turning around some key concepts made the past matter for the present and the future. But beyond that relevance, his work is also boldly interdisciplinary, as his crucial phrase and book title "the content of the form" promises. The statement early on in *Metahistory*, "My method, in short, is formalist," is as provocative—for more traditional historians—as it is relevant for an understanding of what "form," that hard-to-grasp term, can be and do, beyond disciplinary dogma. Here, I affiliate him with Theodor Adorno, whose article "The Essay as Form" (first published in 1958) opens the two-volume edition of the philosopher's writings on literature. By beginning with an essay on the essay, he was thus giving it pride of place in literature. But not as a genre. Rather, unexpectedly, as "form." And whereas much of White's disciplinary transgressions brought him to literature, especially narrative, he did not lock himself up within any of literary studies' subdisciplines, say, rhetoric, narratology, or philology. Nor did he ever simply obey the logic of binary opposition. On the contrary, the only acceptable way to perform historical research always had to be an integration, rather than a contrast, of "facts" and "fiction," as this volume's fifth chapter, "Modern Politics and the Historical Imaginary," among others, argues and demonstrates. And of course, the need to undermine that opposition is most indispensable, as well as problematic, in the context where it came up most acutely, that of Holocaust studies—in this volume's chapter 8, "The History-Fiction Divide in Holocaust Studies," as well as in chapter 12, "Historical Truth, Estrangement, and Disbelief." Perhaps the clearest statement is at the end of the abstract to chapter 15 (included as a note), "Constructionism in Historical Writing": "Stories are not pictures of reality, or even representations thereof; they are presentations in fictional modes of an unobservable past treated as reality." What then follows is the masterly complicating argument that makes the past "unobservable" indeed: the events' "pastness," or historicity, cannot by definition be witnessed by their contemporaries.

That word "turning," with which I began this foreword, is also connected to a word, term, or concept, made stylish in scholarship in the second half of the twentieth century, when in the humanities a specific tendency in the approach began to become more and more prominent. I have witnessed, and participated in, a few of such "turns" myself: the anthropological (or ethnographic) turn, the semiotic turn, the linguistic turn, the cultural turn, the visual turn. . . . What the noun means and the qualifiers qualify is a particular bend, or trend, in disciplinary scholarship eager to exceed the boundaries that the disciplines had built around themselves. This can be seen as an early step toward interdisciplinarity. And even though White has participated in all of them, without boastfully naming them, his analyses demonstrate a particularly intense interest in the linguistic precision that would place his work in the wake of the linguistic turn. Being quite keen on linguistic precision myself, I find his patiently developed critique of sloppy usages of words admirably useful. A most convincing, because self-referential, instance in this volume is the short chapter 13, "At the Limits of the Concept," originally published in 2016 in the journal of the Modern Language Association (*PMLA*). There, he examines and critically discusses the rigid conceptual drive in philosophy, taking that discipline to task for its strong preference for clarity, which entails a rejection of what White call "poeticity." Poetic discourse is not a trap leading to ambiguity and vagueness, as traditional philosophers would have it, but gives a helping hand to that indispensable faculty, the imagination.

This is just one example of White's consistent undermining of "binary reason," the logic that excludes the "other" of a concept. Users of that logic ignore the fact that negative logic, not poetical speech, is what is by definition vague. Weary of binary opposition, White wrote in the final chapter of this volume, significantly titled, given the date (2017), "Is My Life a Story?," a loud and clear refutation of the fact-versus-fiction binary he never ceased to underscore: *"stories are a way of distilling meaning out of fact"* (emphasis in text). The distinction between fact and meaning, which is not absolute but, I would say, complementary, matches what he has written several times: "stories have to be invented; they are not found." To quote one somewhat more extensive instance from White's *Figural Realism* (1999): "Stories are not lived; there is no such thing as a real story. Stories are told or written, not found. And as for the notion of a true story, this is virtually a contradiction in terms. All stories are fictions. Which means, of course, that they can be true only in a metaphorical sense and in the sense in which a figure of speech can be true. Is this true enough?" It is up to us readers to answer that question.

That valuing of creativity and the imagination ("invented") as a necessary element of history, since it consists of story—feminists played with that term (his-)story becoming (her-)story—is what makes White such a key figure in historiography. Although there is not, as far as I know, an "imaginative turn" in the recent history of the humanities, it wouldn't hurt our *sense* of history—"sense" being a typical Whitean term; see chapter 11 of this volume, "Modernism and the Sense of History"—to retrospectively propose that imaginative turn. For, the imagination is a faculty—as Kant saw—of the same caliber as reason—though for Kant reason was the superior faculty. At the beginning of the abovementioned chapter 5, White is even more emphatic: "I regard the study of history or indeed any inquiry into the past as primarily an imaginative enterprise." This is where White takes a Vichian turn, away from Kant.

But White's insistence on the imaginative, fictional, poetical nature of history writing does not take lightly the burden of responsibility in that practice. The two volumes of White's last two decades are titled with the loaded term "ethics" for a reason. Ethics, or the development of, awareness of, and compliance with general norms of what is right or wrong, is with each of us all through our days, in everything we do. It intervenes in all decisions. White calls ethics an issue of "choices." But storytelling, the presentation in whatever medium of a focalized series of events, has two properties that make the ethical aspect of it more specific: it concerns *others*; and it is almost always, at least in part, fictional, even when, or perhaps especially when, it concerns difficult, painful, or extreme situations, and even when the events narrated are real, as facts. The storytelling, fictional as it may be, becomes an experiment, a testing ground for thought about ethics. It has these two features in common with most figurative literature and art.

Let me try to bring together an old ethical question, first with the status of literature as (emotionally) moving, and second with storytelling as focalizing. In the end, these two views join forces, or even melt together. But if ethical decisions are pressing on us almost all the time, then there is another issue that is hard to pin down, define, and theorize. This is *time*. For the lives within which we make those ethical decisions take place now, in the present. And whereas time tends to be considered a formal, structural issue, its bond with memory and the need to consider the future cannot be separated from the ethical. This concerns the ethics of that cultural, literary activity called "representation": the artistic recall—mind the "re-" of (re)presentation as well as of re-call a sign of repetition—of something that, allegedly or really, happened before. And as Judith Butler wrote in her foreword to the first volume, "A fact can only be shown to be a fact if the presentation works with the fact in the service of communicating a reality." So, let us delete the "re-" from "representation" and choose (in White's sense) presentation, as in putting forward, proposing, demonstrating.

The ethics of (re)presentation has been largely determined by debates on the ethics of art and literature in the face of extreme circumstances.

These have invariably taken two opposed positions as their starting point—in short: yes or no; acceptable or not. The first, decennia-old, comes from Adorno's famous warning. As we know since his 1949 indictment of making and enjoying poetry "after Auschwitz," *modesty* is a crucial ethical issue in our relationship to presentation. This is the opposite of *voyeurism*, an exploitative attitude to others, reveling in the pain and grief of others, which can be seen as sadistic; and *curiosity*, as an immodest intrusion compelled by a desire to know what others might prefer to keep confidential. Adorno's statement has often served to provide a simplistic view that can only lead to iconophobia and censorship. But he did not mean it that way, as his later retraction demonstrates.

White's advocating of "poeticity" makes sense of history, an ethical sense. Poetry is a form of discourse one can learn by heart as well as complexify and read aloud in musical cadence and tone. It has a temporality of its own. Reading poetry is usually slower and more detailed than reading narratives such as novels, with equal attention to every word. Poetry has this in common with other forms of art, such as visual art and films, if only we would take it as a guideline. In the wake of White's polemic with philosophy as rigorously conceptual, I posit an equivalence between poetry and other, nontextual presentational forms in view of this mode of reading. In addition, the ethical concern is bound up with the rhythm of the sentence—hence, its temporality, which I consider important for Adorno's ethical commitment, even if the philosopher was perhaps not aware of this.

However, the flip side of Adorno's compelling call for modesty is a forbidding taboo that makes the violence invisible. It is against this taboo that French art historian Georges Didi-Huberman spoke out in his short but influential treatise from 2003 (*Images malgré tout*, translated into English in 2008 as *Images in Spite of All: Four Photographs from Auschwitz*), which is a plea for attention to even the vaguest Auschwitz photographs: "In order to know, we must *imagine*," as his opening sentence has it. And in order to relate to others we do need to know, and when full knowledge is impossible, we still must try to approximate, encircle, or *feel* it. That is what it means to imagine. White's plea for the imagination binds this affective/emotional binding to what we call, but cannot really grasp, "history." That is why the imagination is so important and must be part of an ethical attitude toward the pain of others. Didi-Huberman presents the imagination here as compelling to historical knowledge. It cannot be cast aside as fiction. This, in turn, is why art is important, offering the visual imagination something it *images*.

Taking the element "image" of the imagination, turning it into an active verb that allows an intermediate position between the subject and the object of representation, and thus bringing it to the viewer, both body and mind, is the material practice through which literature and art matter. This is what White must have had in mind when he coined the noun "poeticity" and when he turned "identity" into the verb "identifying." Thus chapter 5 of this volume opens with an epigraph from Walter Benjamin's *Theses on the Philosophy of History*, where the image is even made to overrule stories (*"History does not break down into stories, it breaks down into images"*). In that chapter White gives the visual imagination a strong and serious responsibility for politics.

The readers, viewers, visitors to exhibitions, and other addressees of artworks are in a position equivalent to the linguistic verb form, in Greek, of the "middle voice." This verb form is neither active nor passive but comes close to reflexive, in the sense of mutuality—which, in turn, is close to reflective, in the sense of compelling thinking. The form opens up the empty middle between the comfortable but basically false, because never wholesale, positions of either victim or perpetrator, and makes room for an awareness of complicity and reflection on where to go from there: beyond yes or no. Indeed, this is not only a sensible position, but also one that gives art a vocation on a par with history, through the binding of both to ethics. Art can contribute to facilitating such exercise of the imagination in a way that binds the intellect to the affects, so that understanding implies both, and the two domains can no longer be separated. In addition, this is not only the case in the extreme circumstances of the concentration camps. We keep learning that extremities are still pervasive today, in war zones and other disaster areas. Moreover, the need for expression is also of crucial importance in the intercultural contact zones of the contemporary culture of mobility. There, which is our here-and-now, we need to be both modest and imaginative, in order to *know*, and to *know our place*—to allude to Adorno's call for modesty. White has discussed the middle voice in several texts, and in the second chapter of the first volume of this legacy collection, "Symbols and Allegories of Temporality," it appears again.

The concept of the middle voice, which White examined and advocated for much of his career, also decides how art can contribute to a binary-free, social-political world. The question of an ethically informed political art sits right in the middle of the two positions: of the need for modesty and the need to (imagine in order to) know; not between, but immersed and mired in both. "Middle" expresses that better than "between." For, this is not the binary opposition it is usually taken to be: the middle is not empty; it is a very busy space. Modesty, and the need to speak and hear, show and see: both of these positions move, struggle, and tangle in that middle. Hayden White, as these two volumes demonstrate, is the ideal "middle-man." In this, and thanks to the publication of these books, he remains very much alive.

Editor's Note

Like volume 1, volume 2 of *The Ethics of Narrative* contains both published and unpublished material, including unpublished parts of essays that were omitted from the published version because of space constraints. And as with volume 1, this volume contextualizes these chapters by presenting them in chronological order, with the date of publication or composition indicated after each chapter title; additional contextual information can be found in the notes to each chapter. For details on the genesis of this two-volume project, I refer the reader to my editor's note and editor's introduction to volume 1.

Chapters 10, 16, and 17 were previously unpublished in any form. These essays were originally delivered as lectures, and the occasion for each is indicated in the notes. The sources of the published material are indicated in the acknowledgments. Chapters 3 and 4 were printed in the conference proceedings by the institutes that convened these events and thus feature a more informal, lecture style. Chapters 1, 2, 5, 6, 7, 8, 11, 12, 13, 14, and 15 were published by White as chapters in books or articles in journals (but previously uncollected). Chapter 9, "The Limits of Enlightenment," was published posthumously by the journal *Storiografia* in 2018. Since it was originally given at a conference at Wellesley College in 2014, I indicate 2014 as the chapter's date and include the journal editor's explanatory comment in the notes. There are two published versions of chapter 5, "Modern Politics and the Historical Imaginary," one from 2012 and one from 2008. I have used the 2012 version for this chapter but obtained reprint permission from both publishers (see the acknowledgments). The full version of chapter 7, "The Substance of the Sixties," has been published here for the first time. Approximately one-third of the essay had been omitted from the published version. This is indicated by a section break and in the notes.

In cases where White supplied an abstract for a published article, I have included it in a note at the end of the chapter. All section titles and breaks are by White unless otherwise indicated. Some material from chapter 17, "Is My Life a Story?" (the final lecture White gave before his death), has been omitted owing to its having been published elsewhere, including in chapter 8 of this volume. These details are indicated in the notes to this chapter. Even with these omissions, the essay forms an integral whole that provides a fitting end to this two-volume anthology of White's late work.

All notes are by White except those that are enclosed in brackets and begin with "Ed.," which were added by me. I have kept these editorial notes to a strict minimum.

ACKNOWLEDGMENTS

I would like to thank first and foremost Margaret Brose, Hayden White's widow, who warmly supported this project from the beginning. As I mentioned in the acknowledgments to volume 1, she kindly allowed me to inspect White's files, both paper and electronic, in the summer of 2018, which made possible this two-volume collection of White's late work.

I should also like to thank Mieke Bal for her generous foreword to this volume. And again, I would like to express my gratitude to Mahinder S. Kingra, the editorial director of Cornell University Press, for his steadfast and enthusiastic support for this project and attention to detail in its realization.

The unpublished material appears here by permission of Margaret Brose on behalf of the Brose-White Trust. Versions of fourteen of the chapters have previously appeared in print. I am grateful for permission to reproduce the following material:

Chapter 1, "The Future of Utopia in History," appeared in *Historein: A Review of the Past and Other Stories* 7 (2007): 5–19.

Chapter 2, "Reflections on 'Gendre' in the Discourses of History," first appeared in *New Literary History* 40, no. 4 (2009): 867–77. Copyright © 2009, New Literary History, the University of Virginia.

Chapter 3, "Postmodernism and Historiography," appeared in *Special Public Seminar "After Metahistory: Hayden White on Postmodernism,"* ed. Hiroshi Yoshida, Ryo Shinogi, and Satoshi Sakurai (Kyoto: Report Issued by Research Center for Ars Vivendi of Ritsumeikan University, vol. 13, 2010), 84–99.

Chapter 4, "Anomalies of the Canon in Modernity," appeared in *Author(ity) and the Canon between Institutionalization and Questioning: Literature from High to Late Modernity: International Interdisciplinary Conference, New Europe College, Bucharest, 2–4*

December, 2010, ed. Mihaela Irimia and Dragoş Ivana (Bucharest: Institutul Cultural Român, 2011): 9–21.

Chapter 5, "Modern Politics and the Historical Imaginary," appeared in *The Politics of Imagination*, ed. Chiara Bottici and Benoît Challand (New York: Routledge, 2012): 162–77. This essay is a revised version of "The Historical Imaginary and the Politics of History," which appeared in *Culture and Power: The Plots of History in Performance*, ed. J. Rubén Valdés Miyares and Carla Rodríguez González (Newcastle upon Tyne: Cambridge Scholars, 2008), 55–68. Published with permission of Cambridge Scholars Publishing.

Chapter 6, "Historical Fictions: Frank Kermode's Idea of History in *The Sense of an Ending*," appeared as "Historical Fictions: Kermode's Idea of History" in *Critical Quarterly* 54, no. 1 (2012): 43–59.

Chapter 7, "The Substance of the Sixties," appeared in *Revisiting the Sixties: Interdisciplinary Perspectives on America's Longest Decade*, ed. Laura Bieger and Christian Lammert (Frankfurt: Campus Verlag, 2013), 13–25.

Chapter 8, "The History-Fiction Divide in Holocaust Studies," was published as "The History Fiction Divide" in *Holocaust Studies* 20, no. 1–2 (2014): 17–34. Reprinted by permission of Taylor & Francis Ltd., http://www.tandfonline.com.

Chapter 9, "The Limits of Enlightenment: Enlightenment as Metaphor and Concept," appeared in *Storiografia* 22 (2018): 9–21.

Chapter 11, "Modernism and the Sense of History," appeared in *Journal of Art Historiography* 15 (2016): 1–15.

Chapter 12, "Historical Truth, Estrangement, and Disbelief: On Saul Friedländer's *Nazi Germany and the Jews*," appeared as "Historical Truth, Estrangement, and Disbelief," in *Probing the Ethics of Holocaust Culture*, ed. Claudio Fogu, Wulf Kansteiner, and Todd Presner (Cambridge, MA: Harvard University Press, 2016), 53–71. Copyright © 2016 by the President and Fellows of Harvard College. Used by permission. All rights reserved.

Chapter 13, "At the Limits of the Concept," originally appeared in *PMLA* 131, no. 2 (March 2016): 410–14, published by the Modern Language Association of America.

Chapter 14, "Krzysztof Pomian's Modernist Theory of Culture," was originally published in the jubilee publication *Wśród ludzi, rzeczy i znaków. Krzysztofowi Pomianowi w darze*, ed. Andrzej

Kołakowski, Andrzej Mencwel, Jacek Migasiński, Paweł Rodak, and Małgorzata Szpakowska (Warsaw: Wydawnictwa Uniwersytetu Warszawskiego, 2016), 319–31.

Chapter 15, "Constructionism in Historical Writing," appeared in *Developing New Identities in Social Conflicts: Constructivist Perspectives*, ed. Esperanza Morales-López and Alan Floyd (Amsterdam: John Benjamins, 2017), 1–16, https://benjamins.com/catalog/dapsac.71.

Editor's Introduction

Hayden White, Interpretation, and the Ethics of Narrative

> History reads us moral lessons, whether we would have it or not, simply by virtue of the casting of its accounts of the past in the form of stories.
>
> —Hayden White, *The Practical Past*

> To go on and to ask what the facts might *mean* is to enter an ethical realm where the question of "what can I know?" gives way to the much more uncomfortable question of "what should I do?"
>
> —Hayden White, "Frank Kermode's Idea of History"

This second volume of *The Ethics of Narrative* completes the project of collecting nearly all the published essays and unpublished lectures that Hayden White (1928–2018) composed during the final two decades of his life. This volume is being published in 2023, the fiftieth anniversary of White's seminal *Metahistory: The Historical Imagination in Nineteenth-Century Europe* (1973, republished in a fortieth-anniversary edition in 2014),[1] a work that fundamentally altered the trajectory of discussions of history, philosophy of history, historiography, and narrative expression more generally. Although the basic insights of this monograph guided White's thought throughout his long career, he continued to refine, rephrase, and revise his ideas in his essays and lectures, collected by White himself in four volumes, *Tropics of Discourse* (1978),[2] *The Content of the Form* (1987),[3] *Figural Realism* (1999),[4] and *The Practical Past* (2014),[5] and by me in *The Fiction of Narrative* (2010)[6] and in the two volumes of *The Ethics of Narrative* (2022–23). The essays of this volume thus represent White's "final thoughts," as it were, on the topics that occupied him throughout his life: those relating to historical representation, narrative theory, discourse theory, modernism and historiography, rhetoric and tropology, and the ethical underpinnings of historical writing.

The last element, the overarching theme of this two-volume anthology, is no doubt the least understood in terms of the reception of
White's work. White's 2014 collection *The Practical Past*—which refocuses
his thought in a more explicitly ethical direction—appeared to many to
represent a departure from the tropological formalism of *Metahistory*
and the narratological formalism of *The Content of the Form* that had
heretofore defined White's work. Indeed, the idea of the "practical past,"
which White borrows from the English philosopher and political theorist Michael Oakeshott, has somewhat complicated our understanding
of White's later thought and legacy. Given that White's engagement
with the "practical past" coincides almost exactly with the period of
volume 2 of *The Ethics of Narrative*—indeed, several of the essays in this
volume discuss this concept, albeit not extensively—I shall address it directly in this introduction.

In my editor's introduction to the first volume of *The Ethics of Narrative*, I offered a general overview of the major tenets of White's theory.
I do so briefly again here, for the benefit of readers who may not be familiar with White's work. But I will not repeat myself. I will endeavor to
approach White from a perspective that has been somewhat neglected
in the secondary literature, that of *interpretation*.[7]

Narration as Interpretation

It should be noted at the outset that White does not offer us a theory
of history, the thing itself. He is in fact interested less in history per se
than in how what we call "history" comes into being through a certain
kind of writing, specifically the *narration* of past events taken to have
really happened or, as White often likes to call it, "storytelling."[8] More
properly speaking, then, White's notion of "metahistory," as expressed
in his eponymous tome, denotes a theory of, or an elaborate analytical perspective on, historical *writing* as the condition of possibility for
both theories *of history*, i.e., speculative philosophy of history à la Hegel
and Marx, and "straight history," the empirical, research-driven activity
practiced in today's universities.[9]

While there was great resistance to White's ideas in the discipline of
history—which was loath to come to terms with the formal aspects of
narrative—White's work was greeted with great enthusiasm in literary
studies. This was a function not only of a common interest in literary
form and problems of representation but also, and just as importantly,

of the influence on American departments of literature of the (mostly French) discourses of "critical theory" that emerged in the 1960s and 1970s: structuralism, poststructuralism, and postmodernism. White's assertion that history is identical with historical writing, that the historical referent is *constructed by* discourse (see, for example, chapter 15 of this volume, "Constructionism in Historical Writing") rather than merely reflected in it, that latent (or "deep") synchronic (tropological) structures undergird the manifest (or "surface") diachronic articulations in historical narrative, and that interpretation conditions knowledge (all knowledge emerges only on the basis of prior interpretation) intersected with the avatars of these movements—Claude Lévi-Strauss in anthropology, Roland Barthes in semiology / literary studies, Michel Foucault, Jacques Derrida, and Jean-François Lyotard in philosophy—so much so that White can be considered, variously, as a structuralist, a poststructuralist, or a postmodernist, depending on which aspect of his work is being described. However, despite the obvious affinities, White's intellectual lineage is distinct from that of these French thinkers. It derives more from rhetoric (Vico) than from linguistics (Saussure), more from existentialism (Sartre's *Being and Nothingness* and Heidegger's *Being and Time*) than from phenomenology (Husserl or Heidegger after *die Kehre*), and more from philology (Erich Auerbach) and archetypal or symbolic criticism (Northrop Frye and Kenneth Burke) than from the anthropology of Georges Bataille or the ethical reflections of Emmanuel Levinas or Maurice Blanchot. Thus, even if he ended up in a similar place, White had followed a very different path.

It was the primacy that White gave to the study of narrative that set him apart from most other historical theorists and philosophers prior to the 1980s.[10] White notes in chapter 14 of this volume that

in its representational practices, historiography remains—with more or less opposition—committed to the narrative mode of enunciation and to "the story" as the genre preferred for the presentation of historical truth. The historian narrates—this commonplace remains the *doxa* of historiography from Herodotus to Niall Ferguson; even in the fields of history of art and history of science, it is the full and truthful story of their development that is the ultimate aim of research. The scientist does not tell stories about his electrons, genes, or molecules; she seeks the laws that govern them.

White makes three interrelated points in this passage that define his thought more generally: (1) that historical "truth" is a function not of disparate facts or even of their enumeration in a chronicle, but of the presentation of historical particulars in a specifically *narrative form*; (2) that narrative in historiography is considered a natural, unproblematic, and objective way of articulating historical reality and to this extent remains a blind spot for historical studies; (3) that historical understanding or explanation, even in adjacent disciplines such art history or the history of science, differs from that of the empirical sciences in that it is an effect of *narrative logic*; it does not follow empirical (causal) "laws" and is not observable as such (by definition, it no longer exists); this is why the narrative mode of presentation is inextricable from humanism and from the humanities: it is the default way of presenting objects—texts, artifacts, and events—whose primary mode of being is historical, such that their full elucidation requires studying the past context that produced them in terms of a *meaningful* (as opposed to a merely causal) link between a "before" and an "after"—a story.[11]

White challenges the first point by asserting, provocatively, that there is no such thing as a true story: "all stories are fictions."[12] By this he means not that history is somehow fictional (not fact-based, imaginary) but that it necessarily relies on *fictional forms*, i.e., on preexisting plot-types that cannot by definition correspond to any reality: they function as discrete and culturally derived *interpretations* of historical particulars. In *Metahistory*, White identifies four such basic plot-types in the Western tradition: romance, tragedy, comedy, and satire (underwritten, respectively, by the "deep structure" of the four tropes of metaphor, metonymy, synecdoche, and irony).[13] On the purely formal level, then, White indeed collapses the distinction between literature (fiction) and history. But he also recognizes an obvious dichotomy between them. Whereas in the fictional narrative (literature) events are invented and can be altered by the author at will, the historical narrative (history) is constrained by the facts uncovered by historical research, which are unalterable as to their facticity. Their *meaning*, however, is another matter. For the meaning of the historical narrative is by necessity *voluntaristic* and *pluralistic*: the first is a function of narrative *choices* (plot choice; choosing where to begin, where to end, etc.); the second, of the constantly changing, successive presents that interpret past events: "The constructedness of a historical event is what makes it retrospectively changeable in the light of any new event. And this changeability of the past by the present is what assures us that history names a domain of freedom not enjoyed by natural events" (chapter 15 of this volume; e.g., the European "Thirty Years' War" can only be known as such retrospectively, after the Peace of Westphalia in 1648, and its meaning depends on how later generations see its significance, in light of ever-changing circumstances).

This separation between fact and interpretation is fundamental to White's conception of the historical narrative. As White puts it in "Constructionism in Historical Writing" (chapter 15 of this volume), "What can be added to a set of real events at first seeming to show no pattern at all or a pattern of one kind ('progress,' 'decline,' 'bridge,' etc.) is a plot structure that endows the events with a new meaning while leaving their primary factuality (time, place, intensity of occurrence, end, or beginning) unchanged." For the traditional historian, this "primary factuality" is all that is required to *reconstruct* a historical reality. In the traditional view, history writing simply reflects a fixed and unique story that existed *in reality*. But, as White points out, this is not how storytelling works: there is no story bereft of the conventions that make it recognizable as a story (beginning-middle-end structure, climaxes and denouement, foreshadowing and backshadowing, etc.). Narrative in fact serves to *organize* real events/facts as a way of *explaining* and *giving meaning* to a past that is taken to really have existed, even if this "existence" is simply an effect of the narrative presentation itself—the "mimesis effect," as White calls it, echoing Roland Barthes's *effet de réel*.[14]

With respect to the second point, White here cites a favorite concept of the French sociologist Pierre Bourdieu, *doxa*, meaning that which is accepted unquestioningly, taken as given, not open to dispute or debate—a seemingly perfect correspondence between subjective structures and objective reality.[15] In the doxic perspective White outlines, historical content and narrative form are one: the historical narrative is taken as reflecting the narrative structure of history itself. By dismantling this *doxa* through his relentless attention to narrative form as an autonomous source of meaning-generating structures, White effectively divided historical studies into orthodox and heterodox positions on narrative: an orthodox position (narrative reflects historical reality) that defines historical studies as a discipline as well as popular history (presidential biographies, memoires, etc.); and a heterodox position (narrative creates historical reality) maintained by a small contingent of "historical theorists"[16]—quite a marginal group in historical studies—but also by a much larger group of literary scholars and critical theorists outside historical studies interested in continental thought.[17] The only heterodox position within historical studies to attain establishment recognition was the French Annales school (Fernand Braudel, Lucien Febvre, et al.). Formed in the early twentieth century, it disparaged "event-history" (*histoire événementielle*), i.e., conventional narrative history, in favor of the investigation of very long time spans, the *longue durée*.[18] As White notes in chapter 2 of the present volume, "history—in Braudel's view—is not about stories, but about long-term processes governed by identifiable causal laws and subject to mathematical rather than imaginative (mythological and tropological) correlations." White sees this effort to scientize history by dispensing with narrative as failing to be truly scientific, on the one hand, or truly historical, on the other; for it did not succeed in altering the dominant cultural sense of history-as-story, even if it did serve to raise awareness of the social scientific aspects of historical studies.

Regarding the third point, the disjuncture between narration and objectivity, we must remember that White's principal aim in *Metahistory* was to criticize the scientization of historical studies—a long-term goal of the academic discipline of history since its inauguration in the mid-nineteenth century by Leopold von Ranke (1795–1886). Inspired by the rise and accomplishments of the positive sciences, Ranke advocated for the examination of original sources (archives, ruins, relics) and for a disinterested, objective, and value-neutral approach to the past, to establish "how things actually were," in Ranke's iconic phrase. Ranke dismissed as fanciful and moralizing the kind of historical consciousness inculcated by literary-poetic means, most emblematically the historical novels of Walter Scott (especially *Waverley*, 1814). In "Reflections on 'Gendre' in the Discourses of History" (chapter 2 of this volume), White remarks that "at the origin of scientific historiography, Sir Walter Scott had scandalized the newly professionalized discipline of historical studies by mixing historical fact and fiction in the so-called 'historical romance.'" For White, however, Ranke's scientific realism—the idea that narrative discourse offered transparent access to an objective reality ("how things actually were")—represented a fundamental misunderstanding. White argues that, no matter the historian's actual intention, the historian necessarily *emplots* his/her narrative; that instead of finding the "story" in the facts, as objectivism presupposes, the historian rather *imposes* a story-*form* on (inchoate) facts (facts in their raw, unprocessed, uninterpreted form), establishing and shaping their meaning in the process (so that in retrospect the "facts" appear to drive the story). "Storiness" is not an intrinsic element of disparate facts or events but, as mentioned above, derives from preexisting narrative archetypes and storytelling conventions prevalent in a particular cultural tradition (and which are therefore not "transcendental," in a Kantian sense). White's neologism *emplotment*—made famous by *Metahistory* but introduced slightly earlier[19]—draws attention to the manner in which the historian *selects*, *interprets* and ultimately *values* facts/events according to the extrinsic, nonfactual, and *aesthetico-moral* constraints of narrative form (ennobled as tragic, criticized through irony, etc.). History writing, historical narrative, is thus a *hybrid* of scientifically ascertained *facts* and *value-bearing, fictional* plot-types derived from the literature, legends, myths, and so on, of a given culture.

This idea of the "content of the form" in White's phrase (and eponymous book), the notion that the form used to articulate the historical particulars could affect, shape, and even constitute historical understanding or historical reality, ran counter to the role traditionally assigned to historical interpretation, which typically involved resolving conceptual inconsistencies or factual disputes. Instead, White was proposing that the facts drew their meaning from narrative choices and that fact-meaning depended on narrative-meaning, that is, on the *form itself*. Hence the analytical tools typically used to study literary works also applied to the study of the historical narrative. Insofar as it seemed to subject history to the conditions of literature, White's approach represented an intolerable amalgam for many, if not most, historians, even as it was embraced by literary scholars and other humanists.

The Practical Past

As mentioned above, White's publication, in 2014, of his book *The Practical Past*, based ostensibly on Michael Oakeshott's distinction or opposition between a "practical past" and a "historical past," appeared to many commentators to signal a break with White's focus on the formal aspects of narrative. In reality, the book represented an intensification of many of White's long-established positions; nevertheless, and paradoxically, it also seemed to contradict or at least complicate some of these same positions.

White's reasons for seizing on the idea of the "practical past" late in his career—there is not a single mention of this term or of Oakeshott in any of White's books published before 2010—appear to be linked to his effort to grapple with the history/memory problem: the past as the object of professional historiography versus the past as testimony and witnessing; history in the third person versus history in the first person. The paradigmatic example of this tension is of course the Holocaust.

In *The Practical Past*, White observes that the "historiography of the Holocaust . . . [is] suspended between at least two different conceptions or
ideas of the past, one historical, the other practical, between which there
is little possibility of cognitively responsible reconciliation."[20] Indeed,
White's first mention of Oakeshott or of the "practical past" in print is
in his review-essay, published in the journal *History and Theory* in 2007,[21]
of Paul Ricoeur's *Memory, History, Forgetting* (*La mémoire, l'histoire, l'oubli*,
2003), a book that takes the Holocaust as its principal reference point.
White's first mention of "practical past" in a public lecture (to my
knowledge) is in a keynote address delivered in 2005 titled "Historicality as a Trope of Political Discourse" (collected in the first volume of *The
Ethics of Narrative* as chapter 12). It is probably safe to assume that, even
though Ricoeur's book does not mention Oakeshott, it was Ricoeur's
book, with its foregrounding of the history/memory problem, that was
the impetus for White's late embrace of the notion of the "practical past."

In the present volume, brief discussions of the "practical past" can be
found in chapters 5, 6, 11, 12, and 14. In chapter 6, on Frank Kermode,
White describes Oakeshott's distinction thus:

> In a collection of essays written in the early 1970s, titled *On His-
> tory*, Oakeshott distinguished between the *historical* past—the
> past as it is constructed by historians—and the *practical* past—the
> past that ordinary people carry around with them in the form of
> memories, both accessible and repressed, and to which they have
> recourse when they find themselves in situations in which they
> must act without fully adequate knowledge of where they are or
> sufficient certitude of who they are. For Oakeshott, such situa-
> tions were practical in two senses: first, they are practical in the
> sense of raising the ethical question "What *should* I do?" (in the
> sense of Kant's second *Critique*) and, secondly, they are practical in
> the sense of raising a utilitarian question, "What *can* I do?"

According to White, Oakeshott distinguishes between a kind of professional past, a past by and for historians, and a personal one, a past that,
paradigmatically in the modality of individual memory, is a means
of self-transcendence and ethical introspection in the present. But as
White specifies in chapter 11, while "this distinction between 'the historical past' and 'the practical past' stands in for the older distinction
between a 'historical' or 'scientific' study of the past and all versions of
the past intended for ideological or political uses," we must nevertheless not "assimilate the practical past to ideology." For it is not a matter

of simply distinguishing a nonideological (scientistic) orientation toward the past versus one toward present practical concerns:

> Oakeshott, like Collingwood and Croce (as well as de Certeau, later on), presumes that *all* inquiry into the past is motivated by "present" concerns and problems, however "scientific" the method of analysis may purport to be. So what is at issue for Oakeshott is not the difference between the study of "the past" for its own sake or for itself alone *versus* a study of the past out of *present* concerns and interests. In fact, Oakeshott does not identify study of "the practical past" with *presentism* (as many psychologists who have taken up the term would have it) and the study of "the historical past" with "pastism" or antiquarianism. He distinguishes the two kinds of past on the basis of an analogy with Kant's distinction between "theoretical" and "practical" philosophy: the historical past is theoretical (constructed by an exercise of pure reason), while the practical past is constructed for use by "practical reason," which is to say, ethical consciousness, choice, decision, and judgment. (chapter 11 of this volume, original emphasis)

In this reading, the distinction between the historical and the practical turns on the Kantian distinction between the cognitive (concerning the condition of possibility of knowledge) and the ethical (concerning the condition of possibility of using the will in accordance with a universal moral law). This would seem to imply that the historical past of the historians is value neutral, while only an approach to the past based on individual memory is ethically inflected. But this clearly cannot be the case in the broader context of White's thought, and accepting such a view would effectively undermine White's efforts, since "The Burden of History" (1966) and *Metahistory*, to put into question scientific historiography's putative objectivity and value neutrality.

So, we are left with a conundrum: What exactly does White seek to accomplish with the "practical past" when accepting the opposition on which it is based appears to conflict with the basic thrust of his thought?

For one thing, White is not entirely consistent when discussing the notion of the "practical past." At times (as in an above-quoted passage) it is simply a matter of memory—a *personal, usable* past, not unlike what Sartre discussed under the heading "My Past" in *Being and Nothingness* (a book that was hugely influential on White). At other times, White generalizes the notion to such an extent that its oppositional force is greatly attenuated. For in addition to memory, the "practical past" can also define philosophy of history: "It was this past that Oakeshott called 'practical,' and it was this past that was the object of both philosophers of history (such as Hegel and Marx) and ordinary citizens, politicians, and schoolmasters who naïvely thought that the past could yield knowledge of a practical as well as of a theoretical kind."[22] To the extent, then, that White collapses, in *Metahistory*, the qualitative distinction between philosophy of history and "proper" history (he sees them as mutually implicit),[23] the notion of the "practical past" would have to apply to the latter as much as to the former.

White also sees the "practical past" as pertaining to the construction of national or group identity in traditional political history: "In the twentieth century, history still served communities by providing a genealogical account of the formation of group identities. . . . This genealogical connection is a perfect example of how historians produce historical accounts of the past which serve practical rather than scientific ends. . . . This is the social and political or, I wish to say, ideological function of the 'historical past.'"[24] Here White sees overlap between the practical and the historical pasts, as if they were two different functions of, or ways of conceiving, the same past of the historians rather than two separate species of past.

Finally, White uses the "practical past" to distinguish (twentieth-century) modernism from (nineteenth-century) realism: "Oakeshott thus sets up alongside of 'the historical past' something called 'the practical past,' which is as malleable and manipulable as memory itself, subject to the rule of imagination as much as to reason. Although [Oakeshott] himself does not draw the comparison, the practical past is rather like the past of the modernist novel—the novel of Woolf, Proust, Joyce, Stein, and so on—whereas the typical presentation of the historical past resembles more the realist novel of Balzac or Dickens." Going beyond Oakeshott's distinction in this passage, White redefines the "practical past" to serve his own ends, in this case to emphasize, as he had in previous publications, the necessity of using modernist forms/means to represent modernist events such as the Holocaust—"the paradigmatic modernist event in Western European history," according to White.[25]

Thus, we are left with the problem of interpreting White's conception of the "practical past" in the context of his overall oeuvre. Given his trenchant critique of the putative objectivity of scientific and academic historiography—namely how ethically informed choices of emplotment foreclose any "disinterested" search for the truth—how can there be a true "historical past" in White's thought? As White had written in

Metahistory and reaffirmed countless times, "we are *indentured to a choice* among contending interpretative strategies in any effort to reflect on history-in-general,"[26] and "the only grounds for preferring one [historical account] over the other are *moral* or *aesthetic* ones."[27] To the extent that the historical past is narrated, it is emplotted and is therefore irremediably "practical": an emplotted past is a usable past; it is informed by, and thus constructed to address, the moral concerns and proclivities of the present. According to White's earlier thought, then, there is no "historical past," properly speaking, if by that term one means historical objectivism or scientific neutrality; there is only the "practical past." There is no past-in-itself that could be the subject of the "historical past" except as a conceit of historians alone that evaporates under the kind of scrutiny White has directed at historical writing throughout his life. The "historical past," then, is simply a misconception of what history-as-emplotment must be.

In essence, for White, the debate about the "practical past" is a debate about the competing exigencies of Holocaust historiography. In *The Practical Past*, White notes that the seminal work of Holocaust historian Saul Friedländer, *The Years of Extermination*, is "shot through with ethical as much as scientific concerns . . . a conflict between a scientific and an ethical idea of the kind of scholarship that we must bring to the study of any event with the enduring relevance to our present world as the Holocaust."[28] It is these competing exigencies between factuality and ethical interpretation that White seeks to dramatize in the notion of the "practical past." Given that White wrote an essay on Friedländer's seminal work that has been collected in the present volume, we now turn to a discussion of it.

White and Friedländer: The Holocaust and the Ethics of Narrative

Perhaps the most important pivot point in White's work was the 1990 conference held at UCLA titled "Probing the Limits of Holocaust Representation," organized by Friedländer. This landmark event brought the Nazi genocide to the fore of historical studies, in the context of disruptions wrought by poststructuralist/postmodernist thought. Many of the participants singled out White's work, seen as importing "Theory" into historiography with his *Metahistory* and *Tropics of Discourse* in the 1970s, asking if the ethical imperatives of Holocaust historiography did not militate against the abstract theorizing that put historical truth into question.[29] White's contribution to the conference, "Historical Emplotment and the Problem of Truth," was collected along with those of his critics in the conference volume, *Probing the Limits of Representation: Nazism and the "Final Solution,"* edited by Friedländer and published by Harvard University Press in 1992.[30] In April 2012, for the fortieth anniversary of this publication, a conference titled "History Unlimited: Probing the Ethics of Holocaust Culture" was organized at UCLA, with the participation of both Friedländer and White. Their contributions, in the form of commentaries on each other's work, were published in 2016 in *Probing the Ethics of Holocaust Culture*, also by Harvard University Press (edited by Todd Presner, Claudio Fogu, and Wulf Kansteiner).[31] White's contribution, "Historical Truth, Estrangement, and Disbelief," is reprinted as chapter 12 of this volume.

In their editors' introduction to *Probing the Ethics of Holocaust Culture*, Presner and Kansteiner note that the 1990 gathering at UCLA "was very much about the anxiety of poststructuralism leading to a relativization of the Holocaust." However, Presner and Kansteiner also note that "few intellectuals nowadays are really worried about the possible negative ethical implications of poststructuralism."[32] This is no doubt because the poststructuralist attitude, initially so destabilizing and provocative in the 1970s and 1980s, had been mainstreamed and largely internalized by the 2010s. In addition, the culture of "Theory" that Edward Said had derided in 1983 as a quietist ideology of "pure textuality and critical noninterference" had been transformed in the years 1987–92 into the ethically engaged, politically attuned, and even activist discourses of postcolonialism, gender studies, and critical race theory, among others.[33] The emergent "Holocaust culture" (Steven Spielberg's film *Schindler's List* was released, and the United States Holocaust Memorial Museum was opened, in 1993) was certainly part, and perhaps even to some extent the instigator, of this ethico-political turn; for the pivot points of this turn, the de Man affair and the Heidegger affair, both of 1987, involved the question of Nazism and its legacy in the intellectual history of Theory.[34]

In his contribution to *Probing the Ethics of Holocaust Culture* ("On 'Historical Modernism': A Response to Hayden White"), Friedländer reaffirms his reservations about a poststructuralist approach to history: "We are back at [White's] earliest stance regarding history (not an enumeration of facts, but an interpretation of facts) as a futile search for a nonexistent truth. The quest for truthful interpretation, even as an incremental and discursive process, becomes an 'impossible charge.'"[35]

Of course, for White "truthful interpretation" is an oxymoron if it implies something like objective or scientific truth. And this is not because White simply discards the notion of truth, but because for him epistemological truth must be distinguished from figural truth—figural interpretation—or what White sometimes calls "human truth,"[36] truth as human self-making (this dichotomy roughly corresponds to Heidegger's distinction, in *Being and Time*, between "truth-as-correctness" and "truth-as-world-disclosure").[37] Thus, White believes in *interpretative truth*, truth *as* interpretation (disclosure), but not in "truthful interpretation"; for this latter concept implies, as noted above, that "interpretation" is somehow univocal and corresponds to some stable reality we call history. White believes that, unlike narrative form, *isolated* facts, what he calls (after Arthur Danto) "singular existential statements," can indeed be established and assessed by historians as containing scientific truth-value: "the plot structures used to fashion the different stories are not in the nature of propositions that can be submitted to tests of verification or falsification in the way that 'singular existential statements' can be tested."[38] But there is a fundamental difference between *asserting the existence* of some fact and *explaining or contextualizing* it, that is, determining its specifically *historical meaning*, which only a discursive elaboration can accomplish—i.e., the specifically *interpretative* operation of the joining together of disparate facts into a part-whole relationship, exemplarily via narrative form. In sum, White believes that while historical interpretation is *based on* facts, it is not, and cannot be, *dictated* by them.[39] Thus Holocaust denial or negationism does not involve good-faith arguments for an alternate construction of the term "Holocaust"; it is simply a bad-faith effort to deny the scientifically assessed facts that are conventionally and by consensus included under this rubric.

Friedländer further indicts White's theory for its assertion of the historians' freedom of choice, which Friedländer sees as a kind of straitjacket that threatened the idea of factual representation: "White essentially argued that the *constraints* imposed on the historian by a *limited* and *unavoidable choice* of rhetorical modes of emplotment put into question any 'objective' representation of historical events."[40] In the penultimate sentence of *Metahistory* White avers that the purpose of the book is to show how "historians and philosophers will . . . be freed to conceptualize history, to perceive its contents, and to construct narrative accounts of its processes in whatever modality of consciousness is most consistent with their own moral and aesthetic aspirations."[41] However, this "freedom," often misunderstood by historians either as a license to be loose with the facts or, paradoxically, as a kind of limitation (insofar White delineated only four major modes of emplotment), was in fact neither. The historian is no more "constrained" by the conventions of plot or of realistic representation than by the conventionality of grammar or of language itself.

Friedländer seemingly recognizes this, noting in his response to White that "I merely used the accepted stylistic possibilities of any narration, somewhat like Molière's 'Le Bourgeois gentilhomme' who, quite naturally—as he discovered late in life—was speaking in prose."[42] Indeed, White's point is precisely that the historian, like Monsieur Jourdain, is self-deceived (or unaware) with regard to his actual activity: that he/she is in fact using figures that trump logic, emplotting instead of transcribing, making ethical choices despite pretentions to neutrality. Thus, White endeavors to show how Friedländer, even as he opposes White *in theory*, supports and seemingly exemplifies his views *in practice* on how historical representation actually works: "Friedländer utilizes literary techniques, devices, tropes, and figures to close the gap between truth and meaning in Holocaust historiography without fictionalizing, aestheticizing, or relativizing anything." White might be seen as conceding rhetorical ground by commenting "without fictionalizing, aestheticizing, or relativizing anything."[43] But he is merely asserting that stories are inherently and essentially infused with nonlogical, nonepistemological conventions that, while extrinsic to the realm of fact, nevertheless provide the account with a meaning-structure that produces them as historical. For White, the aesthetics of narrative form are not ornamental or "peripheral," as Friedländer assumes; they are central to the explanatory matrix of historiography and to its ethical basis. In a review of Friedländer's magnum opus published in the *New York Times* in 2007, fellow Holocaust historian Richard Evans observes in a Whitean vein, "What raises [Friedländer's] *The Years of Extermination* to the level of literature, however, is the skilled interweaving of individual testimony with the broader depiction of events. Friedländer never lets the reader forget the human and personal meanings of the historical processes he is describing."[44] Indeed, is not this interpretative tour de force, weaving individual memory (or the "practical past") into the grand sweep of historical narrative, indicative of what White calls "human truth"?

To sum up, I believe one can make three basic points about White's work that are exemplified in the present volume:

(1) White makes a clear distinction between fact and interpretation; thus even if his emphasis on interpretation, in particular on the extrinsic meaning-structure of narrative form, appears, on the surface, to imperil the sanctity of facts, White rather forges a *middle ground* between fact and interpretation that resists reduction to the idea (most common in historical studies) that the story inheres in the facts and to the (Nietzsche-inspired) idea that there are no facts, only interpretations. As Mieke Bal notes in her wonderful foreword to the present volume, "the distinction [in White] between fact and meaning . . . is not absolute but, I would say, complementary. . . . For, this is not the binary opposition it is usually taken to be: the middle is not empty; it is a very busy space."

(2) White contends that the historical impulse is ipso facto ethical or "practical" (in the Kantian sense), no matter the individual historian's intentions. Thus, it is not a matter of whether or to what extent the historian should allow ethical questions to influence his or her writing, but rather, insofar as historiography, *qua* emplotment, *is* an ethical (or ethico-political) enterprise through and through, how does the historian grapple with his/her ethical choices? Appeals to scientific ideals of objectivity, neutrality, value-free knowledge, and the like, are for White simply bad-faith avoidances of historiological responsibility.

(3) All of White's major theses can be seen as manifestations of a guiding premise, namely the paradoxical idea of "choosing the past," which describes both White's earlier tropological-narratological approach (exemplified in the introduction to *Metahistory*) and the existentialist/figural view of the past, which combines Sartre's view of the past in *Being and Nothingness* (and to some extent Heidegger's in *Being and Time* and Nietzsche's in the second *Untimely Meditation*) and Erich Auerbach's interpretation of the *figura*, as outlined in an eponymous essay and in his celebrated *Mimesis* (see especially White's essays "What Is a Historical System?" and "Auerbach's Literary History: Figural Causation and Modernist Historicism").[45] This idea of "reverse causation" or "figural causation" involves interpreting a later event as the *figural fulfillment* of an earlier event from the free-volitional and projectional standpoint of the present. In this sense, all events are historiologically

indeterminate in regard to their interpretation. As Sartre observes in *Being and Nothingness*, "human history would have to be *finished* before a particular event, for example the storming of the Bastille, could receive a definitive *meaning*."[46] In the present volume see chapters 5, "Modern Politics and the Historical Imaginary," and 16, "Primitivism and Modernism," for elaborations of White's views on the figure-fulfillment structure in historiography.

White knew that the great masses of people, those whose attitudes and beliefs make up the soul of a nation, are not convinced by arguments; they are convinced by narratives. Hence the power of history, the power of historical narrative, whether scholarly or popular. Jean-François Lyotard may have proclaimed the end of "grand narratives" but not the end of the *grandeur* of narrative, namely its ability to endow disparate particulars with a sense of overarching purpose, meaning, and destiny, to guide a party or a people in a particular direction. Narratives derive their power not from arguments but by providing a meaning-structure, a *disclosive interpretation*, in which arguments are understood and facts articulated. According to White, the historian must face the burden of history writing, the ethical and existential angst that narrative interpretation—its inviolable freedom—inevitably engenders, rather than avoiding it through bad-faith appeals to objectivity, "letting the facts speak for themselves," and so on. To paraphrase Kant: it was necessary for White to deny objective historical knowledge to make room for faith in history as human self-making.

Notes

1. Hayden White, *Metahistory: The Historical Imagination in Nineteenth-Century Europe*, 40th anniversary ed., foreword by Michael S. Roth (Baltimore: Johns Hopkins University Press, 2014).

2. Hayden White, *Tropics of Discourse: Essays in Cultural Criticism* (Baltimore: Johns Hopkins University Press, 1978).

3. Hayden White, *The Content of the Form: Narrative Discourse and Historical Representation* (Baltimore: Johns Hopkins University Press, 1987).

4. Hayden White, *Figural Realism: Studies in the Mimesis Effect* (Baltimore: Johns Hopkins University Press, 1999).

5. Hayden White, *The Practical Past* (Evanston, IL: Northwestern University Press, 2014).

6. Hayden White, *The Fiction of Narrative: Essays on History, Literature, and Theory, 1957–2007*, ed. Robert Doran (Baltimore: Johns Hopkins University Press, 2010).

7. See especially White's 1973 essay "Interpretation in History," collected in his *Tropics of Discourse* as chapter 2.

8. See Hayden White, "Storytelling: Historical and Ideological," in *Fiction of Narrative*, chap. 20.

9. In the early nineteenth century two related developments presaged a revolution in historical writing: the advent of the literary technique of *realism* and of a concomitant *historical consciousness* (Walter Scott, Balzac, and Stendhal), a sense of the past as conditioning—leading inexorably up to, resulting in—the present; in other words, a sense of the present or recent past as possessing *historical depth*. The past was not simply past—antiquarianism. It also "existed" in the present as its fulfillment—historicism.

10. Louis Mink, whose writings are roughly contemporaneous with White's, would certainly be an exception. See Louis O. Mink, *Historical Understanding*, ed. Brian Fay, Eugene O. Golob, and Richard T. Vann (Ithaca, NY: Cornell University Press, 1987). Recall that the three volumes of Paul Ricoeur's *Time and Narrative*, 1983–85, were composed almost ten years after White's *Metahistory* and in response to it.

11. In other words, not a *chronicle*, a mere list of events in the order of time, but a *narrative*, a retrospective organization of events, creating relations between them. See the first chapter of White, *Content of the Form*, "The Value of Narrativity in the Representation of Reality."

12. Full quotation: "Stories are not lived; there is no such thing as a real story. Stories are told or written, not found. And as for the notion of a true story, this is virtually a contradiction in terms. All stories are fictions. Which means, of course, that they can be true only in a metaphorical sense and in the sense in which a figure of speech can be true. Is this true enough?" (White, *Figural Realism*, 48).

13. I say "respectively" because in *Figural Realism* White observes that "the tropological structures of metaphor, metonymy, synecdoche, and irony (and what I take—following Northrop Frye—to be their *corresponding* plot types: romance, tragedy, comedy, and satire), provide us with a much more refined classification of the kinds of historical discourse than that based on the conventional distinction between linear and cyclical representations of historical processes" (11, my emphasis). On the idea of "deep structure" see White, *Metahistory*, introduction.

14. See White's *Figural Realism: Studies in the Mimesis Effect*, and Roland Barthes, "L'effet de réel," *Communications* 11 (1968): 84–89.

15. See Pierre Bourdieu, *Outline of a Theory of Practice* (Cambridge: Cambridge University Press, 1977).

16. See the website of the International Network for Theory of History (INTH), https://www.inth.ugent.be/.

17. One could put "experimental history" in the heterodox camp as well. See the fascinating essay by Richard T. Vann "Hayden White and Non-nonhistories" in *Philosophy of History after Hayden White*, ed. Robert Doran (London: Bloomsbury, 2013), 183–200.

18. See Fernand Braudel, "History and the Social Sciences: The *Longue Durée*," in *On History*, trans. Sarah Matthews (Chicago: University of Chicago Press, 1980), 25–54.

19. The earliest mention in print would appear to be in "The Structure of Historical Narrative," which was first published in the journal *Clio* in 1972. I collected this essay in White, *The Fiction of Narrative*, as chapter 7.

20. White, *Practical Past*, 76.

21. And collected by me in White, *The Fiction of Narrative*, as chapter 23, "Guilty of History? The *longue durée* of Paul Ricoeur."

22. White, *Practical Past*, 76.

23. "I have suggested that proper history and speculative philosophy of history are distinguishable only in emphasis, not in their respective contents" (White, *Metahistory*, 428).

24. White, *Practical Past*, 98.

25. White, *Figural Realism*, 79.

26. This restatement of Sartre's "man is condemned to be free" simply means that the historian cannot choose not to choose.

27. White, *Metahistory*, 434, original emphases.

28. White, *Practical Past*, 77.

29. See, in particular, the contributions to *Probing the Limits of Representation: Nazism and the "Final Solution,"* ed. Saul Friedländer (Cambridge, MA: Harvard University Press, 1992), by Perry Anderson, "On Emplotment: Two Kinds of Ruin" (chap. 3), Carlo Ginzburg, "Just One Witness" (chap. 5), and Martin Jay, "Of Plots, Witnesses, and Judgments" (chap. 6).

30. White's essay was included as chapter 2 in Friedländer, *Probing the Limits of Representation*, and was subsequently collected in White, *Figural Realism*, as chapter 2.

31. A third conference, to commemorate the publication of *Probing the Ethics of Holocaust Culture*, ed. Claudio Fogu, Wulf Kansteiner, and Todd Presner (Cambridge, MA: Harvard University Press, 2016), was held at UCLA in January 2017 (organized by Todd Presner). The main panel for this conference, a "Book Discussion and Responses," featured Judith Butler, Peter Fritzsche, Karyn Ball, and me (Robert Doran), with responses by Saul Friedländer and Hayden White. This section of this introduction, on Friedländer and White, is adapted from my prepared remarks for this panel.

32. Fogu, Kansteiner, and Presner, *Probing the Ethics of Holocaust Culture*, 3.

33. Robert Doran, *The Ethics of Theory: Philosophy, History, Literature* (London: Bloomsbury, 2017), 159.

34. In 1987 it was learned that Paul de Man (who died in 1983) had written for two newspapers run by Nazi sympathizers in his native Belgium in early adulthood (1939–43); at least one of his articles was explicitly antisemitic. Victor Farias published his *Heidegger and Nazism* in 1987 in French (the English translation appeared in 1989 on Temple University Press). See Jacques Derrida, Hans-Georg Gadamer, and Philippe Lacoue-Labarthe, *Heidegger, Philosophy, and Politics: The Heidelberg Conference*, ed. Mieille Calle-Gruber, trans. Jeff Fort (New York: Fordham University Press, 2016). See also my discussion of this book in Doran, *Ethics of Theory*, chap. 3, "Derrida in Heidelberg: The Specter of Heidegger's Nazism and the Question of Ethics."

35. Saul Friedländer, "On 'Historical Modernism': A Response to Hayden White," in Presner, Fogu, and Kansteiner, *Probing the Ethics of Holocaust Culture*,

76. Martin Jay had expressed a similar view in Friedländer's original *Probing* volume (1992), asking why White did not simply "follow Nietzsche and boldly deny the very existence of an ontological realm of events or facts prior to their reconstruction, thus frankly embracing the radical relativism that haunts White's project and which he wants to exorcise" (Friedländer, *Probing the Limits of Representation*, 97).

36. White, *Content of the Form*, 57.

37. See Martin Heidegger, *Being and Time*, trans. Joan Stambaugh, revised and foreword by Dennis J. Schmidt (Albany: SUNY Press, 2010), §44, "Dasein, Disclosedness, and Truth."

38. White, *Fiction of Narrative*, 232.

39. As White writes in *Content of the Form*, "This is not to say that a historical discourse is not properly assessed in terms of the truth value of its factual (singular existential) statements taken individually and the logical conjunction of the whole set taken distributively. For unless a historical discourse acceded to assessment in these terms, it would lose all justification for its claim to represent and provide explanations of specifically real events" (49).

40. Friedländer, "On 'Historical Modernism,'" 73.

41. White, *Metahistory*, 435.

42. Friedländer, "On 'Historical Modernism,'" 77.

43. Indeed, this seems hard to square with White's dictum, cited above, that "all stories are fictions," or this passage from White, *Practical Past*: "all stories are fictionalizing of the events of which they speak" (82).

44. Richard J. Evans, "Whose Orders?," *New York Times*, June 24, 2007, http://www.nytimes.com/2007/06/24/books/review/Evans-t.html.

45. White's "What Is a Historical System?" (1972) was collected by me in White, *Fiction of Narrative*, as chapter 8, and "Auerbach's Literary History: Figural Causation and Modernist Historicism" (1996) was collected in White, *Figural Realism*, as chapter 5.

46. Jean-Paul Sartre, *Being and Nothingness: A Phenomenological Essay on Ontology*, trans. Hazel Barnes (New York: Washington Square, 1956), 643, original emphasis Or as White himself notes in a similar vein in chapter 15 of this volume: "Thus, whether the Enlightenment was an apex of human life in the West or the beginning of the West's self-destruction remains so far an open question. It all depends on how the Enlightenment is re-made in the present and future."

CHAPTER 1

The Future of Utopia in History [2007]

Discussions of the *topos* of utopia have typi-
cally featured the alleged antipathy between utopia and history. "History,"
Lewis Mumford said, "is the sternest critic of utopias."[1] Mumford
meant, of course, that history—the actual course of events—always
proves the impossibility of utopias. Utopia suggests the transcendence
of the conditions obtaining at a specific time and place, and in that degree the utopian project is doomed. This formulation makes sense for
the modern period in the West, but only insofar as the term "history"
has come to be used to designate a reality lived differently by different
human groups in specific time, place, and structural social configura-
tions. "History" is a congeries of "places" (*topoi*) that, while originat-
ing in and growing out of "nature," are nonetheless distinguishable
from this nature by the system of controls and constraints they posit
as necessary and/or desirable for the living of a specifically human (as
against an animal) life. As a "non-place" (*atopos*), utopia is anything but
historical. Whence Karl Mannheim's famous invocation of "history" (in
Ideology and Utopia) as providing the criterion by which to distinguish
between two kinds of "situationally transcendent" or simply "unreal"
ideas: ideological, on the one hand, and utopian, on the other.

"In the course of history," Mannheim writes, "man has occupied him-self more frequently with objects transcending his scope of existence than with those immanent in his existence."[2] Indeed, "every period of history has contained ideas transcending the existing order, but these did not function as utopias; they were rather the appropriate ideologies of this stage of existence as long as they were 'organically' and harmoniously worldview characteristic of the period (i.e., did not offer revolutionary possibilities)."[3] As long as every imagined paradise was located outside of society, "in some other-worldly sphere which transcended history and embodied these wish-images into their actual conduct, and tried to real-ize them," these ideas remained only "ideological." They might function as paradigms of ideal activity by which to judge comportment in every-day life; they might even serve as a kind of blueprint for human aspira-tion, or even be used to justify reforms and revisions of inherited social systems; but as long as they remained thus sublimated, as ideals never meant to be fully realized in real life, then such ideas remained "ideo-logical." Only when "certain social groups embodied these wish-images into their actual conduct, and tried to realize them, did these ideologies become utopian."[4] What made them "utopian," in Mannheim's estima-tion, was that they were "incongruous," not with "existence as such" but with the "concrete historical form of social existence" obtaining at a given time and place. It is the difference between "existence as such" (which is a problem "that belongs to philosophy and is of no concern" to Mannheim) and "a concrete historical form of social existence" that provides Mannheim with the criterion for deciding what is "realistic" and what is not in both ideologies and utopias.

What I want to dwell upon for a moment is the confidence with which Mannheim postulates the "historically or sociologically real" as the "reality" against which the relative realism of ideologies and utopias, as well as political and social thought in general, is to be measured. He says, "What is to be regarded as 'real' historically or sociologically at a given time is of importance to us and fortunately can be definitely ascertained. For the sociologist, 'existence' is that which is 'concretely effective,' i.e., a functioning social order, which does not exist only in the imagination of certain individuals but according to which people really act."[5] Mannheim goes on to distinguish between a "historical" concept of "history" and the many other approaches to the study of social events, processes, and structures offered by other social sciences: "we may expect that the historian will criticize our definition of utopia as too much of an arbitrary construction because, on the one hand, it has not confined itself to the type of works which got their name from the *Utopia* of Thomas More, and, on the other, because it includes much which is unrelated to this historical point of departure."[6]

Now, a great deal of the criticism directed at Mannheim's pathbreaking book, *Ideology and Utopia*, fixes upon his supposed misrepresentation of the history of ideology (and utopia). Judith Shklar has written that "to understand why the classical utopia declined, not yesterday, but almost two hundred years ago, demands a more detailed analysis of its character than either Marx, Engels, or Mannheim offered. It also requires a return to that historical way of looking at the past which they despised, because it does not try to uncover 'real' patterns, nor to establish laws."[7]

In this essay, I want to reflect on this *topos*, which sets utopia over against history as fantasy against fact, as the pleasure principle versus the reality principle, as myth against reason, not in order to criticize utopianism for failing to pay its debts to history, but on the contrary to challenge the "party of history" for its repression of the utopian moment in history's own makeup and for casting it out of any properly historical reflection on history as a residue either of infantile self-indulgence or of senile imbecility. To put it in the postmodernist idiom, I want to consider history as utopia's Other rather than the reverse, and ask what has been lost in our understanding of that history that is supposed to be the ground and measure of a specifically modernist brand of realism that, against all reason, has brought us to the dystopian situation in which the earth itself is under threat by the very instruments of science, technology, and political economy that were supposed to save it for human use and enjoyment. And this not only because it is commonly thought that, as Lewis Mumford, a great historian of utopias, put it, "history is the sternest critic of utopias,"[8] that "history" in its reality always undermines and explodes the utopian dream world, but because "history" itself has turned out to be that nightmare from which we cannot awaken and, more importantly, turns out to offer very little in the way of understanding our present situation or helping us to escape it.

To say that utopia is now history is, of course, ironic in a context in which it is believed that the principal reason that utopia is now history is because utopia is in some sense history's "Other," by which we mean, not only the opposite of "the past" and a repudiation of that "temporal process" by which and in which the present becomes past, but also a rejection of the kind of knowledge that is supposed to be attainable by a proper kind of "historiological" reflection on this process. But utopia is history's Other in another sense as well—in the sense of being an expression of a memory of a repressed desire, in this case, a desire for the future or rather a future against the claims of a social system that forbids us both to want a future different from our present and at the same time urges us to see in the present social dispensation the future that has already arrived and of which we ought not want better.

Many of the dream-plans of community that are called "utopias" are based on nostalgia for real or imaginary past worlds and express or reflect a melancholic unease with the present. But these are to be distinguished from the future-oriented utopias of modernity, in which the relation between the present and the past is mediated by a promise-fulfillment model of generational affiliation rather than by a poten-tiality-actualization model common to Hegel, Marx, the progressivist historians, and historical school avatars, all at once. Karl-Heinz Bohrer makes a distinction between historical mourning ("*historische Trauer*"), which is a longing for a past we never had, and poetic mourning ("*poetische Trauer*"), which is a longing for something we cannot live without. Bohrer believes—or once believed—that it is poetic mourning that in-forms the distinctively modern (post-Romantic) sense of "presentness" characteristic of aesthetic nihilism. This permits him to forbid any talk of a "poetics" of "history" on the basis of which one might envision a future at once continuous with and disjoined from the past in a rela-tionship of appropriation and sublimation at one and the same time.

Modernist utopias are temporal—in the way that the Christian apoca-lypse and millennium are temporal—but are material, bodily, immanent, and this-worldly, rather than spiritual, soulful, transcendental, and other-worldly, like their Jewish and Christian prototypes. Of course, it is commonly thought that utopian thinking is a secular version of Chris-tian apocalyptical thinking and that utopians are people who hope to be "enraptured" and "swept up," "in the twinkling of an eye," "transported" either to Heaven or some version of the Promised Land. But modernist utopia is rather more metamorphic than apocalyptic: it envisions the kind of transformations worked by the gods on men in Ovid, changes in the attributes of a thing without a change a substance. But with this twist: since modernists do not believe in the distinction between the sub-stance and the attributes of things, they regard a change in appearances as tantamount to a change in substance. In fact, the modernist utopia envisages a humanity in which the aim of human species development is to shed the illusion of substance (and substantiveness) altogether and thereby heal the pain of the *principium individuationis* by abduction. This distinction can help us understand the peculiar attitude towards time and history in artistic modernism that, wherever it appears, rejects not so much "history" as all the ideas of history inherited from the nineteenth century, whether from Hegel and Marx, or from Ranke and Droysen, and their recent avatars, whether the practitioners of professional historiography (which locks thought about time and history within the narrow relationship of present and past or past to present, sternly repressing any thought about the future of our own present time and even any idea that a knowledge of this future on the basis of historical knowledge might be possible) or Bohrer's "aesthetic nihilists," who take pleasure in the knowledge that neither past nor future can match the "thrill" of "suddenness" and intimations of catastrophe.

Much has been made of literary modernism's rejection of history and the historical, of Pound's, Eliot's, Woolf's, Kafka's, Proust's, Joyce's, Svevo's, and Musil's wholesale "flight from history" and into a Schellingian or Heideggerian night in which all cows are black, their supposed "celebration" of the irrational and the uncanny, their abandonment of narrative coherence, their substitution of a fascination with the specters of memory at the expense of the knowledge provided by "history"—all as a way of putting the modernists to the side of the development of a brand of "realism" that was supposedly the sole organon of a progressive and enlightened path to a democratic, socialist, or, failing that, at least a liberal future. Literary and aesthetic modernism is supposed to have been enamored of the Proustian swimming in a dark ocean of involuntary memory, where the anxieties of everyday life under capitalism can be anesthetized by fantasies of Sadean perversion and Huysmans-like longueurs. But this is to misunderstand the profundity of modernism's critique of the banalities of realist historicism. Above all, historicism's foreclosure of any future other than that of the same old bourgeois thing—Benjamin: "the catastrophe would be if things stayed the same." The modernists felt that they had inherited a landscape engorged with ruins of a once vital but essentially barbarized culture—of a barbarism rendered more barbaric (Vico) by virtue of its possession of a science whose power could be turned to any purpose, constructive or destructive, as the case might be. Inheriting a landscape of ruins, the modernists correctly perceived that the problem was to discriminate between what was broken but still useful and what was both broken and, as it were, contaminated, in the way a nuclear test site is contaminated, with waste products that could neither be used nor disposed of without dire risk. The problem was to use these ruins, this waste, these monstrous hybrids and garbage, to build a future that would not resemble the burnt-out landscape and crash-derby mayhem depicted in the Mel Gibson epic, *Mad Max 2: The Road Warrior*.

It was not that the modernists denied the possibility of a future. It was that they recognized how difficult it would be to build a future out of the stuff that had been left to them in the form of a historical legacy that was as insubstantial as it was glossy and that had been packaged to flatter the very servants of power and wealth who had eviscerated Western culture precisely by living up to its ideals.

Antiquarian "utopias" are not anti-historical; they serve to inspire such sublimative practices as professional historical research, archaeology, antique collecting, all of the restorative disciplines and the whole historical museum industry, not to mention the so-called "heritage" movement and Disneyesque historical "theme parks." These should not be confused with what I wish to call "modernist utopias," which come into being contemporaneously with modernity itself, by which I mean "our modernity," the modernity caused by a fully developed, global capitalism that expropriates and absorbs every tradition from our own past and, where the market requires it, the pasts of others. This brand of capitalism sweeps away even the remains of an earlier, commercial, and industrial capitalism, linked as it was to the destinies of specific nations, regions, and even neighborhoods of the industrial cities and in which a craft-like "look" of a commodity could increase its value. Now all vestiges of both an older crafts-world and a somewhat younger "industrial" manufactory, one that still bore the marks of human as against robotic or machine labor, have been relegated to the dustbin of "collectibles," or the museums of industry and technology, whose aim is to promote an interest in the past that will not deflect attention from the present as presenting all the possibilities of need satisfaction.

It is ironic, of course, that I should be able to say, if only in quotation, that "utopia is history," because if there is one thing on which everyone agrees that utopia is not, it is "history." Indeed, it is a conceit of modernity that utopia is radically anti-history, is impelled by a desire to "get out of history," to either escape the burden of historical existence by returning to a condition of Edenic bliss, or to dream of a time and place where the kind of change identified as specifically historical has come to an end; time itself is, as it were, abrogated; politics has been rescinded; and people are permitted to become persons fully without having to undergo the kind of tutelage that modernity was instituted to depose. To be sure, here the word "history" is understood to mean precisely that mode of human existence in which the most arduous and creative forms of human labor cannot possibly result in the achievement of a human community characterized by both "law and order" and "peace and plenty" of the kind envisioned as utopia. Since the early nineteenth century, utopia has been conceived as the antithesis of history: where there is history, there is no utopia; where there is utopia, there is no history.

In the early 1960s, in a symposium sponsored by the American Academy of Arts and Sciences titled "Utopias and Utopian Thought: A Timely Appraisal,"[9] the participants generally agreed that utopian thinking was a poor after-effect of a longing for deliverance that was essentially religious or mythical, a manner of thinking that had long since been discredited, not only philosophically but also practically, by history. A distinguished anthropologist opined that in the best of cases, utopia could mean only "liberation of man's higher faculties" and the aspiration to the "contemplative life." Those utopias that focused on the human body and its needs and desires and envisioned a life of play, "leisure[,] and abundance," he said, were not only childish but "built on forgetfulness." "What [utopia] forgets," George Kateb wrote, "is history," which he immediately glossed as "the record of human suffering." "What it tries to forget," he went on, "is mortality."[10]

Utopia tries, apparently, to forget a great deal more as well. Judith Shklar follows the modern *doxa* on utopia by tracing its anti-historical bent to its origins in religion and metaphysics. Commenting on the archetype of modernist utopian reflection, Sir Thomas More's *Utopia*, Shklar holds that its "Utopia" is inherently anti-historical. She points out that in More's fable, the founder " 'Utopus' simply appears one day and creates utopia."[11] He arrives trailing no origin or past; and his creation does not base its claims to legitimacy on genealogical affiliations with ancestors. The "present" of Utopia is no "heritage" passed down from the past to the present as a precious legacy, to be carried forward, cultivated, and made to grow (Heidegger). And because Utopia is anti-historical it is also, in Shklar's judgment, "profoundly radical." For according to Shklar, what utopia wishes to bring under judgment and what it finds "utterly wanting" in real life is nothing less than "all historical actuality," when utopia brings it before "the bar of trans-historical values." It is this trans-historicality that blinds utopia to the reality of a genealogical tie with the past, and it is this blindness that makes it "profoundly radical" in its essence.

I take it that the challenge to inquire into the future of utopia or the future of utopian thinking, the effort to think of the possibility of radical change in our condition or our situation, in which a rogue state (the United States government of George W. Bush) shows the power to push the world towards a nuclear war, in which a country pursuing the imperatives of a capitalist system gone amuck with the desire to consume has created a veritable "culture of the death drive," in which the very effort to think of change must labor under the specters of heat death, environmental depletion, nightmares of drowning in waste, and of a life lived on the garbage dump—all this might foreclose our impulse even to imagine, let alone wager on, the possibility of a better world for our children and their progeny.

We are told by certain self-described realists of the Left that the fall of the Soviet Union definitively disconfirmed the communism they had once devoutly and even heroically defended. And so too we are told this by those realists of the Right who presume that the victory of the West in the Cold War not only confirms the validity of capitalism as the sole possible way of life from now on but also invalidates any belief in the desirability of a thought that would go beyond the present and dare to think a future beyond the orgy of consumption and waste called advanced capitalism or "the free market economy." Those of us who believe that fundamental changes in our social system—by which I mean, of course, the capitalist social system—are not only desirable but are also necessary for survival are now told that we are crazy, if not criminal, that, in a word, we are, well, utopians.

Apparently, it is OK to try to imagine all kinds of dystopias, wastelands in what is now called in the US "the homeland," and fantasize worst-case scenarios of the kind daily produced by the US Department of Justice, the FBI, and the CIA, in order to justify massive expenditures in arms, military, mercenary, and police forces to protect the citizens from the dangers offered by the new universal and all-purpose enemy: the terrorist. These fantasies are produced by the establishment and disseminated by the media to keep the war machine and the arms industry running, fuel the financial institutions of globalized society, and keep the fate of democracy linked to the future of the "free market economy." But to dare to suggest that we can foresee a time and a condition that would allow us to shut down the war machine itself, is, in my country at least, treated as both utopian and tantamount to treason.

As I surveyed the literature on and about "utopia" in preparation for this article, I was depressed by the consistency with which all of the custodians of "the reality principle," the cultivators of that "realism" that is commended to us as the only possible "real place" from which our thought about our present and its possibilities of becoming a future should be launched, were agreed that "utopian thinking" was and had to be considered to be mere fantasy, "wishful thinking," delusion, dream, or opiate. Utopia, even modern utopia, the realists of our time tell us, belongs at best to the past, specifically the recent past, more specifically the period beginning with the transition from feudal to capitalist society and extending up to our present. Earlier, medieval, and ancient manifestations of the desire for redemption are less than properly utopian insofar as they presuppose an otherworldly dimension, beyond time, space, and materiality, in which humanity, finally alienated from its place of alienation, can at last find peace and rest.

It is otherwise with modern utopias. Modern utopias are born of a reaction to modernity itself. Although this reaction may take the form of an idealized vision of what once had been (pastoral or peasant life, the life of the village, the tribe, or the *ethnos* still connected to nature), it is still impelled to take this bit of redeemed past and "make it new," or re-make it (re-birth it), so as to accommodate it to desires and/or anxieties of a recognizably "modernist" kind. Here I am thinking of the utopian vision that informs Ernst Bloch's putatively "modern" study of utopia itself: *Das Prinzip Hoffnung* (*The Principle of Hope*) is a work that manifests all of the symptoms of the illness it sought to cure.[12] Bloch was disgusted by modernity, but his book is redolent of a desire for what it despises. And this is true of all modern utopias. Modern utopias want to escape not the real world, materiality, or history, but rather that version of these things we call "modernity" itself. This is in accordance with the principle, stated by Fredric Jameson, that each historical period has its own utopia. Consequently, it is important to recognize that if we are asking about the future of utopia, we are also asking about the future of the historical period or *chronotope*—that modern period we inhabit as our present.[13]

Modern utopia seeks escape from modernity, which is one reason why modern utopia is discontinuous with its earlier, religious, and mythical prototypes. The term names a symptom of a specific historical period, namely, those brands of socialism of the nineteenth century, their "extremist" avatars in the twentieth century, which dared to imagine a world that improved upon the techno-capitalist present: the fanatics, the terrorists, the dreamers, the opiated representatives of an earlier, mythic consciousness. This literature, while granting that utopian thinking during the process of Western civilization's transition from feudal, peasant, and preindustrial society to capitalist, bourgeois, and postindustrial society served as an effective and even beneficial instrument (means) of progressive innovation—bourgeois utopianism was a good thing, inspiring the agents of social change to the sacrifice necessary to bring about the bourgeois dispensation—this literature now informs us that this mode of thinking is no longer necessary; or that, in respect to the realities of this dispensation, which is our reality, it is hardly conceivable, much less possible, as an instrument of our liberation from the "discontents," *das Unbehagen*, of our social, cultural, and political moment. In a word, in our time, utopian discourse, the discourse of "what might be" and "what ought to be"—in contrast to the discourse of "what is," "what is the case," reality, the real, things as they are, etc.—this discourse, we are told, is not only no longer desirable; it is not, from the standpoint of that instrumental reason that prevails in our social sciences, even possible. Except, of course, as dream, nightmare, reverie, delusion, sop for the necessary and unavoidable casualties of a modernity that is our fate, our destiny, our *telos*, end, aim and purpose in life, the condition to which we are indentured for "the time that remains," the condition to which all of the other peoples and cultures of the earth are condemned to aspire, whether they wish it or not, if they wish to survive and "develop."

My thesis, then, is this: that modern utopian thinking and its various versions of both theory and practice are of a piece with the rise of the idea of history as a distinctively human mode of being in the world, such that we must consider the possibility that what we mean by "utopian" thinking must be viewed as characterized by a resistance to accepting "history" as defining a specifically human kind of being-in-the-world and historical knowledge or a knowledge of history as the criterion for determining what can count as the criterion for deciding what is realistic and what is unrealistic in any given proposal for a utopian alternative to the lived reality of a specific time and place in human being. If "history" is "reality," if historical knowledge tells us what is real and how this reality came to be what it is and in telling this also establishes its necessity and sets limits on what it is possible to do in and against this reality, then it follows that any utopian project seeking to liberate us from this reality will be adjudged to be "unrealistic," precisely in the degree to which it is "unhistorical." I am reminded of Freud's argument in *Das Unbehagen in der Kultur* (*Civilization and Its Discontents*), namely, that if civilization itself is the cause of the specific illnesses from which we are suffering, then it is delusory to think that more "civilization" of this kind could cure this malady. So, too, if it is "history" from which we are suffering, then it is foolish to think that more "historical knowledge" could liberate us from or cure us of this malady of "historicity." If, as Joyce's Stephen Dedalus tells us, history is that "nightmare" from which we are trying to awaken, then it is foolish to appeal to this "history" as an antidote to the utopian projects that are intended to liberate us from it.

Now, this gives us a way not only of distinguishing between progressive and regressive utopias—in the degree to which they affirm or reject knowledge of history as the instrument for justifying the realism of their projected alternatives to "reality"—but also for justifying utopian projects precisely insofar as they take history as naming the condition they wish to transcend. This allows us also to account for the utopian appeal of Francis Fukuyama's school-boyish exercise in a philosophy of history that proclaims "the end of history."[14] For it is obvious that what Fukuyama proclaims is a way of saying that America (by which he means capitalist society of the American kind) is the realization of the only utopia that can be realistically envisaged as having been fully realized in fact as well as having been dreamed of in imagination. The American way of life, as it is called, is utopia realized in reality. And its victory over its modern and ancient alternatives—the fascist and Nazi and Soviet utopias—confirms both its utopian substance and its transcendent realism as an achieved project that now can look forward only to an immanent development of its concept and its expansion in space—the global space of postmodernity—as a kind of development in place that has nothing "historical" about it.

Popular discourse has absorbed the maxim of the philosopher George Santayana to the effect that "Those who neglect to study the past are condemned to repeat it." We hear this all the time; it is routinely applied as an admonishment to those societies that have failed in their efforts to chart a future different from their past—as if history itself taught that humanity could only lose by trying to change for the better. Everyone forgets what Hegel said in the *Vorlesungen über die Philosophie der Geschichte* (*Lectures on the Philosophy of History*): "Was die Erfahrung aber und die Geschichte lehren, ist dieses, daß Völker und Regierungen niemals etwas aus der Geschichte gelernt und nach Lehren, die aus derselben zu ziehen gewesen wären, gehandelt haben."[15] H. B. Nisbet translates this as: "What experience and history teach is this—that nations and governments have never learned anything from history, or acted upon any lessons they might have drawn from it."

In *Ideologie und Utopie*, published in 1929, Karl Mannheim had already espied the end of utopian thinking and linked its ending to the advent of a new politics of managers, technicians, and intellectuals who, unlike their nineteenth-century predecessors, were "beyond" both ideology and utopia, as they were "beyond" history. Judith Shklar, reflecting on Mannheim's fear that the end of utopia meant something like the end of art and culture of the contemplative and classical kind, suggests that his question "Why are there no utopias today?" is "more a comment on an intellectual situation than a real query."[16] Shklar held that the fact that there are no utopias today indicates that utopia itself is dead, over and done with, no longer even a possibility for serious thought or, as Americans say when they want to indicate that something is really over, totally over, "utopia is now history."

Notes

1. Lewis Mumford, "Utopia, the City and the Machine," in *Utopias and Utopian Thought*, ed. Frank E. Manuel (Boston: Beacon, 1967), 12.

2. Karl Mannheim, *Ideology and Utopia: An Introduction to the Sociology of Knowledge* (1929), trans. Louis Wirth and Edward Shils (New York: Harcourt, Brace, 1946), 173.

3. Mannheim, *Ideology and Utopia*, 173–74.

4. Mannheim, 174.

5. Mannheim, 174.

6. Mannheim, 180.

7. Judith Shklar, "The Political Theory of Utopia: From Melancholy to Nostalgia," in Manuel, *Utopias and Utopian Thought*, 103ff.

8. Mumford, "Utopia," 12.

9. See Manuel, *Utopias and Utopian Thought*.

10. George Kateb, "Utopia the Eternal Human: Utopia and the Good Life," in Manuel, *Utopias and Utopian Thought*, 248.

11. Shklar, "Political Theory," 104ff.

12. [Ed: Ernst Bloch, *The Principle of Hope*, vols. 1–3, trans. Neville Plaice, Stephen Plaice, and Paul Knight (Cambridge, MA: MIT Press, 1995).]

13. [Ed: See Hayden White, "'The Nineteenth Century' as Chronotope," in *The Fiction of Narrative: Essays on History, Literature, and Theory, 1957–2007*, ed. Robert Doran (Baltimore: Johns Hopkins University Press, 2010), 237–46.]

14. [Ed: See Francis Fukuyama, *The End of History and the Last Man* (New York: Free Press, 1992).]

15. Georg Wilhelm Friedrich Hegel, "Vorlesungen über die Philosophie der Geschichte," in *Werke*, vol. 12 (Frankfurt: Suhrkamp, 1970), 17.

16. Shklar, "Political Theory," 114.

CHAPTER 2

Reflections on "Gendre" in the Discourses of History [2009]

> For where there is no law, there is no transgression.
>
> —Saint Paul, Romans 4:15

> You are to keep My statutes. You shall not breed together two kinds of your cattle; you shall not sow your field with two kinds of seed, nor wear a garment upon you of two kinds of material mixed together.
>
> —Leviticus 19:19

Ever since I met him—in the spring of 1969—I have thought of Ralph Cohen as "master of genres."[1] No one has been more assiduous in the cultivation of genre consciousness, no one has been more liberal in the entertainment of different conceptions of genre. Of course, as a literary scholar, Ralph Cohen has been especially interested in the concept and history of the genres of *literary* expression. But he has always treated literary genres as a special case of the more general social and cultural activity of identifying, classifying, and relating the classes and species of things both natural and unnatural.

Up until the end of the eighteenth century, conformity to the "law of genre"—which is supposed to have held that "thou shalt not mix the kinds"—was considered a matter of moral, as well as ontological and aesthetic, necessity. The domain of literary genres was only the most cultivated and sophisticated place where the law was applied, tested, and, when necessary, revised. The law of genre was also supposed to preside over the joining of forms with contents. In literary writing, it was forbidden to join a noble form (such as tragedy) with a base content (such as villainy). But in literature, as in life, Charles Darwin destroyed all that. What Darwin showed, among other things, is that there is no such thing as "nobility" or "baseness," which is to say, no qualitative differences among the kinds that make up "nature." It followed, for

Cohen, that genres had no "natures," which is to say, inherent substances or essences, but were or had to be seen as systems of practical classifications—open systems—subject to mixture, change, and displacement, according to the exigencies of different social and cultural situations. Which was to say that although genres had no natures, they most definitely had *histories*. This meant, among other things, that the best way to study the forms and contents of any mode of cultural expression, and the ways in which forms and contents were fused in any given moment of a society's evolution, was *historically*. Whence, I take it, the origin of *New Literary History*.

The history of genres provides the basis for a history of literature in a way that the other aspects of the literary work of art do not.

But what about "history" itself? If the history of genres provides us with a way of conceiving the history of literature in open and cosmopolitan ways, what happens if we extend this principle to the writing of history itself? Unlike those sciences that take nonhuman physical things as their objects of study and those human sciences that treat human phenomena as physical things, history studies those aspects of the human past that bespeak the differences between human and other kinds of being. It is perfectly fitting, therefore, for history to derive its methods and categories of analysis from that very "culture" that marks the principal difference between the powers of the human species and those of all other kinds. It is, however, difficult to know which aspects of the whole cultural endowment to draw upon for the conceptualization of a possible science of things human. And this is because the human species creates the instruments of knowledge production in the very process of taking the specifically human as its object of interest.

Historical knowledge is a case in point. A specifically historiological interest in the past appears to have been a product of a particular culture arising at a particular time and place and with the kind of mindset that made this particular kind of interest in the past worth cultivating. The modes of analysis and explanation utilized in the elaboration of a specifically "historical" way of studying the past were drawn from a stock of techniques and attitudes common to all of the divisions of the cultural heritage shared by the peoples of this time and place. This is why early historical thinking, as manifested in Herodotus and Thucydides, has been variously interpreted as having been influenced or even inspired by Greek myth, Greek medicine, Greek rhetoric, Greek drama, Greek law, Greek philosophy, and so on. At the same time, these divisions of Greek cultural production have been held to be informed by the same general interest in the past as that which has turned out to be specific to the kind of interest in the past called "historical."

On this view, Greek culture in general can be supposed to have been implicitly "historical," while that division of it called "historiography" consisted of those discourses of Greek antiquity in which this "historical" component predominated as the guiding principle of research and representation. And this intimate connection, not to say genealogical relationship, between "historical writing" and the other divisions of Greek culture in various times and places can be seen as accounting for the various "genres" of historical writing that appeared right from the beginning of its "history" in the differences seen to exist between the "storyteller" (logographer) Herodotus and the Hippocratean diagnostician of the *polis*, the retired *strategos*, Thucydides.

As a field of knowledge production, historiography has always vacillated between the poles of representation (which is to say, classification, nomination, and presentation) and explanation (which is to say, analysis, nomothesis, and demonstration). These poles themselves have their own histories, or can be viewed as describing different kinds of trajectories in their evolution. What can be said to count as an adequate representation of history and the phenomena met with therein changes from time to time and place to place as the specifically "historical" interest in "the past" spreads, first, in the West and then, along with Christianity, capitalism, and the physical sciences, to the rest of the world. And so too for what can be said to count as an adequate explanation of the changes that historical things undergo over time and the kinds of continuities that can be thought to characterize them. But in the conceptualization of the complex skein of relationships between modes of representation and modes of explanation in the "career" of historiography in the West, we can begin to grasp the nature of the relationship between two kinds of genre: mythic-rhetorical-dramatic-literary, on the one side, and logico-deductive-argumentative, on the other.

My thesis is that historiography uses the genres of myth and literary writing to initially characterize and thereby identify specifically historical phenomena as undergoing the kinds of development best described in the *narrative* mode of representation. As thus envisaged, the genres of historiography would be as numerous and as various as the genres of myth and narrative literature to be found in any given moment of a culture's "history." These genres (and of course their mixtures) would be perceivable on the surface of the historiographic discourse: (1) as the *story* that is told about the object of interest in the past; (2) the *figurations* by which persons and events are worked up to serve as the *kinds* of characters, situations, and actions met with in the mythico-literary endowment of a time or epoch; and (3) the kinds of *emplotment* used by the composer of the discourse to endow the story told with a specific kind of cultural significance or meaning.

I presume that there is no such thing as a "story-in-general," unless by that term one means some archetype or paradigm by reference to which one might be justified in saying, "Well, yes, this is indubitably a story"; but then would have to add, "But what *kind* of story it might be, I cannot tell." The *kind* of story—the genre or genres to which a given story might belong—is determined by the plot structure, which, gradually elaborated over the time of the story being narrated, allows one to recognize it as a tragedy, a romance, a pastoral, an epic, and so on. To be sure, we have plenty of "plot-types" on hand in any given moment of a culture's evolution, derived by abstraction from stories actually told or theorized as possibilities of emplotment on the basis of the analysis of such abstractions.

The *conscious* use of generic conventions and plot-types to serve as explanations of historical phenomena was perfectly respectable for most of the history of historical writing. Prior to the early nineteenth-century effort to transform historical studies into a science and to substitute the nomothetic-deductive mode of explanation for the ideographic-descriptive mode of narrativization, historiography was treated as a branch or department of rhetoric, which is to say, as a compositional practice licensed to *impose* upon the facts known about the past, structures of *meaning* derived from religion, myth, common sense, philosophy, and all manner of "serious" literature. Historiography belonged to the so-called moral sciences, which were more concerned to exemplify and validate the *doxa* of "society" than to analyze its possible flaws, contradictions, and weaknesses. As such, it contributed to what was regarded as the society's fund of wisdom (*sapientia*) as well as to that other, more pragmatic, more instrumental body of knowledge designated as *scientia*. Insofar as historiography contributed to the latter kind of knowledge, it did so by, as it were, testing the adequacy of the genres of narrative presentation to the known facts about human comportment in the past.

The effort to transform historiography into a modern science changed all that. For modern science has no truck with the idea that "meaning" inheres in things. Scientific "meaning" is indistinguishable from the determination of "what is the case." In science, truth and meaning are coterminous: the "meaning" of a statement of fact is the adequacy of its predication to a real, rather than a possible or imaginary, referent.

Consider the idea of "tragedy," or the notion of a tragic circumstance, a tragic life, a tragic death, and so on. Does tragedy inhere in a set or series of real events in such a way that a merely truthful, diachronic representation of them would necessitate their emplotment as a tragedy? A number of philosophers, most notably Paul Ricoeur, but also others, beginning with Aristotle, have thought that the depiction of a real set of events as a tragedy would be truthful if that set of events manifested the aspects of a tragic mode of being-in-the-world. A tragic life would be a life that had actually been lived as manifesting the characteristics of the *kind* of life conceived in Western culture as "tragic." People can be conceived, Ricoeur argued, as living their lives as narratives and, as it were, self-emplotting their lives insofar as they base their actions on the kinds of moral principles that make possible the experiencing of "tragic" conflicts.

I am less interested in assessing the plausibility of this view of the origin of the literary genre of tragedy (or indeed other plot-types) than in accounting for its use in historiography down to our own time. For although the effort to transform historical studies into a science entailed the elimination of narrative as a mode of explanation and indeed even as a mode of truthful representation of historical reality, narrative, narrativization, and narrativity have continued to serve as the dominant mode of presentation of historical phenomena down to our own time.

The leader of the Annales school of historians, Fernand Braudel, insisted that if history was to become a science, it had to eliminate narrative or *le récit* from historiography. If historical phenomena were to be treated scientifically, Braudel insisted, historians had to forswear any interest in the kind of event (such as political events) that lent themselves to presentation as an element of a story.

History—in Braudel's view—is not about stories, but about long-term processes governed by identifiable causal laws and subject to mathematical rather than imaginative (mythological and tropological) correlations. If history has no story, neither has it any plot or plot structure. The kind of structure that history does have, he concluded, is that of "levels" of short-term (political), middle-term (social and cultural), and long-term natural processes (climate change, epidemiological processes, population growth and dispersal, et cetera). At the short term, there is very little possibility of discerning real structural determinations, and at this level, therefore, there is no possibility of a science of politics (at least, none that can be based on historical knowledge).

The fact that stories, cast in terms of various mythical and literary genres, continue to be told about this level of historical existence merely indicates the "literary," which is to say the *fictional*, nature of this kind of historiography. So, here "genre" is equivalent to "fiction," and the manifestation of the use of literary-generic categories for the organization and presentation of historical phenomena would be considered evidence of a "fictionalization" of history—the one mistake that any modern historian must want to avoid.

It is well known and generally recognized that modern historiography wished to substantiate its claim to scientificity by its effort to remove "fiction" from its presentational practices. At the origin of scientific historiography, Sir Walter Scott had scandalized the newly professionalized discipline of historical studies by mixing historical fact and fiction in the so-called "historical romance." The hybrid form realized in Scott's *Waverley* series had violated "the law of genre" instantiated by the passage from Leviticus used as my epigraph above, the law against any mixture of the kinds (genres).

In the period in which Scott was working out his sinful enterprise, the history was considered to be a manly (or masculine) genre (it was a story about men, written by and for men, and related in a "virile" or manly way) and the romance a womanly (or feminine) genre. It might be thought that the wedding of a masculine genre with a feminine genre could be considered not only the "natural" but also the "proper" thing to do. All one would have to do was find the proper authority to preside over the union. But because the genres were not only gender coded but also class coded—insofar as men and women were assigned different class-coded functions—the wedding of the history with the romance effected by Scott carried with it the connotation of a cross-class union. In fusing history with literature, fact with fiction, and in accordance with the principle that, in a union of the strong with the weak, it would be the stronger that would be diminished, Scott could be conceived to be depriving "history" of its masculinity. It was this presumed masculinity of the history genre that permitted it to claim the status of a "kind" of science throughout the rest of the nineteenth century and well into the twentieth.

This was in accordance with what happened in the field of literary writing that, contrary to history's interests, continued on the way to developing a new genre, the novel, in which the *mixture* of the kinds, of genres, plot structures, voices, modes, and meanings was the rule rather than the exception. In supplanting the romance as the regnant kind or paradigm of artistic prose discourse, the novel metamorphized into a kind of androgynous *mélange* or carnival of fact and fiction, history and poetry, reality and illusion, and, in modernism, became a kind of laboratory for testing the extent to which a reality that was considered to have no essential meaning could be given such by the kind of auto-poietic means that the human species had utilized to drag itself out of "savagery" and into "civilization."

Now while professional historians were in the process of eliminating fiction from their discourses, most of them continued to use narrative as the favored mode of presentation of their "facts." The idea was that narrative was a kind of neutral form and a "container" well suited to contain the events serving as their referents, under their aspect as elements of a temporal sequence, without adding anything to the events themselves in the way of meaning. Most did not see that "narrativity" was itself a meaning, that to indicate that a series of real events could be truthfully depicted as having a given plot structure was to play into the myth of meaningfulness that modern sciences had dispelled as a precondition of seeing the world "scientifically."

Meanwhile, and not unironically, the novel was undergoing a transformation not unlike that proposed by scientifically minded historians who wished to eliminate "narrative" or "narrativity" from the literary representation of a "reality" being comprehended as "historical" in kind. The genealogy of the modern novel is still a matter of dispute among historians of Western culture. But as Erich Auerbach appears to have established beyond a shadow of real doubt, the modern novel appears to take shape during a long process in which "literature" (a term that takes on the meaning of artistic writing only near the end of the eighteenth century) gradually took on the task of "representing reality," and "reality" itself came to be identified as a complex interplay of natural and cultural forces of which a specifically historical (or "historicist") mode of existence was the product. Auerbach showed that nineteenth-century realist writing took "history" as its subject matter and extended the idea of history to encompass the present as well as the past. To treat the present "historically" meant to seek the forms as well as the contents of reality as inhering in things rather than as existing in another world or in some canon of literary masterpieces bearing the authority of Holy Writ. To treat the world "historically" was to recognize that it was in constant evolution and development.

Although it is often thought that Darwin's theory of biological evolution influenced historical thinking by providing a scientific basis for
dealing with social change and development, it is just as true that historical thinking influenced Darwin inasmuch as he "historicized" a "nature" that, until his time, had been viewed as an endless reproduction
of the Same. Darwin's ideas about mutation and adaptation permitted
scientific belief in the transformation, metamorphosis, and transub-
stantiation of species of all kinds, artistic and social as well as biological
and organic. After Darwin, it became possible to view genres of all kinds,
but especially genres of speech, discourse, and writing, as "historical" in
the sense of having their beginnings in time and culture, as transmuting
over time and displacement, and as being subject to change by human
agency whenever circumstances required it.

In many respects, the modernist novel—called by many "the genre
of genres," the polymorphous genre—since it can be seen as a field of
meaning production on which the utility of genres is tested in the fire of
representation and the very possibility of generic coherency is brought
under question, represents the moment at which historical writing and
literary writing both transcend their status as "fictions." In a famous
essay, "Metacommentary," Fredric Jameson traced the evolution of
the modernist novel as a process in which the traditional elements of
storification—event, character, and plot—were progressively suppressed
or sublimated in order to make the "subject" of the novel an account of
its own rise and disintegration, leaving the "fragment," and its random
collocation with the other bits and pieces of "tradition" left over from
the demystification of the world effected by scientific (instrumental)
rationalism, as the principal "content" of the novel.[2] And indeed, as
Jameson never ceases to reiterate, what we must mean by literary modernism is a writing practice that is deemed all the more realistic the
more the traditional modes of narrativization and the genres peculiar
to traditional narrativistic writing are suppressed. Jameson equates this
suppression of narrative and its genres with a repression of a sense of
history peculiar to modernism's ideology.

But there is nothing in "history"—understood as the process of
humankind's efforts at self-creation over time—to necessitate the employment of the narrativistic mode of representation and the genres of
tragedy, comedy, romance, farce, and so on, to endow the facts of the
matter with a "meaning" proper to those facts taken *seriatim*. On the contrary, ever since Herodotus, "history" has been set over against "myth"
in the manner of the modern opposition of "truth" to "lie" or "error."

The modern opposition of "history" to "fiction" represents at the level of critical self-consciousness an advance over the opposition of "truth" to "lie." But when it comes to the representation of a process such as that of "history," the earlier stages or phases of which are no longer open to perception or inspection, then surely such a representation would be more profitably characterized as a "fiction" than as a truth or fact.

And here those who are interested in history, and who are particularly fascinated by those parts of human being that were once "present" but are now "past," might take a page from the ways in which the modernist novel gets beyond the fact-fiction dichotomy.

It used to be thought that the modernist novel—as represented by Joseph Conrad, Marcel Proust, James Joyce, Virginia Woolf, Franz Kafka, and so on—represented a retreat from the program of the realist novel understood as the effort to map the present as "history." But again, Auerbach's *Mimesis* showed that the modernist novel, exemplified in his treatment by the work of Virginia Woolf, far from abandoning history, extended its concept to include the depths of human consciousness opened up to inspection by Freud and psychoanalysis, although in a way anticipated by earlier novelists such as Gustave Flaubert, poets like Charles Baudelaire, and philosophers of culture like Giambattista Vico—and, it might be added, historians like Jules Michelet, Friedrich Schiller, and Nikolai Karamzin. In making of the writer's own efforts to capture human reality in symbols the central or manifest subject of the novel, the modernist writer effectively changed what had been thought of as a literalist transcription of reality into "poetic statement," which, rather than report or transcribe "reality," performed the kind of linguistic operations that made the human kinds of creativity possible. This is to say that the modernist novel makes of language itself *a*, if not *the* principal subject of reflection and/or representation.

But the notion of language informing literary modernism is not that of the philologists of yore, in which each word is considered to have a proper (or literalist) and an improper (or figurative and ambiguating) use, and "literacy" consists of knowing the rules governing when to switch from one to another usage. On the contrary, modernist writing employs procedures theorized by linguists working with a semiological theory of language. Here it is not the word but the sign that is taken as the basic unit of representation, such that the referential function of language use is thrown awry by: (1) the presence in every sign of a split between its signifier function, on the one hand, and its signifying function, on the other; (2) the discovery that every signified is itself only a signifier that has been given the function of a signified; (3) the acknowledgment that signification, or the endowment of both words and things with meaning, is a purely free or at least unbound activity proceeding as much by "free association" as by putative "laws" of grammar, syntax, and logic.

Since language could now be taken to be a "natural" phenomenon, as a thing among other things, rather than as that aspect of *Homo sapiens* that distinguished it from the rest of nature, it could be studied scientifically rather than simply "interpreted." And since language was a free or at least an unbound activity, it could fall to the literary artist to experiment with its forms, modes, genres, and aspects in exactly the way that the poets in the Western tradition had been doing since the time of "Homer."

Thus, when it comes to the use and abuse of "genre" in modernist writing, it has to be said that "anything goes."

This dictum has important implications for understanding what is currently happening in the treatment of "history" in our time. First, it can be seen that modernism's fixation on "history" comes into its own in the postmodernist novel, which, above all, tends to take "history" as its favored content (when it is not experimenting with overtly "fantastic" modes of literary representation). The "historical novel" is a dominant genre of postmodernist writing, but this dominance is shared with the fantasticist forms of science fiction, gothic tale, vampire and ghost story, monster story, and the like, but also develops into what we might call "historical fantasy," in which the fantastic is sought in the records of remote times and exotic places. Second, the postmodernist novel does not so much dissolve as, rather, transcend the distinction between history and literature by articulating, in a way different from that of the past, the concept of "fiction." In a famous essay, Linda Hutcheon dubbed the dominant forms of postmodernist writing "historiographical metafictions."[3] She wished to give a generic name to the writings of such authors as Thomas Pynchon, Toni Morrison, Günter Grass, Norman Mailer, Philip Roth, W. G. Sebald, J. M. Coetzee, and a host of others whose aim seems to be to show how what had been seen as the "order" of history could be shown to be as illusory as the "order" of "society" had proven to have been after Nazism, Stalinism, Fascism, and Maoism.

The irony in all this is that as postmodernist novelists proceed with their "disemplotment" of "history," an operation Jean-François Lyotard has called "the rejection of the *grands récits*" as a possible mode of representing "history," the novel approaches nearer and nearer to the kind of "historiography" favored by the heirs of Braudel and the structuralists. Disemplotment is also dethematization, so that the postmodernist past is as zany and farcical as any Marx Brothers movie. Indeed, as Roland Barthes argued in a famous essay titled "Le discours de l'histoire," avant-garde historical writing could be legitimately called "novelistic" (*romanesque*) insofar as it was understood that the "novel" (*roman*) being referred to by adjectivalization was the modernist novel in which events were indeterminate, characters indiscernible, and plots virtually nonexistent.[4]

On this view, the genres of a specifically modern literature would have been purged of all of their earlier metaphysical idealism, "brought down to earth," as it were, and used only to demonstrate the extent to which "historical reality" is no more substantial than any creature of "fiction." This is not quite the same as asserting that history or any other kind of reality *is* a fiction. It is rather to say that we may very well be able to come to a specifically historical understanding of reality only by way of the various fictions we impute to it.

Notes

It is thought that the Old French term *gendre* is the origin of the terms "gender" and "genre" in English. Some lexicographers give "son-in-law" as the meaning of *gendre*. In any event, the term "gender" was used to indicate both sexual kind and literary or discursive kind until the end of the eighteenth century. Thereafter, the term "genre" was used for literary kind and the term "gender" for sexual kind. The so-called "law of genre," instantiated by the quotation from Leviticus in my epigraph, has it that the "kinds" shall not be mixed, while the corresponding "law of gender" would have it that a proper marriage could only be between two persons of different genders, never between two persons of the same gender. Both the law of genre and the law of gender have the same end or purpose: to make sure that what has been separated into different kinds shall remain separated but that whatever within a given kind is different will be permitted—under the appropriate circumstances—to unite and reproduce properly.

In *The Elementary Structures of Kinship*, Claude Lévi Strauss argues for the parallelism between the rules governing the proper use of language and those governing the proper use of women in primitive societies. There appear to be rules governing the proper way of mixing the Same and rules governing the proper ways of mixing the Different. Literary and discursive "genres" can be seen as formalizations of such rules for the mixing of forms, the mixing of contents, and the mixing of a given kind of form with a given kind of content. The systems of prescriptions and prohibitions governing such mixtures are dealt with in Lévi-Strauss's well-known *Introduction to a Science of Mythology*, trans. John and Doreen Weightman (London: Jonathan Cape, Random House, 1970).

[Ed: See also Jacques Derrida, "The Law of Genre," trans. Avital Ronell, *Critical Inquiry* 7, no. 1, On Narrative (1980): 55–81.]

1. [Ed: Ralph Cohen (1917–2016) was the founder and longtime editor (1969–2009) of the journal *New Literary History*, in which this essay first appeared.]

2. Fredric Jameson, "Metacommentary" (1971), in *Ideologies of Theory* (London: Verso, 2008), 5–19.

3. Linda Hutcheon, *A Poetics of Postmodernism: History, Theory, Fiction* (New York: Routledge, 1988).

4. Roland Barthes, "Le discours de l'histoire" (1967), in *Le bruissement de la langue* (Paris: Seuil, 1984), 153–66. [Ed: Roland Barthes, "The Discourse of History," trans. Stephen Bann, in *Comparative Criticism: A Yearbook*, vol. 3, ed. E. S. Shaffer (Cambridge: Cambridge University Press, 1981), 3–20.]

CHAPTER 3

Postmodernism and Historiography [2009]

Postmodernism is a term that names, first, a certain epochal self-consciousness, a sense shared by many artists and intellectuals of having to work and create in a situation deprived of the certainties of twentieth-century modernism. Indeed, postmodernism arose on the ruins of the search for certainty, objectivity, foundations, and even truth itself that had underwritten the West's belief in "progress" since the time of the Enlightenment. Thus, the term "postmodernism" can be defined more by what it has denied, rejected, or simply abandoned of the philosophical and social endowment of the Enlightenment than by any positive cognitive content or utopian aspiration of a distinctively modern kind.

On the other hand, however, the term "postmodernism" also refers to a number of cultural movements arising after the 1950s, in architecture, literature, film, art, psychoanalysis, philosophy, and the human sciences in general, which purport to transcend the limitations, prejudices, and illusions of an artistic modernism of the kind represented in architecture by the International Style; in literature by T. S. Eliot, Ezra Pound, James Joyce, Franz Kafka, Virginia Woolf, Marcel Proust, Gertrude Stein; and in art by the historical avant-garde, namely Surrealism, Cubism, and Abstract Expressionism.

The two kinds of postmodernism share a suspicion of every kind of foundationalism: epistemological, ontological, ethical, and esthetic. This rejection of foundationalism includes the ideas—epistemological, ontological, ethical, and aesthetic—that have underwritten and authorized the kind of knowledge produced by historical research since the middle of the nineteenth century. This does not mean that postmodernists are uninterested in the past, in history, and its interpretation. On the contrary, many postmodernists believe that a specifically postmodernist idea of "history" provides the only basis for the kind of knowledge required by an emerging global society and the new cultural media that have made it possible. However, this postmodernist "history" has little in common with that posited as the basis for modern, scientific historical research. In fact, it is much closer to premodern conceptions of history, understood as a reserve of exempla to be drawn on for practical (political, pedagogical, ideological) purposes and as a discourse rather than a discipline.

Postmodernists—in architecture, the arts, literature, cinema, and philosophy—tend to view the past as a vast, inchoate, fragmented, decontextualized, and synchronic congeries of forms, media, genres, and ideas that can be treated as *objets trouvés* in the manner of Duchamp's "Fountain" (the inverted urinal that he signed "R. Mutt," exhibited in an art-space, thereby effecting its transformation into a work of art). For postmodernists, the "past"—irredeemably absent and accessible only by way of spoors, fragments, and traces—is the place of memory, reverie, and fantasy, and therefore of poetic inspiration, rather than a space of past human actions that can be recovered and represented more or less accurately "as it really was" (for scientifically oriented, modern professional historians). Postmodernists are much more interested in the meanings that, by means more or less artistic, can be produced by reflection on pastness than they are in truth understood as a finite set of true statements about discrete periods of history attested by a documentary record. There are few postmodernist histories because postmodernists reject what professional historians would recognize as scientific historiography.

Indeed, postmodernist treatments of "the past" are to be found predominantly in artistic works: "historical novels" (such as *Libra* and *Underworld* by Don DeLillo; J. M. Coetzee's *Foe*, John Banville's *The Untouchable*, Philip Roth's *American Pastoral* and *The Plot against America*), epic films (Daniel Vigne's *Le retour de Martin Guerre*, Richard Attenborough's *Ghandi*, Tony Richardson's *Charge of the Light Brigade*, or Oliver Stone's *JFK*) and documentaries (Claude Lanzmann's *Shoah*, or Alain Resnais's *Nuit et brouillard*), site constructions (such as Christo's "wrapping" of the Reichstag), comics (like Art Spiegelman's "Maus" and "Towers"), the paintings of Anselm Kiefer (or installations by Christian Boltanski), and museological revisionisms (such as Daniel Libeskind's "Jewish Museum" in Berlin), or witness literature (such as Primo Levi's *Se questo è un uomo*),[1] rather than in such attempts to write historiography in a postmodernist mode as Simon Shama's *Dead Certainties* and Carlo Ginzburg's *The Cheese and the Worms*.

Much of the postmodernist experimentation in the representation (or rather, the "presentation") of the past derives from dissatisfaction with traditional scientific history's inability or reluctance to deal effectively with the "extreme" events connected with the totalitarian regimes of the twentieth century: the Holocaust specifically, but also "industrialized genocide" in general, the use of atomic weaponry (Hiroshima, Nagasaki) and other arms of mass destruction (firebombing, antipersonnel mines, long-distance rocketry), world population explosion and migration, new kinds of diseases (AIDS), globalization, etc. A universal demand on the part of populations that had hitherto been treated as peripheral to the great events of history for representation of their experiences of such extreme events spawned new genres of testamentary and martyrological (witness) literature, video, and film. Therewith, the older opposition between history and memory was brought under question, and history as the corrector of memory soon came to be thought of as "history the suppressor of the memory of the oppressed."

Walter Benjamin's brief on behalf of the anonymous and the neglected of history received wide recognition as a critique of professional historiography's identification with history's "victors," interest primarily in the actions of great men, and association with centers of power and patronage.

Movements on the margin of professional writing, such as feminism, women's history, postcolonial studies, cultural studies, "history from below," and oppositional historiography, contributed to the general and growing disinterest in professional historical research, demeaned for its specialization, its preference for micro-phenomena, and its search for truth as against the desire for meaning.

The demand for meaning, interest in the oppressed of the past, call for inclusiveness in history's subject-matter, rejection of specialization, fascination with the experience of "witnesses" to the extreme events of history, and, finally, the belief that these extreme events augured the advent of a new kind of historicity—all this promoted attitudes towards the past and the study of it that correlated badly with the principles of "scientific historical research" inherited from the early twentieth century.

Within philosophy of history, which is to say, the philosophical study of the possibility and limits of the kind of knowledge produced by professional historians, such attitudes converged with the outcome of debates that had been going on since the 1930s and 1940s involving idealists (Collingwood, Croce), positivists (Popper), existentialists (Heidegger and Sartre), phenomenologists (Gadamer, Merleau-Ponty, Ricoeur), and a group whom I wish to call historicists (Raymond Aron and Ernst Bloch, Isaiah Berlin and Friedrich Meinecke) over whether history could ever properly be called a "science" at all. More relevant for the moment is the extent to which this debate bore upon certain questions and topics peculiar to its postmodernist aftermath: topics having to do with language, discourse, and narrative, on the one side, and questions having to do with the canonical view on the relation between history and literature, on the other.

Postmodernist treatments of the past and history (not all treatments of the past are "historical") are typically criticized by historians (when they deign referring to them at all) for espousing such beliefs that the past has no reality, that history is (nothing but) a text, that the principal problem of historical representation is that of narrativization, that, when it comes to representing the past, there is no important distinction between fact and fiction, and that, finally, historical phenomena are best made sense of by storytelling rather than by model building and causal analysis of chains of events.

It has to be said that, with a few exceptions (Richard Evans, Keith Jenkins, and Ewa Domanska being the most notable), these notions about postmodernism are more lamented than documented and responded to with scientific rigor by professional historians. To sympathetic representations of certain postmodernist ideas (by Ricoeur, Hartog, Derrida, Foucault, and myself, for example), professional historians tend to respond with warnings of the social dangers of the relativism and skepticism inherent in them. Two ideas especially are subject to the most criticism: the relation between history and literature; and the concept of the world as a text.

Discussions on the relationship between history and literature go back to Ranke's famous criticism of Sir Walter Scott for mixing historical fact with fiction. Historical studies were transformed into a science by excluding a number of discourses and practices commonly mixed with historiography prior to Ranke's time: theology, philosophy, rhetoric, and romance. These exclusions were implemented in the interest of committing historical studies to a truthful, by which was meant a factually accurate, representation of the past. It had the effect of dividing Western culture's efforts to comprehend its past between those of professional historians, concerned to establish facts about the past, and a host of others—philosophers, novelists, poets, and, increasingly, social scientists—who were more interested in the meaning of those facts for the understanding of the present as they were in their significance for understanding the past. This issue arose in the post–World War II years with respect to the Holocaust or Shoah.

As the Nazi genocide of the Jews receded into the past, becoming in the process a distinctively "historical" event, survivors of it especially became concerned less with the fact of its occurrence than with what it felt like to experience such an event and what it implied about the society (presumed to be enlightened, humanistic, humane, and rational) that had been responsible for this event or, in many instances, had either aided in its execution or simply stood by and let it happen without significant resistance. With the exception of a few manifestly pathological pseudo-historians, scientists, and scholars (known as revisionists), no one could really deny that the event had occurred, but the occurrence of it and the way in which it had been carried out brought under question most of the basic presuppositions of that scientific and humanistic culture on which the West had prided itself since the Renaissance. The growth of a large body of "witness" testimony, about the Holocaust but also about other genocides, about the experience of decolonization, about migration, and about the horrors of modern warfare, showed that "artistic" writing (such as Levi's *Se questo è un uomo*) or cinema (such as Landsmann's *Shoah*) were infinitely better suited to conveying the "shock" of new, contemporary experiences than were the dry, measured, and antiseptic tones of the conventional historical narrator. Result: the return among postmodernists of a desire for the artistic representation of history as a means of dealing not only with the past but also with the present as history.

"The present as history": In *Mimesis*, his magisterial account of the growth of realism in Western literature, Erich Auerbach argued that the basis of modern literary realism—from Stendhal, Balzac, Dickens, and, later, Gogol and Tolstoy, Mann, Proust, and Woolf—lay in the treatment of the present as history. This is to say that, whereas in the past, history had been about only the past, in the early nineteenth century "the present" was added to "history," which now became, according to Koselleck, a kind of causal force in its own right, such that people could now speak about "historical forces" and "historical processes" that changed that stable present from which one had formerly viewed a past "over and done with" into a heaving, moving, violent platform from which one could never confidently view either past or future.

It was in this sense that the literary realism of the nineteenth century had taken as its referent—its ultimate referent, to be sure—historical reality, which it proceeded to map out and examine in depth in ways that professional historians, fixated on war, politics, and great men, could never have imagined. This was the real legacy of Sir Walter Scott, dismissed by Ranke as a romancier, but actually the inventor of a mode of studying the past in such a way as to show its relevance to the present as a relation of figure to fulfillment. And this interest in history as the ultimate referent of "serious" literature remained alive in literary modernism—in Proust, Joyce, Eliot, Pound, Woolf, Brecht, Stein, Musil, etc. The point was that history had to be endowed not only with truth but also with meaning—which meant symbolization.

Now, the important point about literary modernism is that the opposition between factual and fictional discourse gives way to a simple difference among various kinds of writing. The principal distinction is between literary writing and utilitarian writing, wherein the latter is distinguished from the former by the "set" (*Einstellung*) towards the message that deflects significance from the referent to the code in which the discourse is articulated. On this view of the matter, the distinction between factual and fictional writing has less to do with the reality or unreality of the referent than the degree of "literariness" (the use of literary devices) manifested in the presentation. Thus, there can be literary writing that is factual (a historical work such as Huizinga's *Autumn of the Middle Ages* would be an example) and literary writing that is fictional (Joyce's *Finnegans Wake*, for example).

But if by "factual" writing one means writing that has the "real world" for its referent, then a work such as Thomas Mann's *Buddenbrooks* or *The Magic Mountain* or Robert Musil's *The Man without Qualities* are quite as "factual" as anything written by social historians in the modern age. And so too for a work such as DeLillo's *Libra*, Norman Mailer's *Castle in the Forest*, Banville's *The Untouchable*, or J. M. Coetzee's *Disgrace*. Like Tolstoy's *War and Peace*,[2] these works seek to grasp the historical substance or the essence of an age, a period, a time. In order to do this, they must, unlike the writer of a report on what has been found in an archive, narrate and emplot the events to which they refer, thereby giving them dramatic weight and symbolic depth.

Narrativity in historiography, increasingly disdained by modern scientific historians as mere rhetorical flourish, ornament, or ideology (Braudel), thus returns in postmodernist historical novels as the paradigm for mediating between being (factuality) and value (meaning). All of which returns us to the distinction between history as a science and history as a discourse, and the relation of postmodernist notions of the text and textuality to the conceptualization of "history" (as both an object of study and of representation).

Parerga: Postmodernist historical thought is present oriented and is primarily interested in the past only insofar as it can be used to serve the present. Thus, Jean-François Lyotard is only half right in finding the origin of postmodernism in the rejection of the great schemata (*grands récits*) of universal history, which purported to disclose history's direction, aim, and meaning. Professional historians and philosophers of history had dismissed these great schemata as myth and ideology long before Lyotard reported their abandonment. But postmodernism goes further and rejects not only the *grands récits* of providence, progress, the dialectic of the World Spirit (Hegel), Marxism, etc., but the *petits récits* of professional historians as well; both kinds of historiography are deemed irrelevant to the practical needs of our epoch. Central among these needs is "coming to terms with" a past "that won't go away," especially the past of the Nazi genocide, which belied the myths of progress, enlightenment, and humanism sustained by professional historians in the service of the state and bourgeois society since the time of the French Revolution.

For postmodernists, "the historical past" of the professional historians is an abstraction that never existed except in history books, was never experienced by anyone (except, possibly, certain deluded historians), and is meaningful ultimately only to professional historians themselves. What interests postmodernists is the past that continues to exist in the present, but less as heritage and tradition than as phantasm, memory, the "return of the repressed" (*le retour du refoulé, l'après-coup*), ghost, enigma, threat, or burden. This past must be *perlaboré*, its burden lifted from the present, so that living men can go into the future without the old delusions.

Here historiology helps the *travail du deuil* (work of mourning) that follows upon the dissolution of the great myths of Christianity, humanism, progress, Marxism, substantive rationality, capitalism, metaphysics, the heroic subject, and the bourgeois historiography. Therewith it becomes possible, postmodernists aver, to use as a place of fantasy, pleasure, a play of forms, even of utopian possibility. This formulation of the post-modernist notions of the past and history is framed in vaguely Freudian terms in the interest of highlighting their potential therapeutic func-tion (as against the merely didactic function of traditional, professional historiography). This formulation also allows one to account for what the critics of postmodernism take to be its fallacies, errors, and outright delusions.

First, postmodernists question professional historians' presumption that they alone have the authority to decide what history is, how it must be studied, and what uses can legitimately be made of historical knowl-edge. Postmodernists, per contra, tend to believe that nobody owns his-tory, that anyone has a right to study it for purposes both theoretical and practical, that the past of history and the past of memory are quite different things, and that finding out what happened in the past is less important than finding out "what it felt like" for the patients as well as the agents of past events. This is why postmodernists favor the genre of the "testimony," the use of experimental, even surrealistic literary de-vices and mythological plots, favor cinematic "special effects" and po-etic tropes and figures, and encourage a mixture of documentary with "fictional" techniques for the presentation (*Darstellung*) of a past more indeterminate than clear in outline, more grotesque than heroic in its stature, more malleable than fixed in its form. Disregard for the propri-eties of professional historiography exposes postmodernists to charges of relativism and skepticism, which are often treated more as sins than as possible intellectual positions. Relativism, it is alleged, leads to episte-mological and moral anarchy and is therefore to be resisted on ethical as well as cognitive grounds. So, too, skepticism is to be opposed on moral as well as cognitive grounds: it is supposed to lead to Pyrrhonism, nihil-ism, and chaos. It is as if historical truth were the only kind of truth we had, and any attenuation of it would shake the foundations of civiliza-tion itself.

To these charges postmodernists reply: it is true that postmodern-ism is skeptical of professional historians not only because their work is boring or, alternatively, sentimental, but because they seem themselves to be in the pay of special interest groups—the state, wealthy patrons, corporations, the university itself. Moreover, their purpose seems to be to keep nonprofessionals from poaching on their turf, as if the past were a piece of real estate and access to it consigned to professional scholars alone. Finally, one can distinguish between a metaphysical skepticism that denies the possibility of any kind of knowledge and a skepticism about the kind of knowledge produced by a specific group, such as of a gild of professional scholars whose methods resemble those of lawyers or, in the worst cases, astrologers, while trying to pose as "scientists" pure and simple.

And so too for the charge of relativism, which is typically equated with the idea that all points of view are equally valid (or invalid), that there is no possibility of choosing among them on rational grounds, that, therefore, "anything goes" in thought and action, and that, as a consequence, ethical principles are a fraud and morality an illusion.

Finally, postmodernists maintain that all knowledge is not only "knowledge about" particular things but also "knowledge for" particular social groups and cultural projects. Thus, the validity of any given presentation of the past and history is to be assessed in terms of its utility for the group for which it has been produced.

The criterion is pragmatic or pragmatist, and it holds as much for the natural sciences as it does for the human sciences. Historical studies have their own histories, they vary from time to time, place to place, and group to group. Which is why histories formulated on the basis of religious beliefs—such as Saint Augustine's *City of God* or Jean Froissart's *Chroniques*—are not less for their failure to conform to the criteria of contemporary professional historiography. And so too for the idea or vision of history to be found in literary, poetic, and other kinds of artistic media. If, as Ricoeur argued, historical consciousness is a product of a particular kind of experience of temporality, then the representation no less than the analysis of this experience requires all the resources that art as well as science can provide. Indeed, the effort to change the subject of history, to imagine a different past from that constructed for dominant groups of the industrial age, and to provide a historical basis for critiquing the immediate past and escaping from the institutional constrictions it has placed upon the present, all this seems to be taken more seriously by literary and cinematic, video and computer artists, than by professional historians.

The vision of a future idea of history is to be found in a postmodernist art that is more conceptual than mimetic, more "writerly" than "readerly," more interested in the symbol than in the algorithm. Postmodernist writing, for example, transcends the conventions of traditional, narrativistic, and fabulistic storytelling. This did not mean that postmodernists had any greater faith in the *petits récits* of professional historiography. For postmodernism also rejects the version of the past and history produced by professional historians and the discourses of *l'humanisme universitaire.* They reject humanistic history's naïve faith in empiricism and trust in the "document," its belief in a "subject of history" as an "action hero," conqueror of inferior peoples, and carrier of civilization. For postmodernists, professional historians study the past as a thing-in-itself, write for other professional historians, derive no lessons of any use to the present, and seek to repress imaginative uses of history in the service of life (as in Nietzsche's second *Untimely Meditation*).

Like Foucault, postmodernists are less interested in the past as a thing-in-itself than as a means of comprehending the present. Where history offers no insight into the present, it is condemned as mere antiquarianism. For postmodernists, truth is a semantic, rather than an epistemological issue. Statements about the past and about their relevance for comprehending the present have less to do with what is said than with what is meant in what is said. Consequently, the significance of an utterance—whether about the present or about the past—cannot be separated from the context within which it is uttered. This idea of truth opens postmodernism to charges of relativism: cultural, moral, epistemic.

Postmodernism's suspicion of the possibility of deriving universals from the study of history exposes it to charges of skepticism. It should be noted, however, that skepticism about the possibility of knowledge regarding things no longer perceivable is one thing; skepticism about the very possibility of knowledge of anything, absent or present, is quite another.

Postmodernists do not deny that we can have knowledge of the past. Their point is, rather, that we must use the imagination along with reason in the construction of that knowledge. And by imagination they mean not merely fantasy, dream, reverie but also *poiesis*, after the manner of Vico, the Romantics, and Michelet. Only thus can the ethical claims of memory—individual and collective—be reconciled with the epistemological claims of reason.

Academic or university historiography is too "disinterested" to bridge the gap that postmodernists perceive to exist between the truth of past facts and the meaning of this truth for the understanding of modernity. Like Foucault, postmodernists are interested in the past not as an end in itself but for what it can tell us about the present. This means that the establishment of the facts about the past must be followed by the interpretation of them: for above the level of atomic facts—such as dates and specific occurrences about which there can be no doubt—there arise questions about the past and history for which there can be no factual answers.

When it comes to the meaning of the big events of modern history—the French Revolution, capitalism, industrialism, Nazism, even the Shoah—events so important to our own identities that we cannot not confront them, there can be no definitive answers. But of the making of interpretations, there is no end. We can only multiply interpretations and thereby undermine any dogmatic claims about the past, history, and human nature thereby. Since the past is by definition no longer open to perception, we can never be certain that any description of it or of any of its elements is adequate to it. In this respect, the past differs from the present, which, in principle, is observable. But what we mean by the present is as much a construction of thought and imagination, fantasy and hope or fear, as the past. Thus, caught between two abysses—a past that is dead and a future that is still unborn—we must choose to live in ambiguity, ambivalence, and despair.

The world appears to postmodernists in the manner in which Heidegger and Sartre presented it in the 1930s. Neither philosophy nor science can help us. Whence the postmodernist recourse to art, literary writing, and the poetic imagination for dealing with the aporias of historical existence.

In conclusion, let us consider some of the various ways of viewing history:

(1) Since its beginnings, history has aspired to the status of a science according to standards of scientificity currently prevailing in the time and places in which it has been practiced. Since science itself has a history, which means that what it consists of is constantly changing, history's effort to become scientific is also constantly changing. This is why the different ways that historians construe the past and its relationship to the present appear to be incommensurable. While some historians typically see continuity and regular progress in history's millennial effort to become scientific, others just as typically register its continual failure to do so. None of this matters very much as long as a given society feels itself to be unproblematically connected to its (or the) past. It is when the past is felt to be a burden on the present, a debt rather than a legacy, that history

may come to be thought of as a fake or pseudo-science and demands for its supplementation by "real" science, religion, art, or metaphysics called for.

(2) Real historians, it is alleged, are interested in the truth and nothing but the truth about the past, without any ideological preconceptions or intentions, and in a spirit of objectivity and neutrality towards their subject-matter. Their principal activity is research, particularly in archives and especially in "original" sources or documents. They sift evidence, analyze data, construct arguments, and offer proofs about what happened in some domain of the past insofar as the record allows. The facts of the matter preexist the historian's investigation of them; he (or more rarely, she) "finds" them rather than invents them. The recent past and present are not proper subjects of history because a certain time must have passed before one can know how certain processes "came out," eventuated, or concluded. So, too, one should not undertake to investigate any aspect of the past before the relevant archival materials have been made available. When the research is finished, the historian writes up his/her findings in a sober and severe style. No levity or rhetorical flourish can be allowed; irony is reserved for those amateurs and laity who think that "history" can be written by anybody, that the past is a general human legacy, and that anyone has the right to study it as best they can.

(3) When it comes to claims to producing real knowledge (as against information) about the past, history must moot certain, potentially disturbing enigmas of temporality, the aporias of memory, and the paradoxes of desire. (It must get on with the task of finding out "what happened" in the past and of presenting it in an appropriately domesticated form, so as to feign that death is not terminal and that the fruits of prior human labor are not totally lost to human memory.) Enigmas of temporality: the sense of at once being, having been, yet to be, and ultimately not be. Aporias of memory: the sense that the past is in me and yet is absent from me, that I can recall this past and, at the same time, lose it, that, in the end, I cannot trust memory but, at the same time, I cannot escape it. Paradoxes of desire: the sense that I want what I do not have and have what I do not want, that I want what I cannot have and have what I ought not want, that I do not know what I want and do not want what I know.

(4) In this essay, "history" refers to Western and for the most part modern Western notions about the past, the relation between past and present, and the uses to which historical knowledge can be put. Although all cultures and societies have an interest in the past, only a few of them have developed a specifically "historical" approach to its study. And although Western historians have claimed that a specifically historical way of studying the past and its relation to the present has universal validity, it would seem that such a way, mode, or idea presupposes notions about human nature, sociality, production, value, and meaning that are identifiably Western in kind. And indeed, Western notions of historicality have spread only to those parts of the world in which other, specifically Western beliefs and institutions—such as Newtonian science, humanism, Christianity, capitalism—have already taken root. It should not, however, be thought that "history" in the West designates a single, monolithic orthodoxy regarding what it consists of, how it should be studied, and the ends to which it can legitimately be put. Western historical sciences want to be "scientific," but since modern Western historical thought has always fallen short of the ideals of science prevailing at any given time in its development, it has generated a number of different ideas of history conforming to the intellectual and artistic ideologies predominating at any given moment in its evolution.

Times of social, economic, and political crisis provoke debates between representatives of these different ways of viewing history and about programs for the reform of historical thinking and its practices. It can hardly be denied that the West and (because of the dominance of Western institutions and practices worldwide) the rest of the world are currently undergoing transformations so extreme as to bring traditional institutions and values under question everywhere. It is therefore eminently understandable that historical thought and institutions should be subjected to the same criticism that is being launched against the other aspects of the intellectual and artistic endowment of the West.

As a would-be science, historiography neither foresaw the crisis of modernism nor provides any advice about how to overcome it. Insofar as current calls for the revision of historical thought are based upon a sense of radical change and transition to a new, hitherto unimaginable world-system, these can be termed "postmodernist."

Notes

[Ed: This is the text of a lecture given at a "Special Public Opening Symposium" at Ritsumeikan University, Japan, titled "After Metahistory: Lecture on Postmodernism by Professor Hayden White," on October 22, 2009.]

1. [Ed: See "Figural Realism in Witness Literature: On Primo Levi's *Se questo è un uomo*," in volume 1 of White, *The Ethics of Narrative*, chap. 9.]

2. [Ed: See "Against Historical Realism: A Reading of Leo Tolstoy's *War and Peace*," in volume 1 of White, *Ethics of Narrative*, chap. 15.]

CHAPTER 4

Anomalies of the Canon
in Modernity [2011]

> What if there were, lodged within the heart of
> the law itself, a law of impurity or a principle of
> contamination? And suppose the condition for
> the possibility of the law were the *a priori* of a
> counter-law, an axiom of impossibility that would
> confound its sense, order, and reason?
>
> —Derrida, "The Law of Genre"

Everyone knows, I presume, what a canon is
or ought to be. A canon is a set of rules, principles, doctrines, images,
or texts incarnating, representing, or containing what are held to be absolute values of the class of objects to which they belong. If the objects
in question are, for example, sacred writings, the canon will consist of
those books that have been determined by the relevant authority to be
of unimpeachable holiness. If the class in question is law, the canon
consists of those statutes, prescriptions, and prohibitions deemed to be
absolutely inviolable, so as to constitute a paradigm of the very essence
of legality itself. A constitution, which can be considered to be a document that specifies what can count as a genuine law within a given domain, would be an example of a canon. So, too, the Mosaic Code or the
Ten Commandments would have the same function in ancient Hebrew
religion. In the legal canon, the law of the law or the lawness of the law
shines forth as a measure of the very idea of legality. In literature and
art, the canon is thought to consist of certain works and writings that
contain or manifest the essence of art, certain classics that serve not
only as examples of art but also as paradigms against which the artness
of any putative artwork can be measured.

Our stated topic,[1] however, is not so much the canon, canonicity,
or even exemplarity as, rather, the relationship between "Author(ity)"

and "the Canon," an ambiguous disjunctive conjunction that allows us to construe this relationship pretty much as we wish. Are we to be concerned with the *authority* of the canon, which is to say the authority that authorizes the canon, or are we to think about the *canon's authority*, its aura of holiness or its status as paradigm *ne plus ultra*? Moreover, we are asked to deal with these matters within the context of another conjunction, namely, institutionalization and questioning that, I surmise, has to do with the fact that the canon, any canon, in any field, has the power of an institution—an administrative power, a power of command and demand like the law, so that the very possibility of questioning the canon, of adding to it, or subtracting from it, is thrown into question. Finally, all of this is to be begun from within the field of "literature" and the transition of its practices from High to Late Modernity.

Now, contemporary discussions of the canon or canonicity began in earnest after the forces unleashed by the 1960s had pretty much lost their force, and it became obvious that certain fields of cultural production needed some principles by which to assess what was creative and what was destructive in their pretended practitioners. The principal casualty of the 1960s was authority itself—"Question Authority" was a favorite *graffito* of the time. This demotion of authority was liberating in the arts, sciences, politics, and sexuality, but was deadly to the priesthoods, the professorates, the judiciaries, and moralists of every stripe who had formerly spoken for and in the name of canons. It is not surprising that when the dust settled, it was the judiciary, the professorate, the priesthood, and moralists of every stripe who began to raise the question of the canon or a canon by which to give form and order to fields that threatened to fall into anarchy. There was no significant call for a canon in literary writing or the arts, but there was such a call among professors of literature, conservative judges and jurisprudents, the priesthoods, and defenders of patriarchal sexual domination. Peter Goodrich, in a work entitled *Oedipus Lex*,[2] points out that the law typically and consistently seeks to control three things: property, women, and language. It will not be surprising to find that those who want a canon usually want a law, and that the law they want is the kind described by Goodrich.

In a field like literary studies who, other than professional scholars of literature, needs a canon? Only conservative writers—writers who wish to work within the confines of a tradition—speak about a canon. No avant-garde writer needs or wants a canon. No, it is the critics and scholars who want a canon. For a radical writer or thinker, canons exist to be broken.

The paradigm of the idea of canonicity was for the greater part of European history the Christian New Testament, which, although it took a discrete number of years to constitute itself, served as the model of every institution claiming the authority of divine law for millennia afterward. And although this canon was regarded as self-constituting and self-authorizing, the secular history of its formation is a story of conflict between orthodoxy and heterodoxy in which the question of the canonicity of the canon was often the center of debate and discussion. Thus, while this canon of canons constituted itself, the question of what really belonged to the canon, and what did not, required the authority of the Church for its determination. On this issue, it was a conflict between reductionists and expansionists: reductionists like Marcion of Sinope who wanted to admit to the canon only a fragment of one gospel and a few of the letters of Saint Paul, or an expansionist like Montanus who, on the basis of his own receptivity of the Holy Spirit, wished to expand the canon indefinitely and infinitely. It is obvious, then, that not only the elements or items in the canon require someone or some institution to interpret them, but the canonicity of the canon itself requires interpretation. It is the same with modern political constitutions, but with one difference: constitutions can be amended, while a canon requires interpreters.

Of course, to speak about a *canon* in a field like literature, painting, music, even architecture, is to speak metaphorically. For, whatever other connotations the term *canon* may carry with it—list, collection, catalogue, etc.—the baseline of its meaning is "law." In the field of jurisprudence, a canon would be both a given statute and an instantiation of the power of the law to engender itself, a law of the law. A law, any law, differentiates and hierarchizes. Every law says, "This and not this" and in doing so, sets up the possibility of saying, "And not *not* this." Which creates the category of the permitted but still suspect, since whatever is positive in "And not *not* this" is the result of a negation of a negative. "Not *not* this" creates a gray zone in which the border between what is legal and what is not legal tends to dissolve. A canon in literature does not say that a specific genre, kind, or category is illegal; it says that certain kinds of genres are not *not* legal without being exactly *il*legal. Any group can agree on a set of masterpieces, on the one side, and a vast congeries of works that have nothing in common with these classics, on the other. It is the *tertium quid* that requires critics, judges, and commentators.

In a field such as literature or in the arts in general, wherever there is a demand for or a defense of a canon, it is a demand or possibly a wish for law. In literary studies, the canon of classics defended by critics and ordinary readers carries the authority, if not the force, of law. In this talk I am going to consider some of the anomalies that inform demands for or defenses of a canon for culture in general, or for any of its various domains, within a framework in which the notions of art in general and literature specifically have lost whatever substance they were once believed to possess. The end of a belief in substance is what, it can be argued, informs (or deforms) modernist and especially postmodernist conceptions, not only of art and literature but also of the law and politics as well.

I

In a polemical Prologue to his book *An Appetite for Poetry* (1989),[3] the late great literary critic Frank Kermode presented an argument for the desirability of a canon of literary classics against those who, at the time, seemed to regard canons as instruments of the "cultural racism" of "white males," made up of "static monuments" to "political oppression," utterly "totalizing" in their psycho-social effects. He pointed out that canons—even religious ones—change over time, are responsive to the body of commentaries produced by their devotees and their critics, and contain as many self-deconstructing texts as "totalizing" ones. And while granting that canons do embody traditions, he notes that, without some equivalent of the notion of tradition, there would be no need for "the special form of attention elicited by canonical texts; and so, incidentally, no room for such special forms of attention as deconstruction." He concludes by stressing the contradiction involved in wishing, at one and the same time, to abolish the canon and reform it by admitting to it *indiscriminately* the work of anyone or any group just because they have been oppressed, marginalized, or otherwise mistreated by dominant constituencies. And he remarks on the fatuity of thinking that either of these goals—destroying the canon or elevating the oppressed to membership in it—could be accomplished by "doing theory" rather than by writing literature or practicing literary criticism.

But Frank Kermode does not stop at criticism of those who oppose a canon for literature. He also points out what has been missed in literature by those whose theoretical or simply prejudicial "foreunderstanding" of texts of all kinds blinds them to what is distinctive of literary texts in particular. It is, Kermode says, "poetry" that gives to literary texts the kind of density and fascination lacking in ordinary, everyday, and technical writing, but also in the kind of "bad" literature and art purveyed by the mass media.

Kermode was not, then, defending the canon and the notion of canonicity on the ground of pragmatic convenience, in the way that conservatives and reactionaries of all stripes are inclined to do. He was not saying that, if we have no canon, culture is doomed. He was defending *the* or *a* canon on the basis of what he took to be an obvious fact, namely, that readers both common and specialized return again and again to those texts in their traditions they deem worthy of the kind of "attentive" reading that *poetic* writing always elicits, demands, or otherwise authorizes.

Kermode uses the term "poetry" and the adjective "poetic" in a technical way. The literary work will be more or less "poetic" in the extent to which what Roman Jakobson and the Czech formalists called "the poetic function" predominates among the several functions activated in every act or scene of communication. The poetic function Jakobson defined as the particular "set" (*Einstellung*) towards the message by which to endow it with value or worth and to give it what Freud called an *unheimlich* (uncanny), hyper-semantic valence.

For Frank Kermode, then, as I understand him, the canon of literature or of any art would consist not of a list or catalogue of classical forms or (thought-or-value) contents, but rather of works in which poeticity or the poetic function predominated. Here poeticity would be manifested in the difficulty with which the work resisted any facile distinction between its form and its content, indeed, the way in which content could be seen as form and form as content. Nor is poetry to be understood as a contrary of (opposed to) prose, any more than poetic utterance is to be opposed to rhetorical, or conceptual, or logical discourse. Nor is it to be understood as "figurative" as against "literal" speech. Poetry, or the poetic, is not conceptually opposed or opposable to anything. It takes its rise on the boundary between what Kermode calls "easy opinion," on the one side, and the enigmas of human existence that always recede to just beyond the advancing frontiers of our scientific knowledges, on the other.

In other words, a canon of literature, or the literary, or of literarity would consist of those works that are not only written poetically but, in being so written, provide us with rules, principles, procedures, models, or paradigms for *reading* poetically as well. And because poetic writing is not only always new but also authorizes a new *kind* of writing, it always brings under question any tendency towards a dogmatic conception of what writing or literature has to be in order to be recognized as "good." Literary writing is always at the edge of what has hitherto been established as normative, just as it is always "at the end of the era" in which it has been produced. And this is why the canon of literature (the literary canon), unlike the canons of religion, of the law, and of politics, has nothing to do with any notions of the sacred, morality, legality, or propriety, except insofar as these are brought under question by the law of invention exercised in every instance of poetic utterance.

Now, in spite of the relative modesty of Kermode's proposal, it can be easily seen as an example of a tactic by which a priesthood, professorate, or any other "academy" justifies its own claim to a certain kind of (what Pierre Bourdieu calls) "symbolic capital," by virtue of the putative difficulty of its chosen objects of study. Kermode's argument for a canon of literary classics turns upon his belief in the desirability of designating a corpus, more or less generously defined, of classics that can be held to possess the quality of "poeticity." These writings require a special kind of reader, not because ordinary readers cannot appreciate their special qualities, but because these works invite the cultivation of an "appetite" for the very extraordinary qualities these things seem to possess. In a review of Harold Bloom's idiosyncratic choice of classics for a world canon of literature, Kermode makes it quite clear that what Bloom (and he) are defending is not just "literature" but also aesthetics or more properly "the aesthetic." The identification of the poetic with the aesthetic is one of the linchpins of modern ideologies of literature. But there are many who think that this identification is unjustified, that the idea of the poetic is much more extensive than that of the aesthetic, that "aestheticism" is itself a Platonizing ideology that deprives *poiesis* of its radical power; so that the current crisis of the canon or canonicity might well be a symptom of a deeper crisis, a crisis of the aesthetic. For if the poetic is subordinated to the aesthetic as its law and authority, what is the justification of this subordination? Unlike the aesthetic, the poetic is a principle of action and making, while the aesthetic is a principle of patience and reception. Even T. S. Eliot professed to believe that poetic genius showed itself in the poet's capacities of self-abnegation and willingness to serve as an instrument or medium of tradition rather than a creator in her own right.

II

Here I am going to change the subject or rather swerve to another topic I believe to be relevant to the question of the kind of authority a canon can lay claim to in a post-aesthetic period of art history. I want to raise the question of the relevance to our discussion of "authority and the canon," of a question asked—poetically, to be sure—by Jacques Derrida in a famous essay precisely on canonicity and the law—in this case, the "law of genre," which, to be sure, he defined as "the law of the law of genre," and which he glossed as "the law of the genre of the law," and which, it turns out, is nothing but the idea that there must be law if only to permit a difference between degrees of impurity.[4] Every law is a law of genre; and since there is no such thing as a pure genre, there is no such thing as a pure law.

Saint Paul famously said, "There is no sin before the law," by which, the glossators hastily point out, he did not mean that there had not been any impure acts before the revelation of the Law, because indeed, given the lesson of the Fall of all men in the fall of Adam, there could have been nothing but impure acts before the Law came to establish the distinction between ordinary, everyday impurity and the kind of impurity caused by "transgression" of the law.[5] What the law provided was a canon by which to distinguish between different kinds of impure acts, ordinary or common, on the one hand, and specifically forbidden or illegal, on the other. It was this distinction that led Derrida to formulate a question that brings us—or at least, me—up short in my thought about canons, canonicity, and that law of which every canon is supposed to be a pure instantiation. Derrida: "What if there were, lodged within the heart of the law itself, a law of impurity or a principle of contamination? And suppose the condition for the possibility of the law were the *a priori* of a counter-law, an axiom of impossibility that would confound its sense, order, and reason?"[6]

In other words, suppose that, at the heart of every canon of every law ever conceived or promulgated, lay—necessarily and inevitably—the presupposition that the law in question was impossible to fulfill.

Awakening on the morning of "one fine day" to find two officers of the court standing by his bed to inform him of his impending trial (*Prozess*), Franz Kafka's Josef K. asks of what he has been accused. To which the officers of the court reply that he is accused of being guilty. K., law abiding citizen that he is, undertakes to find out how he can be guilty of something when he has hardly ever thought of doing anything. His visits to and investigations of the law lead only to the discovery that the law exists to confirm the guilt of everyone falling under its jurisdiction. This is a poetic insight, since it shows that the dream of innocence is nothing but a sublimated inversion of the nightmare of contamination.

K.'s study of the law, its institutions, and its practitioners yields no insight into its origin or authority. He discovers, if anything, that the law is there to goad him into confirming his own guilt for being guilty and forcing him to "justiciate" himself.

The question of a canon of literature would then be a question of the relation of poetry (or the poetical) to the law. "We have art in order not to die of the truth"—that is Nietzsche. But that means that, if the law is the truth, then we have poetry in order not to die of the law.

Something like this insight seems to lie behind or within Kermode's distinction between religious, legal, and political canons, on the one side, and modern cultural or artistic canons, on the other. The impurity of canons would provide a justification for the kinds of changes that canons undergo by those geniuses who perceive the need for a change of canon in response to historical change. This would account for Kermode's insistence that traditions transform themselves in the way that T. S. Eliot, in a famous statement about "Tradition and the Individual Talent," proposed in 1919. Traditions and the works that constituted their "classics" changed at the behest of poetic talents who had grasped their need of revision due to the impurities that still remained even within the most nearly perfect of their classical instantiations. (Eliot was speaking about literary traditions, classics, and canons, not religious ones.) Literature too fell under the law of the law, or the law of the impurity of every genre of literary or artistic expression, however canonical it appeared to be.

But this idea of an impurity or lack or want of some sort in the literary canon allows one to distinguish between premodern and modernist canons on the basis of the presumed revisability of the latter as against the resistance to change characteristic of the former kind of canon. Indeed, insofar as the very idea of canonicity takes its rise—in the West at least—in the example of the New Testament, the canon of which was declared closed by the Church as early as the fifth century AD, it is easy to see how the modern canons could be seen to differ from ancient ones by their openness to change. But—and here comes the difference between modern or modernist notions of canonicity and their postmodernist counterparts—as any game theorist knows, it is one thing to change the rules of a game, and quite another to conceive a game without rules altogether. And I think that this latter conception is what underlies and authorizes the anti-canonicity of postmodernist art and literature.

Pierre Bourdieu is a prominent advocate of the idea that modern art differs from its premodern, academic, or traditionalist counterpart due to the differences between traditionalist rule-*governed* activity, on the one hand, and modern rule-*changing* activity, on the other. In his studies of Flaubert (*The Rules of Art: Genesis and Structure of the Literary Field*) and Manet (*Manet: A Symbolic Revolution*) as well as the idea of "cultural capital" ("Cultural Reproduction and Social Reproduction"),[7] Bourdieu argues that modernism is created by Flaubert in literature and by Manet in painting by their transformations of what could count as "literature" and as "painting" as against the dogmas prevailing in the societies in which they worked, dogmas sustained by institutions (the State, patrons, market, and audiences) with interests in keeping things *un*changed. Flaubert not only changed conventional notions about what could and could not serve as the subject-matter of literature and the range of forms (genres) in which this subject matter could be presented; he also changed the rules for determining what could count as "literature" and what could not. For example, Flaubert successfully substituted the idea of "style" for that of "taste" as the dominant attribute of any writing aspiring to the status of "literature." And so, too, for Manet in the history of painting, or at least the history of painting in nineteenth-century France: Manet successfully challenged the prevailing "academic" conception of what could legitimately serve as the subject matter of artistic painting and the notion of the style or technique of presentation in which such subject matter could be properly presented.

Bourdieu emphasizes that these changes were not a result only of the "genius" of the innovators: that both Flaubert in literature and Manet in painting had themselves been masters of the canons they would overturn and, more importantly, belonged to a network of other artists as interested as they were in changing the rules of the game in which they played. Finally, both artists enjoyed the receptivity of newly established social groups and institutions—especially the connoisseur and "capitalistic" art market—in whose interest it was to break the hold of the French Academy and the state on ideas regarding what "proper" art consisted of. All this combined or came together at a time and place that permitted a change from the rules of the game prevailing in one "field" of cultural production to a new set of rules that both changed the game and the way it could be played for the foreseeable future.

Thus, according to Bourdieu, it is not that modern art and literature are anti-canonical (any more than Lutheranism was anti-canonical) as, rather, that they have different rules of the game and consequently different canons than the older "academic" kind. To be sure, modern art and literature are constituted as such on the awareness that canons can not only be revised but completely overturned and new ones put in their place. And this gives to experiment and innovation a kind of license that the older, academic canons did not. But the modernity of modern art consists in its openness to change and innovation, as against the rigidity and dogmatism of the older, academic establishment. This does not mean that modern art and literature are totally alienated from the past and tradition. Bourdieu stresses that neither Flaubert nor Manet could have effected their revolutions without solid grounding in the traditions of their fields and a respect for the substance of the rules of the game they were intent on changing. Respect for the classics of the traditions they wanted to change is what allowed them to find in certain representatives of the older conventions models worthy of imitation or innovators whom they could claim as precursors. Thus, the canons of modern art and literature differ not so much in what they oppose in the *tradition* as, rather, what they *value* in it and, above all, what of it they do not *not* reject in its *history* (cf. Mieke Bal, *Quoting Caravaggio: Contemporary Art, Preposterous History*, on Caravaggio and postmodernist art).[8]

Now this all very well and, to me, quite convincing in the way it dialectically mediates the differences and similarities between modern art and literature and their academicist and dogmatist predecessors. But Bourdieu's efforts to link up—genealogically, as it were—a genuinely revolutionary, an anti- and a postmodernist artist like Marcel Duchamp with the tradition inaugurated by Manet and his cohort in the 1860s is not convincing to me. I speak of Duchamp as "genuinely revolutionary" because Duchamp—in both his thought and his practice—not only sought to change the rules of the game called art but succeeded in very large part in dissolving the distinction between art and nonart shared by every artistic movement in the West since the invention of "aesthetics" in the late eighteenth century.

Back in 1983, the art historian Hal Foster published an anthology of writings titled *The Anti-aesthetic: Essays on Post-modern Culture*,[9] which defined postmodernism as an anti-aesthetic movement—not, be it noted, a movement against art, but a movement against aesthetics or the aesthetic per se. The idea was that one could account for the originality of the current avant-garde only on the assumption that through it art had broken free of the idea of the aesthetic, which was little more than a sublimated form of religiosity and, as such, a way of subordinating art to morality. The detachment of art from aesthetics was, as thus envisaged, an even more radical revolution in art than those effected, in Bourdieu's account, by Flaubert and Manet in the constitution of a distinctively *modern* artistic practice.

At the same time, and in fact within the same year as Foster's book, Arthur Danto proclaimed "the end of art" precisely insofar as postmodernist art, which he dated from Duchamp's display of *Fountain* in the 1917 Society of Independent Artists in New York, erased the distinction, not between the aesthetic and the unaesthetic, but between the artwork and every other thing found in nature or culture that could be presented as being not *not*-artistic in kind.[10]

I hope I have made a point here. Duchamp, at least on Danto's account, constitutes every object in nature and culture as candidate, not for the status of art or nonart, but for that of the not *not*-artistic. It is not a denial or negation of a putative positivity by which Duchamp will try to de-constitute the difference between art and its other. It is rather by a privative definition that he will deflate the ontological claims of an art claiming the status of divine. Duchamp recognizes no ontological difference between Michelangelo's *Pietà* and a wine bottle drying rack (*Bottle Rack* [*Porte-Bouteilles*], 1914). What Duchamp will call the *objet trouvé* or "ready-made" will have the quality of being not unartistic, as against those things in the world that are not *not* unartistic. It is a thoroughly democratic conception of the world and the things found in it— differences in form and function, but not of quality.

Now, insofar as a number of avant-garde writers, from Dada and Breton, Gertrude Stein and Apollinaire on, picked up this idea and undertook, for example, to destroy the authority of grammar or syntax, not to mention semantics, in writing, we can say that the spirit of Duchamp informs an idea of literature as *not not-literary*. This idea is quite different from the idea of the literary that informs the work of such writers as Conrad, Woolf, Proust, Eliot, Joyce, Svevo—the whole first generation of modernists who still share a nostalgia for and connection with the models of Flaubert and Baudelaire. They are still "aesthetical" and believe in style as what distinguishes literary from non-literary writing. They are quite different from Stein, Kafka, Beckett, Burroughs, and Faulkner, who anticipate postmodernist writing in the consistency with which they violate all of the rules of "fine writing." Kafka writes with a sense of the nastiness of writing, not so much the immorality as the perversity of it. Kafka has an overpowering sense of the materiality of the body, indeed the animality of it. Writing, for Kafka, like memory for Freud, stinks.

I do not have time to go into the ways in which postmodernist writers—from Pynchon to Sebald, from Roth to Toni Morrison, from Mailer to DeLillo, like their counterparts in the arts, from Venturi to Gehry, from Beuys to Christo, from Cindy Sherman to Laurie Anderson, from David Lynch to Quentin Tarantino—work within the presupposition of the non-canonical, because they work without any presupposition of "the law of the law" and especially the law of the aesthetic. Phrases such as "simulacrum," "authentic fake," "copy without an original," "wrapper without a content," "the novelesque," the "neutral," the "androgyne," and so on, seem to be invoking the more bizarre moments of Dada, Surrealism, and Futurism. But in my view, they differ radically from the slogans of the historic avant-garde in their indifference to the authority of "art" per se. It is as if the postmodernists have grasped the impurity at the heart of the law of the law, the law that allowed the establishment of "art" as an "autonomous" domain of cultural production in which the very idea of the law would be affirmed in its negation.

The principal enemy of postmodernist poetics is a capitalized art market that does not so much wish to "commodify" art as establish it as another instance of "exchange value." Postmodernist artists and writers do not, it is true, promote the idea of the "use-value" of art as a countermeasure to "exchange value." It is the concept of "value," or the idea of value-in-itself, that they bring under question. For in the same way that, for Duchamp, every object could be said to be as much artistic as non-artistic, so too for the law, the law of the law, the law of genre, and the law of the canon—none of these *have* value except insofar as they can enter that domain once reserved only for "works of art" of undeniable nobility, authenticity, and gravity but now known to be just another space presided over by connoisseurs who find their own taste incarnated in the works they pretend to value as the work of genius.

Notes

1. [Ed: White notes in the text that "this is a version of the notes I used to keynote the conference of which the other essays in this collection were the proceedings." This conference, "Author(ity) and the Canon between Institutionalization and Questioning," was held at the New Europe College in Bucharest, Romania, on December 2–4, 2010.]

2. [Ed: See Peter Goodrich, *Oedipus Lex: Psychoanalysis, History, Law* (Berkeley: University of California Press, 1995).]

3. Frank Kermode, *An Appetite for Poetry* (Cambridge, MA: Harvard University Press, 1989).

4. Jacques Derrida, "The Law of Genre," trans. Avital Ronell, *Critical Inquiry* 7, no. 1 (1980): 55–81.

5. "What I shall call the law of the law of genre . . . is precisely a principle of contamination, a law of impurity, a parasitical economy. In the code of set theories, if I may use it at least figuratively, I would speak of a sort of participation without belonging—a taking part in without being part of, without having membership in a set" (Derrida, "Law of Genre," 59).

6. Derrida, "Law of Genre," 57.

7. [Ed: Pierre Bourdieu, "Cultural Reproduction and Social Reproduction," in *Knowledge, Education, and Cultural Change: Papers in the Sociology of Education*, ed. Richard Brown (London: Routledge, 1973), 56–68. See also Pierre Bourdieu, "The Forms of Capital" (1985), in *Handbook of Theory and Research for the Sociology of Education*, ed. J. Richardson (New York: Greenwood, 1986), 241–58; and Bourdieu, *The State Nobility: Elite Schools in the Field of Power*, trans. Lauretta C. Clough (Stanford, CA: Stanford University Press, 1996).]

8. Mieke Bal, *Quoting Caravaggio: Contemporary Art, Preposterous History* (Chicago: University of Chicago Press, 1999).

9. Hal Foster, *The Anti-aesthetic: Essays on Post-modern Culture* (Port Townsend, WA: Bay Press, 1983).

10. Arthur C. Danto, *After the End of Art: Contemporary Art and the Pale of History* (Princeton, NJ: Princeton University Press, 1998).

CHAPTER 5

Modern Politics and the Historical Imaginary [2012]

> History does not break down into stories, it breaks down into images.
>
> —Benjamin, "On the Concept of History"

We are asked to consider the relation between politics and the imagination, or, to put it more precisely, politics as a struggle for the imagination.[1] In this paper, I want to examine the extent to which history, considered as both a mode of being in the world and as a kind of knowledge about the world, has been used in that struggle. Let me say at the outset that I regard the study of history or indeed any inquiry into the past as primarily an imaginative enterprise. Bachelard once said that we can study only what we have first dreamed about.[2] This may or may not be true, or may be true of some things and not of others. In any event, insofar as dreaming belongs to the imagination much more than to the rational faculty, Bachelard is telling us something important about the relation between certain kinds of knowledge (or knowledge production) and certain kinds of objects of knowledge.

Historical knowledge or knowledge of history has to do with a domain of existence—the past—that must be imagined before it can become an object of knowledge. For—obviously—one cannot perceive past things directly or invest them immediately as possible objects of rational cognition. They first must be conjured up as *possible* objects of knowledge. Historians conjure up images of possible objects of study by reading both the work of other historians and/or documents relating to a particular time and place where possible "historical" events may have occurred. This means that one must have some general idea of "historicality" by which to identify or distinguish a specifically historical event from other kinds of events or things.[3]

Not all events of the past are historical in kind. Indeed, most of the events of the past would not qualify as historical at all. Unless, that is, the concept of event is applicable only to the kinds of occurrences that appear to be something other than "natural." In fact, it is not at all clear that the concept of "event" has any necessary function in the classification of natural or physical processes. There once was a time when all the things we call events—natural, cultural, supernatural—were thought to be effects of the actions of supernatural beings or forces. Then, when agency was imputed to human beings, natural events consisted of all of those occurrences apprehensible by human beings but not attributable to human causes.

Narrative and the Politics of History

In the nineteenth century it was a commonplace widely honored that held that "history was past politics" and that "history" itself—the mode of existence and the consciousness of this mode of existence—came to birth only with the invention of the state (the Greek *polis*) and the apparatus of record-keeping, discipline, and control needed for the maintenance of the state. This was Hegel's view, at least. But even in the twentieth century Heidegger and Arendt held that "history" and "politics" were born on the site (*Stätte*) of the Greek *polis*. Arendt especially came to view history as an alternative to politics, a contemplative domain in which the more activist impulses of politics could be avoided. But Hegel and the later Arendt (in *The Human Condition*) added a third component to the history-politics connection, and this was *narrative*, considered by Hegel to be the discursive mode best suited to the representation of that reality made possible by the discovery of the relationship between history and politics.

Now, the belief that narrative is the discursive form adequate to (indeed, necessary for) the representation of the dynamics of the relationship between politics, on the one side, and history, on the other, reveals something about the imaginary nature of the history-politics nexus. It is no secret that narrative is a mode and a form common not only to the literary genres of epic, fable, romance, and legend, but also to dream, delusion, myth, and legend. In other words, narrative is the mode and the form in which desire, in the genres of the adventure, the quest, and the test or *agon*, reaches discourse as wish-fulfillment fantasy. As thus envisaged, narrative is not only a possible container of a more basic substance or meaning, but is a meaning-substance in its own right, what Frank Ankersmit memorably called a "narrative substance," a model, paradigm, or structure of temporal coherence.[4] Narrative can show how beginnings eventuate in endings consonant with them or, conversely, how an event apprehended as an eruption from the depths of being can be provided with a genealogy that authorized its occurrence early on. The relationship of "before and after" has been recognized as an ontologically significant categorem since Aristotle and as a ground on which the adequacy of narrative form to historical process can be presupposed. "Once upon a time" is common to both folklore and historical consciousness.

But every narrative account of anything whatsoever must posit the before-and-after nexus as a matrix for arranging what would otherwise be only a *series* of events into a *sequence*. Narrativization of a series of real events makes beginnings, middles, and endings out of what would otherwise remain only "one damned thing after another." It endows events with meaning by distributing them into the past-present-future of the general past. The psychological effect of narrative is to dramatize social, cultural, or personal processes by endowing them with the aspect of the dominant meaning-producing systems in a given community or group. In that Greek culture in which "history" was first performed or recited (by Herodotus, even before it was conceptualized), myth, drama, philosophy, and medicine provided different paradigmatic scenarios that could be used to emplot events and identify agents and agencies adequate to the social purposes of historiography.

History is, of course, something quite other than "the past." It presumes a crucial relationship between the past and the present and, more specifically, the notion that every present (including that in which the historian is operating) is at once a fulfillment of a past and the prefiguration (or anticipation) of a future that is latent in it. It is commonly thought that Hegel's notion of the future is teleological, and so it is insofar as Hegel posits an end to history that is both necessary and inevitable. But it is commonly overlooked or, if perceived, not sufficiently stressed, that the end Hegel postulates is more like the end of a story than the end of an argument or a deduction. That is to say, like the end of a story, the end of history is not knowable from within any place in the sequence of events and actions that make up the literal or manifest level of a series of historical occurrences. That history must have an end,

Hegel doubted not at all. That we might be able to grasp the *general* nature of this end, he believed for good reasons. That we might be able to discern where and when it would end, he held to be a nonsensical illusion. Narrative was the mode of discourse best suited to the presentation (*Darstellung*) of the "poetry" in "the prose of the world," which was to say, the creativity in the work of destruction carried out at the "slaughter bench" of history.

Hegel originally coined the phrase "die Prosa der Welt" (the prose of the world) to characterize the Roman state and to distinguish it from its more "poetic"—by which Hegel meant brilliant, idealistic, evanescent, and short-lived—Hellenic counterpart, the Athenian *polis*. Rome represented a politics different in kind from that of Hellas by virtue of its practicality, rusticity, literal-mindedness, and, above all, success in expanding in space and perduring in time, while, unlike China and India, providing a place for the personal life of individuals and families alongside of the public life of assemblies, armies, and rulers. The poet Petrarch would later say, "What else then is all history, but the praise of Rome," thereby indicating the appeal of Rome (the *translatio imperii*) to the "imaginary" of every subsequent polity in the West.[5] The political past of Europe, Hegel maintains, takes its rise not in Greece but in Rome. "[The] extreme prose of the spirit we find in Etruscan art, which though technically perfect and so far true to nature, has nothing of Greek Ideality and Beauty: we also observe it in the development of Roman Law and the Roman religion."[6]

As thus envisaged, the political imagination of Europe has its object of interest in Rome. The space of the political imagination is infinite in extent, its time endless, and the whole governed by a law that protects both the community and the citizen from an all-devouring *Fatum*.[7] "Rome was the fate that crushed down the gods and all genial life in its hard service, while it was the power that purified the human heart from all particularity."[8] The political past per se is Rome, and only Rome, because Rome is the secular principle par excellence. Its story provides the plot of every political story that follows afterward; "before" is to the rise of the polity as "after" is to its fall. This pattern of rise and fall is what political history or the history of politics is all about; it is political history's primal scene. This primal scene is sublimated and domesticated by being narrativized, by being made into a story that not only renders what happens on that scene comprehendible but also in the process assigns a value to it.

But how does narrative, which, by common consensus, is merely a form of discourse, one that can be filled with any content, assign a value to that which it contains?

The conventional answer to this question is that the process of narrativization transforms what would otherwise be a series of events into a story, a sequence of events that assigns events different plot-functions (for example: beginning, middle, end) but also provides connections between the plot elements so as to produce an explanation (or at least an explanation-effect) by the endowment of endings with teleological force (which is rather like saying that the ending of a story explains by being presented as the *telos* latent in the story all along). But narrativization does more than that to a set of events construed as a field of action about which a story can be told. Narrativization dramatizes events, the individuals involved in them, and the kinds of conflicts that can appear in them. Narrative presupposes a scene (chronotopically organized) in which certain kinds of characters can appear, certain kinds of events can happen, certain kinds of acts are possible.

Narrativization, moreover, presupposes a limited array of possible scenarios for the emplotment of what can happen in that scene. In the West, there are a limited number of scenarios for the emplotment of sets of events: epic, tragedy, comedy, pastoral, farce, and so on. In other words, narrativization provides a frame for a field of events (real or imaginary, or both) that, by means of thematization, sets limits on what can possibly happen in that scene and what can possibly be said and thought about it. By thematization, narrative systematically posits a domain of possibility, on the one side, and, at the same time, excludes or forecloses certain other possibilities of what can be said about the phenomena being represented.

Hegel recognized that the professional (or scientific) study of the past must educe more time-anxiety and concern (*Sorge*) than it did pride in and satisfaction with human achievement. In fact, it was precisely the scientific study of the past that, because of the image of disconnection and incoherence that it inevitably created, produced a kind of horror of it. Thus, in the Introduction to his *Lectures on the Philosophy of History*, Hegel (or his editor) writes that a merely factual account of the events of the past presents a picture of fearful aspect because the individuality of historical phenomena does not lend itself to transcendental summation or synthesis. When we cast a glance back over the spectacle of "human passions" that history presents to us and "observe the consequences of their violence, the unreason that is associated not only with them, but even—rather, we might say *especially*—with *good* intentions and righteous aims; when we see arising from them all the evil, the wickedness, the decline of the most flourishing nations mankind has produced, we can only be filled with grief for all that has come to nothing." Moreover, "since this decline and fall is not the work of mere nature but of the human will, our reflection may well lead us to moral sadness, a revolt of our good spirit (if there is a spirit of goodness in us)." And this allows us to say, "without rhetorical exaggeration, that a *merely truthful* account of the miseries that have overwhelmed the noblest of nations and polities and the finest exemplars of private virtue forms a most fearful picture and excites emotions of the profoundest and most hopeless sadness, counter-balanced by no consoling outcome."

Hegel is here describing the moral or psychological effect of a merely factual account of the historical past, an account that must, if it be truthful, relate a story of universal ruin and desolation, productive at best of feelings of melancholy. In other words, Hegel regards the simply truthful account of the human past as nugatory. It gives lots of information; the information admits of no more general consideration; and its incoherency is depressing.

The human tendency, Hegel continues, is to "draw back into the vitality of the present, into our aims and interests of the moment" and to "retreat, in short, into the selfishness that stands on the quiet shore and thence enjoys in safety the distant spectacle of wreckage and confusion."[9]

Of course, Hegel does not himself fall into this condition of melancholy. On the contrary, he says, in the face of the image of such universal ruin and abjection, we cannot but ask what end or purpose this spectacle of destruction and ruin inevitably summons up before our minds. He then proceeds to lay out his theodicy of history, which purports to demonstrate that this spectacle of unreason and folly secretly, latently, or implicitly figures forth the march of reason in the world and reason's grasping in consciousness of its own possibility and actuality. *It is at this point that Hegel moves from the discourse of the past imaginary to its investment by the symbolic system.* In calling his philosophy of history a *theodicaea*, Hegel openly signals the therapeutic purpose of sublimating the anxieties and care that the products of scientific historiography must arouse by any account of the past in "merely truthful" terms. Because, as Hegel indicates in his distinction among original, pragmatic, and critical historical thinking, scientific history cannot but come to the recognition of its own limitations as an aid to practical reason. "Nobody ever learned anything from the study of history," he says, "except that no one ever learned anything from the study of history." Here Hegel anticipates Michel Foucault when the latter says that, quite apart from that history studied scientifically for which the nineteenth century is renowned, there was another history, a history of things that resisted coordination with the history of mankind. It is this other history—dominated by the law of entropy, which ultimately claimed the authority of Darwin as well as that of Sadi Carnot—that progressively overtakes and overrides the optimistic version of mankind's heroic production of itself. And it is this other history—which Nietzsche espied on the horizon of Europe's imperium, and which authorized his own nihilism—that underwrote the nihilistic politics of the twentieth century.

The explicit and self-styled science of history that contributed to the establishment of the legitimacy of the nation-state, that compiled its genealogical line of descent from its origins in the land and the people, and that constructed the master-narrative of its development over time, this history was accompanied by its metaphysical shadow, which destabilized the very effort to set limits on what could possibly be known about the past by inscribing change, destruction, and entropy into the foundations.

In modernity, of course, politology has taken a somewhat jaundiced view of history. Modern political economy, political science, sociology, and so on, were constituted as "sciences" in part in terms of their abandonment of the historicist way of thinking about politics. So, in a sense, political philosophy, theory, or speculation can be broken down into two kinds: (1) that which regards history as fundamental to an understanding of politics and the political; and (2) that which regards history and historiology as irrelevant to an analysis and comprehension of the political per se.

Here Foucault's work may be taken as exemplary of the most advanced thought on this issue. Foucault's *Les mots et les choses* (translated as *The Order of Things*) culminates in a discussion of the role and function of history among the human and social sciences. First, he dismisses the conventional view of a fundamental conflict between the scientific history of the early nineteenth century and the grand philosophies of history of Hegel, Auguste Comte, Marx, Herbert Spencer, Spengler, and so on. Foucault insisted that these two enterprises, far from indicating a belief in and reverence for the past, actually manifested a deep anxiety about a present that had become unanchored from every religious and metaphysical foundation and now floated in those "infinite spaces" that had so agonized Pascal. By the end of the eighteenth century, Foucault maintains, it had been discovered that

> there existed a historicity proper to nature; forms of adaptation to the environment were defined for each broad type of living being, which would make possible a subsequent definition of its evolutionary outline; moreover, it became possible to show that activities as peculiarly human as labor or language contained within themselves a historicity that could not be placed within the great narrative common to things and men.[10]

And the result of the historization of the cosmos in all its parts was that "the whole lyrical halo that surrounds the consciousness of history [in the early nineteenth century], the lively curiosity shown for documents or for traces left behind by time—all this is surface expression of the simple fact that man found himself emptied of history,"[11] that the "historical scholarship" focused on the hysterical collection of "facts about the past" was a manifestation of an effort to fill up a void that had suddenly opened out before men who had thought it possible to make history, divine its future, control it and give it direction. This new History, this history behind or below or ahead of the manifestly "historical" data served up by scientific historians, is the *antitype* of a historical knowledge that had been meant to show time's, and therefore man's, fullness of being.

Thus, Foucault avers:

> Obviously, [this] History . . . is not to be understood as the compilation of factual successions or sequences as they may have occurred; it is the fundamental mode of being of empiricities, upon the basis of which they are affirmed, posited, arranged, and distributed in the space of knowledge for the use of such disciplines or sciences as may arise. . . . History, as we know, is certainly the most erudite, the most aware, the most conscious, and possibly the most cluttered area of our memory; but it is equally the depths from which all beings emerge into their precarious, glittering existence.[12]

"The emergence of history as both knowledge and the mode of being of empiricity" marks the advent of our modernity. The emergence can be dated: "the outer limits are the years 1775 and 1825," but there are two successive phases in this process of emergence. In the first of these phases, "men's riches, the species of nature, and the words with which languages are peopled, still remain what they were in the Classical age." They are subjected only to a reordering in the mode of temporality. "It is only in the second phase that words, classes [of things], and wealth will acquire a mode of being no longer compatible with that of representation."[13]

This leads Foucault to conclude some one hundred and fifty pages later in his book:

> History constitutes, therefore, for the human sciences, a favorable environment which is both privileged and dangerous. To each of the sciences it offers a background, which establishes it and provides it with a fixed ground and, as it were, a homeland; it determines the cultural area—the chronological and geographical boundaries—in which that branch of knowledge can be recognized as having validity; but it also surrounds the sciences of man with a frontier that limits them and destroys them from the outset, their claim to validity within the element of universality. It reveals in this way that though man—even before knowing it—has always been subjected to the determinations that can be expressed by psychology, sociology, and the analysis of language, he is not therefore the intemporal object of knowledge which, at least at the level of its rights, must itself be thought of as ageless. Even when they avoid all reference to history, the human sciences (and history may be included among them) never do anything but relate one cultural episode to another (that to which they apply themselves as their object, and that in which their existence, their mode of being, their methods, and their concepts have their roots); they apply themselves to their own synchronology, they relate the cultural episode from which they emerged to itself. Man, therefore, never appears in his positivity, and that positivity is not immediately limited by the limitlessness of History.[14]

Foucault's notion of a doubly articulated historicity provides a kind of equivalent of the psychoanalytic concept of psychic phenomena as possessing a surface-depth structure, not so much in the mode of a (logical) explicit-implicit relationship as, rather, a (tropological) manifest-latent relationship. This provides a way of comprehending how political discourse can invest the "imagination" of the multitude by techniques of "coaction" quite different from those used in traditional rhetorics to construct a secondary content that gives value or quality to what otherwise might appear only as fact or quantity.

Actually, history, historical knowledge, and historiology would seem to be relevant to the comprehension of political structures and processes only in the extent to which political groups and institutions might have an interest in establishing their own identities in *genealogical* terms, were committed to governance in accordance with tradition and precedent, or actually thought that the best way to approach current problems came by way of a comprehension of how peoples in earlier times had dealt with similar or analogous ones. Of course, the public appeal to history for models, examples, ideals, precedents, or alibis and exoneration, presumes that knowledge about the past is quasi-scientific, or at least is as "secure" as the kind of evidence brought by lawyers before courts of law. The fact that historical knowledge can be considered as "scientific" only in the most tenuous sense of the term, or that the authority of legal evidence is commonsensical or conventionalist at best, means that any appeal to the past itself must be cast in terms that engage not only the intellect but also other faculties as well, for example, the kind of faculty that is commonly called "the imagination" as well as those of the will and intellect. But what could one possibly mean by the term "imagination" at this moment in "history"?

The Imaginary, Althusser's Process of Interpellation, and Freud's *Zensur*

To consider politics in its aspect as participant in a struggle to engage, discipline, control, and educate (the) imagination requires a preliminary, if only provisional, specification of what we might mean by imagination, what or whose imagination is being invested, and what instruments of control are available at specific times and places in the history of political institutions for the exercise of that control. But put this way, we are immediately confronted by the curious fact that by the term "history" we do not indicate a clear and unambiguous referent. Are we speaking about "the past"? Whose or which past? Are we speaking about a process of development peculiar to certain peoples and geographical areas of the world and not to others, so that others will not be considered to have a history or to exist in history? Are we speaking in the manner of Hegel and Heidegger about a certain mode of being-in-the-world, a mode of existence in which a people or group lives as if it were an agent of its own making, exercising a certain degree of freedom in this operation, and is capable of, or fatally compelled to, assume responsibility for its own identity? Moreover, it is a troubling fact that "history" or "historical consciousness" or "historical knowledge" has functioned more or less effectively over time as one of the instruments deployed by dominant social groups in the effort to "control the imagination" of the multitude, or at least of elites destined to control the multitude—what American ideologues during the Cold War called "winning the hearts and minds" of men. Finally, we must address the troubling fact that the notion of "imagination" is strangely resistant to definitive analysis whether considered (1) as a faculty operating in the service of emotions, the will, or reason; or (2) as a zone or level of what Freud called the "perception-consciousness" system whereon the relation between soma and psyche is negotiated in the process of transforming instinctual impulses into drives (*Triebe*).[15]

In my view, this question was addressed most provocatively in the 1960s and after by Louis Althusser who, in his synthesis of Marxist and Lacanian thinking about ideology, elaborated the concept of "Ideological State Apparatuses" and focused on the process of "interpellation" as the device by which political regimes transformed individuals into "subjects," by inducing in them an "identity" or "subjectivity" that was not only "submissive" but that, at the same time, produced a sense of pride and self-esteem by the pleasure taken in the awareness of its own self-imposed submissiveness. For Althusser and his group, the question that concerns us regarding the politics of imagination centers upon the relation between the notion of legality itself and the notion of what constitutes for the individual a proper identity. The law creates, as Saint Paul wrote in the Epistle to the Romans ("There is no sin before the law"), the conditions under which sin or immorality becomes possible. Where there is no law, there is no sin or crime. Where there is no law, there is neither "normal" nor "proper" human behavior. So it is the law that establishes the condition for distinguishing between the properly human and the non- or un-human. The problem, insofar as politics is engaged in a struggle for the imagination of the individual, is to find a way of inducing the individual to internalize a figure of the law to serve as the simulacrum of that conscience (or inner voice) that disciplines the ego in its efforts to serve the ends of instinctual gratification.

Althusser presents the scene of interpellation as a primal or phantasmatic scene in which the individual is interpellated (addressed and summoned, in the manner of Josef K. in Kafka's *The Trial*) into the juridico-political system, to assume a relation of subordination and self-policing that constantly scans inner impulses for evidence of their possible impropriety. Althusser and his group did not consider the function of historical consciousness/knowledge in this operation (first, probably, because their idea of history was that of Marxist scientism, and, second, because since they thought that historical knowledge was scientific, it had to address itself to consciousness rather than to the unconscious or the *Imaginaire*).

To put the matter in these terms is to question at least implicitly the whole philosophical discourse about the imagination deriving from Kant, who considered imagination as a faculty, which, since it is only pre- or para-rational, constitutes a problem for both pure and practical reason. It is inclined to deviate from its proper function of providing images for consideration by intellect and to degenerate into fantasy, "fancifulness," or playfulness. From the standpoint of an interest in a political investment of the imagination, the imagination must be disciplined on at least two levels: the conscious level at which what Hobbes called "command" operates; and the unconscious level where what he called "coaction" (persuasion, or seduction) has to be used.

In the case of Hobbes, when he spoke of coaction as one of the two instruments to be used by the sovereign in the work of compelling assent of the citizenry, he meant—in spite of the dangers they presented to reason and authority—both rhetoric and symbolic language. Here he agreed with Aristotle on the necessity of investing both the body by force or violence and the spirit by techniques of persuasion and seduction. And the famous second half of *Leviathan*, in which the author analyzes the Christian commonwealth, on the one side, and the Kingdom of Satan or the Forces of Darkness, on the other, shows affinities of Freud with Hobbes, insofar as the former, too, grasped the necessity of inverting the psyche of the individual at the level not so much of *pre-* as rather that of *un*conscious desire, anxiety, and remorse.

Freud was fascinated by the "politics of imagination," from *Beyond the Pleasure Principle* to the late *Totem and Taboo*. But it was especially here that he elaborated the relationships obtaining between the wish-fulfillment fantasies (*Wunscherfüllungen*) manifested in dreams and reveries and what he claimed to have discovered of the "phantasmatic" material of the "primal scenes." These concepts, regarding a dimension of the psychosomatic system at a level below that of preconsciousness (where memory and recall operate), generate a notion of imagination utterly different from anything conceptualized by Kant and his avatars (including, I think, Cornelius Castoriadis).[16] The principal difference between most philosophical definitions of the imagination and a psychoanalytical one lies in the tendency of the former to conceive imagination as pre-intellective, which is to say, preconscious and tending towards irrationality, which means that it must be controlled, educated, disciplined, and regulated by essentially rational and conscious means. Thus, while philosophical thinking has tended to divide imagination into two modes (a priori and constructed, primary and secondary, constructive and reconstructive, productive and reproductive, passive and active or "radical," and so on), Freud, for example, abandoned the notion of imagination as a mental *faculty* in order to consider it as a zone of transition between consciousness and the unconscious, where thinking in images and rebus-like combinations was subjected to the repressive and sublimative operations of the *Zensur* (censorship).

Like earlier theorists of the imagination, Freud distinguishes between primary and secondary psychic processes, but he extends this difference into what had been considered the voluntative and the rational faculties as well. The psychodynamic functions formerly considered to originate in the imagination were now located in a zone of relationship between dynamically unconscious repressed thoughts and images (as the latent content of the dream, for example) and the manifest level of waking consciousness, where various kinds of parapraxis betrayed effects of mechanisms very much like those that, in *Die Traumdeutung* (*The Interpretation of Dreams*), he called *Traumarbeit* or "Dreamwork" (the four operations of *Dichtungsarbeit, Verschiebungsarbeit, Symbolismus,* and *sekondäre Bearbeitung*).[17] These operations of condensation, displacement, symbolization, and secondary elaboration or revision, it turns out, correspond to the tropes of neoclassical rhetoric, in which they were treated as discursive instruments for the production of figures of both thought and speech that would invest the emotions, giving a certain slant of passionate intensity, while, on the literal level, the discourse addressed and informed reason and practical understanding. Indeed, in correlating the tropics of discourse with the mechanisms of the dreamwork, Freud discovers a way of reconceptualizing what might be meant by "a politics of imagination."[18]

This brings us back to Althusser and his Lacan-inspired concept of the transformation of the individual into a subject by interpellation, understood as an effect of a simulacrum of the "voice of the father" speaking as, or in, "the name of the law." Calling the individual into and before the law engages it at the level of primary process thinking and the *phantasmata* of "primal scenes" of separation anxiety, concern, care (*Sorge*), and wish-fulfillment fantasies of "the fullness of life." Freud gives us a way of understanding not just how what used to be called "imagination" works, but also how it might be manipulated to produce the compliant citizen, the self-policing legal subject.

Freud's substitution of the theory of the drives for the older notion of imagination had the advantage of getting beyond discussions of this "faculty" as being not so much active on one level and passive on another as, rather, operating on the borderline between the psyche and the soma, in which the active-passive relation was projected into or onto consciousness to account for the split or schizophrenic nature of both will and reason, each in its own way. In "Die Triebe und seine Schicksale" (translated into English as "The Instincts and Their Vicissitudes") Freud posits the active-passive relationship along with the axes of the subject-object and the love-hate relationships as modalities of the two operations of "reversal" (of love into hate and the reverse) and "turning back upon the self" (of transforming the subject into an object and the reverse) that produce the sado-masochistic and the voyeur-exhibitionist syndromes.

If this kind of topography and dynamics of the psyche appears somewhat antiquated today, it is in part because we are dealing with a politics of the imagination still conceived primarily in terms of "primary modernist" verbal and auditory technologies of interpellation—the technologies of the first industrialism. What has happened since the second technological revolution—the electronic one—is that the technologies of communication have so increased the phatic capacities of the messaging system as to have transcended the conventional exigencies of messaging—conveying information or a command—altogether. Now the imagination can be invested much more completely than anything that the oral-oratorical performances could have done, allowing the political machine to invest the subject directly at the level of the phantasmatic, which is to say, primary process consciousness where wish-fulfillment fantasy and anxieties arise in the context of the primal scene(s). Again, as in Kafka's vision of modernity, the state no longer has to argue anything; it merely commands on the assumption that everyone is guilty and is deserving of whatever the state wishes upon them. It is the implantation of guilt in the consciousness of the citizen that the state is able to effect by its self-presentation as the custodian of the Law. "There is no sin before the law," the Apostle teacheth. Nor is there any imagination. Before the law appears, the subject is neither inside nor outside of the city, because there is no city before the law.

The Historical and the Politics of Imagination

Now we must ask: What is the role of the historical in this more general politics of imagination? Here it is necessary to stress that in posing that question one is not trying to identify the ways in which the academic study of history has been used to support or to undermine the claims of the modern state to represent the moral or at least legal substance of the nation through "patriotic" or "nationalist" historiography overtly supporting the claims of a certain class or classes to hegemony. As Foucault has pointed out, history, or, more specifically, the work of constructing a specifically "historical past," has "performed a certain number of major functions in Western culture: memory, myth, transmission of the Word and of Example, vehicle of tradition, critical awareness of the present, decipherment of humanity's destiny, anticipation of the future, or promise of a return."[19] These functions produced what, following Michael Oakeshott's (*On History*) lead, we may call "the practical past" of Western culture, that past that is drawn upon by politicians, lawyers, judges, policemen, antiquarians, archaeologists, philologians, accountants, educators, and ordinary educated people in the course of their daily affairs any time they feel compelled to advert to what Reinhart Koselleck calls "the space of experience" of their cultural endowment, to connect a present world with some aspect of a past one, recent or remote. This practical past is differently configured, differently populated, differently structured, and differently shared than is the new "historical past" constructed in the nineteenth century and after by those disciplinized scholarly communities, located for the most part in the universities, with explicit rules, licensing regulations, review procedures, and so on, for the scientific or at least *wissenschaftliches* study of the past.

To be sure, the scientific practice of history has its own "imaginary," with its own "dreams" that manifest the deep psychological levels of consciousness that would seek to invest "the past" as a source of a kind of knowledge that is held to be "desirable in itself" or "a good in itself," a knowledge that has no practical use in or for the present, but the accumulation of which had been conceived to be worth a lifetime spent in cold, drafty, and dusty archives that offer small prospect of contact with living human beings. Foucault indicated the importance of the distinction between the "practical past" of memory, casual knowledge of the past, intimation of an origin, concern for a heritage, and anxiety of legitimacy, on the one hand, and the interest by professional scholars in "the historical past" they were concerned to identify, retrieve, and reconstitute on the basis of a scientific study of documents and monuments alone, on the other.

But Foucault, like many other historians of history, identifies this other past as a construction of the discourse of philosophy of history, after the manner of Hegel and Marx (and Darwin), analysts of the concept of history as revealed in professional historical scholarship, but that is probed for what it might reveal in the way of history's *meaning*.

Modernist rhetorics differs from traditional counterparts by the terrible power of the technological means used to package sensorially overdetermined messages for delivery to social constituencies. It is these means—represented above all by the kinds of "special effects" met with in contemporary cinema—that, in the disparity they manifest with respect to the verbal and conceptual content of a message, produce the kind of "sentimental" politics that modern totalitarian regimes have typically favored and deployed. European commentators on American society are characteristically bemused by the rise of fundamentalist religiosity in American politics, seeing it as being at once a paradox for a modern enlightened society and a threat to the rationality of political thought and practice that is considered to be a necessary precondition for the working of democratic political institutions. In my view, however, religiosity is only one of the many forms that fundamentalism can take when the technical means at hand permit the investment of the psyche of the citizen at the level of "imagination," understood as the zone of consciousness at which primal forces such as the pleasure principle and the death drive rage unchecked by any concession to waking rationality or pragmatic concerns about the care and treatment of bodies. Figures such as "the terrorist," "the weapon of mass destruction," "suicide bombers" (and above all, "the female suicide bomber," the wife, grandmother, and girlfriend suicide bomber), "the hijacked jet airplane," the "cell" or "virus" implanted in the inner arteries and veins of "ordinary" (Western) society—such figures are given a vivacity and palpability by the techniques of modern media that make the hellfire and brimstone sermons of the pre-electronic preacher pale by comparison.

Indeed, these techniques make of "the preacher" (imam and ayatollah as well) himself a larger-than-life player on the political stage. These figures not only directly address the topic of death and destruction, entropy and apocalypse, the end of days, the rapture, and the last things; they also seem to *embody* the messages they circulate. Small wonder that the politician who cannot approach to a similar condition of figural embodiment will have little chance of capturing the heart (or imagination) as well as the mind of the citizen.

Freud's idea of the primal scene—the site of psychic consciousness where what was once meant by imagination arises—is the place where bodily anxieties are gathered and the first efforts at their sublimations are attempted. The primal scene is the place where the sleeping ego, deprived of its ego defenses, contrives an imaginary scene, where fantasies of the unknown origin, separation from the body of the mother, loss of the object of possible gratification, mutilation (genital, ocular, and otherwise), loss of identity, and so on, are organized into a "scene" on which a drama unfolds of which the subject is at once both (imagined) observer and (imagined) actor. In the dream state, and also in reverie, these scenarios play themselves out more or less completely as either anxiety-ridden farces, wish-fulfillment romances, or some phantasmagoria that threatens the dreamer by its failure of plot resolution. These scenes, in Freud's formulation, constitute the bases of what he calls "the dream content" over against the manifest form of the dream, which he calls "the dream thoughts."

The technique of "coaction," which Althusser dubbed "interpellation," combines address to the individual's (or group's) conscious moral sensibilities and intellectual commitments, and at the same time to its unconscious anxieties and wish-fulfillment fantasies. Unlike the military *command*, in which the coactive or symbolic element is present as "what goes without saying," or is simply presumed, commands directed from centers of power and authority to civilian or lay individuals intended for subjectivization must engage anxieties of identity and fantasies of fullness activated by the ambiguities and contradictions of a life to be lived as an individual who is *also* a member of a group. This means that the command (masked as a recommendation, suggestion, advisement, or simply appeal) must be cast in such a way as to remind the individual of the law, norm, rule, or protocol in reference to which the desired response on the part of the individual is felt to be *both* necessary or inevitable *and* freely chosen, at one and the same time.

Notes

1. [Ed. This essay was published in an anthology titled *The Politics of Imagination*, ed. Chiara Bottici and Benoît Challand (New York: Routledge, 2012), 162-77. The beginning of the book description reads, "*The Politics of Imagination* offers a multidisciplinary perspective on the contemporary relationship

between politics and the imagination. What role does our capacity to form images play in politics? And can we define politics as a struggle for people's imagination?"]

2. [Ed: White used this quotation from Bachelard's *The Psychoanalysis of Fire*, "One can study only what one has first dreamed about," as the epigraph to his *Metahistory: The Historical Imagination in Nineteenth-Century Europe*.]

3. See Hayden White, "What Is a Historical Event?," in *The Practical Past* (Evanston, IL: Northwestern University Press, 2014), 41–62.

4. See F. R. Ankersmit, "Statements, Texts, and Pictures," in *A New Philosophy of History*, ed. F. R. Ankersmit and Hans Kellner (London: Reaktion Books, 1995), 223.

5. Francesco Petrarca, quoted in Benjamin G. Kolb, "Petrarch's Prefaces to *de viris illustribus*," *History and Theory* 13, no. 2 (1974): 134.

6. G. W. F. Hegel, *Lectures on the Philosophy of World History*, trans. H. B. Nisbet (New York: Cambridge University Press), 374.

7. Hegel speaks of "the universal *Fatum* of the Roman world" (*Lectures*, 413) as what must be overcome (*aufgehoben*) in Christianity, which, thus understood, is the vision of that liberation from "history" (*Lectures*, 419) of which Saint Augustine is the theorist.

8. [Ed: White neglected to put quotation marks around this sentence. Source: G. W. F. Hegel, *Lectures on the Philosophy of History*, trans. Ruben Alvarado (Aalten, Netherlands: WordBridge, 2011), 290.]

9. Hegel, *Vorlesungen über die Philosophie der Geschichte* (Frankfurt: Suhrkamp, 1986), 34–35.

10. Michel Foucault, *The Order of Things: An Archaeology of the Human Sciences*, trans. Alan Sheridan (New York: Vintage, 1994), 367.

11. Foucault, *Order of Things*, 369.

12. Foucault, 219.

13. Foucault, 221.

14. Foucault, 371.

15. Cf. Sigmund Freud, "Die Triebe und seine Schicksale" (1915) ("Instincts and Their Vicissitudes"), in which the drive is defined as an instinctual impulse endowed with a possible object cathexis or, more precisely, a vague image of a possible object of satisfaction. In order, then, to address adequately the question of the relation between politics and the imagination, we must ask what exactly is being invested when politics or politicians or politologists seek to address the subject at the level of, or in the zone of, the perception-consciousness system called "imagination."

16. [Ed. See Cornelius Castoriadis, *The Imaginary Institution of Society*, trans. Kathleen Blamey (Cambridge, MA: MIT Press, 1987).]

17. Sigmund Freud, *The Interpretation of Dreams*, trans. James Strachey (New York: Basic Books), chap. 6.

18. Cf. Émile Benveniste, "Remarks on the Function of Language in Freudian Theory," in *Problems in General Linguistics* (Coral Gables, FL: University of Miami Press, 1971), 74–75.

19. Foucault, *Order of Things*, 367.

CHAPTER 6

Historical Fictions

Frank Kermode's Idea of History in
The Sense of an Ending *[2012]*

> The critics should know their duty.
>
> —Frank Kermode

Frank Kermode's *The Sense of an Ending: Studies in the Theory of Fiction* is recognized as a masterpiece of literary theory (or theory of literature);[1] it is not always recognized that it was also a philosophy of history. Kermode's book is ostensibly about time, temporality, and the ways in which literature deals with the problem of how things end. Throughout the book, there is an implication that, in real life at least, things always end badly, less with a bang than with a whimper. The hope that everything will come out all right in the end is a delusion that fosters such myths as the Apocalypse, the Millennium, Utopia, the Return to the Promised Land, and the Resurrection of the Body, not to mention Renaissance, Reformation, Enlightenment, and all the other providentialist interpretations of history in the history of thought about time. The idea that when the end comes, everything will "light up" with meaning, Kermode consigned to the never-never land of Myth. Yet he recognized that human beings, caught up in what Paul Ricoeur called the "aporias" of temporality,[2] could not avoid the problem of how to end, and in literary fictions he found images of endings—of individuals, of projects, of civilizations, of history, of the cosmos itself—that could make the effort to live worthwhile. Like myth, fiction provided meanings useful for facing the anomalies of a life lived in the company of others. But unlike myth, fiction undercut the authority of its own meaning-giving capacity. In much the same way that the "poetic function" in language use diverts attention from the message to the process of production, so too what might be called "the fictive function" in literature forces awareness of the extent to which all meaning is invented rather than found and can claim authority as truth only as long as it is useful for life.[3]

The medievals thought that the Book of Creation manifested meaning at four levels of existence: historical, allegorical, moral, and anagogical or mystical. At the first (historical) level, things happen, events occur, conflicts arise—in an orderly space and an order of time—and their happening, or *that* they happened when, where, and as they did, *is* their historical meaning. At the same time, however, the events that happen in time and space are figures or images that mask, even while they manifest, their substantive natures. So, at a second level, worldly events have another meaning, which is their relationship to the substance of Creation itself, figurations of their status, place, and value in God's plan for the world. An event such as a battle, or a personage such as a king, enjoys an individuality that derives from its place in a hierarchy of being, each stage of which possesses a value quite other than that of the individuals who occupy it. Next, the conflict among the *kinds* of authority possessed by persons and other kinds of agencies reveals a moral dimension deriving from the difficulty of assigning proper value to persons, offices, and places in worldly time and space. It is the manifestation of this moral dimension that allows us to derive lessons or principles from reflection on the conflicts and contestations of real life. And finally, there is the anagogical or mystical meaning posited by Dante as ineffable because of its non-sensory and extra-rational nature, apprehensible as the necessary and sufficient causes of that relationship between things and meanings that makes love possible, hope credible, and faith authoritative. Any representation of this complex of meanings will be poetic and thus fictive insofar as it captures the form of the *whole* in images and, at the same time, forces awareness of the inadequacy of any image to the faithful presentation of its ineffable "content."

Now, there is a sense in which Frank Kermode's approach to the study of literature inverts this medieval schema, putting myth at the first level, fiction at the second, history at the third, and "reality" (something like the Lacanian *réel*) at the fourth or anagogical level. "Reality," or the cosmic slide into entropic silence and energic slackness, is, for Kermode, formless, meaningless, chaotic, and (therefore) ineffable in the way that the mystical "Great All" or "Great Nothing" can be held to be. At each level, however, a different kind of meaning can be discerned in or projected onto phenomena: total or totalizing meaning at the level of myth; provisional, hypothetical, or practical meaning at the level of fiction; documentary or evidentiary meaning at the level of history; and the non-meaning of entropic drift at the fourth or "anagogical" level.

I admit that I have extracted this structure from Kermode's much more subtle and slippery discussions of the fate of poetry in modernity. For Frank Kermode was not only a student but also a devotee of modernism. He identified with the project of what he called the "first modernism" of Conrad and James, Eliot, Pound, Wyndham Lewis, Lawrence, Woolf, and Joyce, who had heroically faced the crisis of meaning willed to them by their Victorian progenitors. These first modernists had wrestled with this crisis by sublimating both the Romanticist and the Realist programs of the nineteenth century for the renewal of art into a putatively new kind of *poiesis* that rejects "history" in order to return to the archaic origins of both art and life. Thus, although Eliot, in his famous review of *Ulysses*, wrote that his generation had rejected the "narrative method" in favor of the "mythical method," Kermode, viewing the first modernism from within the second one, purported to have seen what was really involved in our own modernist modernism from the beginning: namely, a dissociation of fiction from myth and rejection of myth's last avatar in literature, narrative.

Pre-modernist fictions of the end are all bound up with narrative and narrative form. In the traditional narrative mode of discourse, everything is pointing to the end, to the way things come out, the way they conclude *and* the way they cast a light back over what had happened since the beginning and *make* sense of what had happened afterward. The decline of what Eliot called "the narrative method" in modernist modernism signaled the end of any interest in "the end," or at least of any effort to make sense of "the sense of an ending" in the way that myth and, in its own way, literary fictions had been doing since the invention of "art" in Hellenic times.

The first chapter of *Sense of an Ending* is entitled "The End." Men die, the (Aristotelian) tradition has it, "because they cannot join the beginning with the end." Kermode accepts this aphorism as a challenge and then goes on to say: "What they, the dying men, *can* do is imagine a significance for themselves in these *unremembered but imaginable events*" (my emphases). They can and do create myths of the beginning of all things (and of the pasts from which they have sprung) and myths of the end of all things (of the future towards which they are tending), myths of genesis, on the one hand, and of apocalypse, on the other. Such myths, of "unremembered" (and "unknowable") but "imaginable" events, allow us to join an *imagined* beginning with an *imagined* end that pro-retrospectively—that is to say, pre-posterously—endows the time between beginning and end with meaning.[4] If the meaning with which the "middle" of a life course is endowed retrospectively is theological or metaphysical, the result is mythic or mythological. If the meaning is at once produced but is in some way indicated as being *only* imagined or feigned, as being not true but only possible, it is fictional or, as Kermode would have it, *fictive*.

By fictive, I take it that Kermode meant something like "that which has been made" rather than "found" in nature and which bears the signs of its manufacture on its surface, at the plane of expression whereon the interaction between the form of expression and the substance of expression produces the effect of *poiesis*.[5] It is easy, Erich Auerbach remarked,[6] to tell the difference between legend and history: the story told in the former runs far too smoothly—its formal properties override the effort to *refer* to any reality external to itself. Kermode revises this idea of the relation between the form and the content of the *historical* story. Every historical narrative swerves from the task of referring *only* to past reality to that of making a *story* out of what would otherwise be a senseless *series* of events, without discernible beginning and end, and therefore without the kind of meaning that is needed for humanity to imagine the possibility of making a something out of nothing.

The myth of the end of the world—apocalypse—Kermode took to be paradigmatic of the mythological version of the end of all things. But the mythic version of the end does more than tell of it; it justifies it morally. Thus, the "Apocalypse" *predicted* in the book of Revelation depicts not only the *destruction* of all things but also the *justice* of this destruction. The mythical apocalypse foretells not only an end, but an end that is at the same time a fulfillment, the *telos* towards which the whole of creation had been tending since the beginning. Thus, the mythic version of the end of all things is *pre*determined: although it may be impossible to predict who or what may be redeemed at the end, that *some* will have been redeemed and some not, is already and has always been *given*.

Fiction pulls the thorn of predetermination by stressing the fundamental principle of narrative, which is to allow the events of the story to unfold from beginning to end by dialectical interplay between purposiveness and contingency, so that, as Kermode puts it, "the end comes as expected, but not in the manner expected."[7] Whence the peculiar

satisfactions and popular appeal of histories cast in the mode of a narrative.[8] Whence too the peculiar satisfactions and appeal—at least to
an elite of modernist readers—of stories that are meant to frustrate
narrativist expectations, stories that end but do not conclude. Such
stories—Robbe-Grillet serves as Kermode's exemplary writer here—take
the fiction of fictivity to such length as to end in a kind of myth of the
impossibility of fiction itself.

One problem for Kermode, then, was how to save the substance of
narrativity, the fiction of how ends could retrospectively endow beginnings and middles with meaning, without lapsing into apocalypticism,
on the one hand, or nihilism, on the other. Much of *Sense of an Ending* is
taken up with this task in its examination of the literary masterpieces of
the two modernisms, first and second.

But instead of trying to summarize and analyze the ways in which
Kermode goes about saving the idea of literary fiction from its association with myth and mythmaking, I want to examine what I have characterized above as the third level of Kermode's version of the medieval
fourfold hermeneutic: the historical. History was important to Kermode because it was the dimension of existence wherein humankind
manifested its drive or instinct for meaning—and its recurrent failure
to achieve it definitively. This is quite a different conception of history
and the historical from that of modern scientific historians. For the latter, history is simply given as the record of the things done by human
beings that distinguish them from the rest of animal nature. The historian's question is: what happened? And his/her determination of what
happened—the establishment of the facts of the matter—is the only answer to that question he/she requires. To go on and to ask what the facts
might *mean* is to enter an ethical realm where the question of "what can
I know?" gives way to the much more uncomfortable question of "what
should I do?" Science gives way to ideology.

But Kermode was driven by the thought that literature's purpose in
a universe without purpose was to interrogate the complex relation between knowing and meaning, epistemology and ethics, or more mun-
danely, experience and expectation, with an imaginative freedom denied
to philosophy and history alike.[9] He required an idea of history to provide both a base of human reality against which to measure the extent
to which imagination might resist the hard lessons taught by experience
and to provide a matrix for charting the course of literature's emergence
out of myth and the development of its distinctively fictive capabili-
ties over time. Much of Kermode's work belongs to the field of literary

history (or history of literature—there is a difference), and one of the questions repeatedly asked in *Sense of an Ending* is: how is history possible and what does the fact that literature has a history tell us about the nature of literature itself?[10]

This gesture toward the historicity of literature signaled Kermode's rejection of New Criticism's myth of the timelessness of great literature and the recently established "archetypal" criticism of Northrop Frye, which purported to discover the "content" of literature in sublimated versions of the forms and contents of the great myths of antiquity. Kermode was able to posit the possibility of a purely fictive content for literature by theorizing literature's subject matter or ultimate referent as that "history" that had rejected both myth and fiction in favor of accounts of the deeds of human beings whose "meaning" was nothing other than the "fact" of their occurrence. The fact that these deeds could be plausibly presented in the form of "stories" argued more for the literarity of historiography than it did for the adequacy of the story-form for representation of historical reality. Storytelling, or the narrativization of a series of real events, argued rather more for the adequacy of literature to the exigencies of realistic representation than for the fictive nature of the events being represented.

Kermode was well aware that the scientific status of historical studies had been undermined by the debate over "historicism" and the complicity of historians of various stripes with those fascist regimes that had sought to purify the human race by exterminating the parts of it that "history" itself had supposedly condemned to extinction. But Kermode's idea of history had little in common with the ideology of most modern, professional historians. For professional historians of his time, historical studies has the human *past* for its object of study, the truth of fact as its aim, and the dispelling of error, lies, *and* fictions about the past as its purpose. Although many professional historians presented their findings in the form of stories, most of them preferred the genre of the research report, in which an event or other entity is set within its original context to demonstrate why and how it appeared when, where, and as it did, how it "conformed" to, or was consonant with, its own time and place of occurrence, and why its development over time displayed a kind of meaning peculiarly "historical" in kind. For this kind of historiography the diachronic aspect was present simply as an account of how the event under study emerged in its context and changed it in order to become one with it. As thus envisaged, the whole of history is a congeries of such contextualizations, more like a satellite photograph or map of a landscape than a drama erupting on a "scene," or Bakhtinian "chronotope" already pre-figuring the kinds of actions that can possibly occur within its confines.

Kermode, by contrast, regarded "history" not so much as "the past" as, rather, a domain of existence in which humanity came to conscious-ness of itself, fashioned itself, endowed itself with various meanings, and temporarily sustained itself, from time to time and in different places, against the general cosmic drift into entropic dispersion. It is—surprisingly to me—a very Heideggerian way of looking at history.[11] On this view, "history" is only a part of the past, that part of it manifesting the peculiar power of human kind to make something—form, pattern, meaning—out of chaos or nothing.

Kermode was fully aware that historians wished to deal in facts, es-chewed grand interpretation, and contented themselves with small and regional truths rather than large and universal ones. But he also thought that the kind of order or meaning that historians purport to have found in their study of the past—an order of sequence, periodicity, and connectivity—had more in common with the kind of order found in myth and literature than with the kinds found in science or, for that matter, law. To him, historiography was a species of the genus fiction, to which myth and literature also belonged. Like myth and literature, his-tory relieves us of "time's burden" by imposing upon the facts of reality the kinds of "plots" found in myth but purged of dogmatism and bear-ing signs of both their provisional and their purely transitory nature, in the manner of literary works. These plots or plot-types not only "defy our sense of reality," but also provide us with models or paradigms of the kinds of responses to the human condition that alone permit us the hope without which distinctively human actions remain impossible.[12] This is why Kermode was interested more in narrative history than in its social science counterpart. And this is why he wanted to demonstrate his-tory's similarity to literature rather than its presumed opposition to it.

Thus, in Kermode's view, far from being—as many historians be-lieve—the *antidote* to myth and an *opponent* of literature, history is one with their therapeutic purposes. The modern historian's belief in the truth of fact and in the authority of the written document keeps history grounded in a reality that myth disavows but literature sublimates into intimations of order. But the order that historians present as inhering in the facts—an order of sequence, continuity, and periodicity—derives from the same longing for meaning that inspires the great myths of genesis and apocalypse, the myths of crisis, transition, and peripeteia, the myths of creation *ex nihilo* and the myths of a final destruction in universal conflagration, flood, and plague. The historian's order may be more local, less grandiose, less metaphysical, more banal than that spectacularly presented in myth; but this historian's "order" comes from the same province of human consciousness as myth. It is saved from full mythologization by the historian's devotion to fact and to that part of past reality that has left evidence of its existence in the form of documents and monuments. Nevertheless, history remains "mythical" in the extent to which it still aspires to an apprehension of meaning as adequately representable in a *narrative* or, more specifically, in a presentation of the human past or some part of it as a story with a *plot* that "may relieve us of time's burden" by defying our "sense of reality."[13]

Kermode does not spend much time analyzing historical writing in order to demonstrate the fictional element in it. But in *History and Value* (1988), he pauses long enough to explicate a passage from A. J. P. Taylor's *English History, 1914–1945*, to show how a certain element of fictionality is required to transform what otherwise would have been a dry chronicle of events into a proper history, an account not of how things appeared to be, but of "how things *essentially* were."[14] But what is the difference between "the way things were" and "the way things *essentially* were"?

In his comment on the passage from Taylor's *English History*, Kermode speaks of Taylor's *identification* of the union members who joined the general strike of 1926 in solidarity with the miners with those soldiers in World War I who selflessly went to war "in defense of Belgium in 1914." The two historical events—the strike and the war—are connected "metaphorically" and conflated "rhetorically," according to Kermode, to allow Taylor to show that the "workers deserve more than a passing tribute." This metaphorical strategy, Kermode says, allows the historian to insert a suggestion of "nobility" into the description of the facts of the matter. We do not object to this insertion of this opinion into the account of the facts, Kermode says, "because we know very well that historians, like non-modernist novelists, usually feel free to have opinions and even emotions." Then, Kermode goes on to generalize:

> just as works of fiction need not consist entirely of fictional discourse, works of history need not consist entirely of historical discourse, and may well contain expressions of opinion, compassion, distaste, etc., of the sort often to be found in works of fiction. In this case, for instance, we noted a certain wonder at the altruism of the workers, *treated in the pastoral mode* [my italics] as if they were *others*, members of an admirable but alien culture.[15]

I have emphasized "treated in the pastoral mode" because it suggests that it is a literary and not strictly factual trope that provides a sense of "how things *essentially* were."

I have emphasized "essentially" because I think that this term holds the key to much of what was at issue in the post–World War II discussion of the relation between history and literature. For historians of the era in which Kermode launched his *Sense of an Ending*, "history" was differentiated from "literature" on the analogy of the *difference* between fact and fiction. Fact itself was defined as either identical with "event" (one spoke of "study of the facts") or as a kind of statement about events. (Arthur Danto: "A fact is an event under a description.") "Fiction," considered as the "substance" of literature, was thought to be a product of "imagination" and therefore as fixed on "imaginary" events, happenings, persons, and so on, that had never existed and because of their "fantastic" natures never could exist. This idea of fiction or the fictive has been so consolidated over the course of the twentieth century that literary scholars (such as Dorrit Cohn and Wolf Schmid) have come to insist that a work of fiction is so removed from reality that even if there is an undeniable reference to a real historical person or event (such as, say, "Napoleon" or "the battle of Borodino"), the thing referred to must also be taken as *fictional*. Indeed, the principal distinction between fiction and other kinds of literature, it is held by many even nowadays, is that the work of fiction does not, because it cannot, *refer* to anything in the world beyond its confines. Such an idea of fiction would, of course, rule out *ab initio* any notion that historical discourse could legitimately contain any element of the fictional. For history is nothing if not a discourse dominated by the referential function, even though its referents are by definition no longer available to any kind of direct perception.

In *Sense of an Ending*, Kermode opines that, in modernity, "historiography has become a discipline more devious and dubious because of our recognition that its methods depend to an unsuspected degree on myths and fictions."[16] This idea was underwritten in Kermode's mind by Popper's demonstration that history could never lay claim to the status of a genuine science. Popper had shown, or purported to have shown, that history, properly practiced, dealt with individual events occurring in specified time-space locations, on the basis of evidence that precluded any properly scientific analysis of causation or possibility of prediction, and that historians were advised to concentrate on the telling of stories (narratives) about how things came to be in given times and places, in the way they did and not otherwise, and in the form of plausible sequences of events arranged in proper narrative (rather than a strictly chronological) order.

It has to be said that, in the 1960s and 1970s, philosophers and historians interested in the problem of historical explanation brought to the discussion of this topic rather primitive notions of both story and narrative. A narrative was considered to be a *form* of discourse peculiarly suitable to the representation of series of events of the kind called "historical" (rather than "natural" or "supernatural"). Historical events were supposed to differ from natural events by virtue of their predominantly diachronic (rather than synchronic) nature. Historical events, as Aristotle had taught, were either earlier or later in a series, or came before or after some "crisis" in a system that changed, reversed, or inverted its "natural" order. As thus envisaged, sets of historical events could be realistically represented as having the form of stories, the "followability" of which provided an "explanatory effect" (an effect of "comprehension" or "understanding") in lieu of a properly scientific or causal explanation. It was not recognized that if a story produced an explanatory effect, it was because the events presented as describing the form of a story had been removed from the domain of reality and endowed with the form of myth or, as Kermode argued, fiction.

To be sure, there was plenty of opposition to the idea of explanation by storytelling, and not only because historical stories shared with myth a common form and mode of presentation. Stories were regarded as a substitute for a properly scientific mode of explanation, represented by the so-called nomothetic-deductive model prevailing in the modern natural sciences. Moreover, both the rise in historical studies of the so-called social history, which borrowed its methods from the social sciences, and the idea of historical causation as a long, impersonal, and serial process amenable to description by statistical correlations were inherently hostile to storytelling. The leader of the Annales group, Fernand Braudel, famously attacked the use of stories to represent historical processes because, in his view, stories aestheticized reality or substituted an attractive *form* for the reality they purported to present to view. And in a brilliant essay on "The Discourse of History" ("Le discours de l'histoire," 1967), Roland Barthes dismissed the old-fashioned narrative history as manifestly mythifying reality by virtue of its form alone.[17] But more was at issue than the fate of narrative historiography; the attack on narrative and narrativity extended to literature in general and the idea of the cognitive authority of *poiesis* or poetic utterance itself.

The idea was that literature, poetry, and art in general should restrict themselves to fantasy and entertainment and leave reality to the sciences.

Already in the early 1960s, a debate was taking shape over the proper modes and models to be used in the representation of such ethically fraught events as the Holocaust and other "crimes against humanity." To treat such events as occasions for artistic performances threatened them with aestheticization, relativization, and even trivialization.[18] And thus insofar as storytelling had to be considered an art or at least a craft, then it had to be eliminated from any putatively realistic and/or ethically responsible representation of events that had caused a kind and degree of suffering hitherto unknown to history.

In *Sense of an Ending,* Kermode referred to the Holocaust a number of times.[19] He used the Holocaust mostly as an example of the dangers of taking a myth such as antisemitism literally and then launching programs designed to test the "truth" of its propositions in such "scientific" milieux as the gas chambers of Auschwitz.[20] Citing Hannah Arendt, Kermode opines that "the philosophical or anti-philosophical assumptions of the Nazis were not generically different from those of the scientist, or indeed of any of us in an age 'where man, wherever he goes, encounters only himself.'" He then poses the question, "How, in such a situation, can our paradigms of concord, our beginnings and ends, our humanly ordered picture of the world satisfy us, make sense? How can apocalypse or tragedy make sense, or more sense than any arbitrary nonsense can be made to make sense?" And answers it by juxtaposing *King Lear* against "the Third Reich," to distinguish between two kinds of fiction that, although superficially alike in their fictiveness, produce different orders of effect: "antisemitism is a fiction of escape which tells you nothing about death but projects it onto others; whereas *King Lear* is a fiction that inescapably involves an encounter with oneself, and the image of one's [own] end."[21] But there is another difference as well, a difference in the degree of self-consciousness with which myth and fiction hold to the "lies" they tell as if they were "truths."

Kermode gets from Wallace Stevens, Ortega y Gasset, and Hans Vaihinger the idea of myths and fictions as "consciously false" constructions—lies that not only know themselves to be such but send out signals of their "pretend" nature along with suggestions of their purely practical utility.[22] But, Kermode maintains, myth presupposes the truthfulness of its constructions, whereas fictions—or at least, literary fictions—sustain and constantly force us to remember that they are only constructions, products of our imaginations, and are to be taken as neither true nor false, but as instruments for multiplying the possibilities of ways we can have of relating to our world. Hence, Kermode's dictum: "Fictions can degenerate into myths whenever they are not *consciously* held to be fictive."

I want at this point to go on to consider the implications for Kermode's understanding of history of his idea that historiography needs fiction, and fiction, in turn, is to be taken as "conscious falsehood," or in any case not to be taken as "true." To do this, I need to digress for a moment into a consideration of the ways in which the mapping out of problems in terms of antithetical conceptual poles generates a semantic field capable of explicating the structures of mixed cases, such as the psychoanalytical case of "madness in insanity" or "insanity in madness." So it is with the polar isotopes, "true" and "false." Kermode challenges us to see such fictions as *Lear* or Stevens's "Man on the Dump" as "consciously false," when he might be said to have wanted to characterize them as neither true nor false (the traditional view of fictions) but as "not untrue" in the sense that they present a vision of the world that is more virtually than actually true.

No world-image, no imagined cosmos or cosmos presented as real, can meet the test of truthfulness required by a semantics that presupposes the true to be the *opposite* of the false, the false to be the *contradictory* of the not-false, and the not-true to be *implicandum* of everything that is in the least bit false. Out of the opposition of true (+) to false (–) we can thus generate a hierarchy comprised of true (+) at the top, the not-false (– –) following, the not-true (– +) below that, and the false (–) at the bottom. The two middle terms (the not-false and the not-true) can be instantiated by the glass containing a liquid of half of its whole volume. Whether we choose to call the glass half-full or half-empty determines the value to be placed on the volume of water in the glass. Everyone knows that anything that is half-full is better than its half-empty twin, because fullness is everywhere valued more highly than emptiness.

And so it is, I believe, with Kermode's efforts in *Sense of an Ending* to present literary fiction as superior to the fictions of science, religion, philosophy, and history, by virtue of its hybridization of the true and the false in such a way as to permit, without contradiction, the imagination of an element of the false in any putatively true representation of reality, on the one hand, and an element of truthfulness in any figment of the artistic imagination, on the other. As Freud taught us to see the element of sanity in every kind of madness and a kind of madness in any putatively perfect sanity, so, too, Kermode grasped the "secret" of modernist literature in its search for the real in the illusory and the illusory in the real.[23] Thus, in a crucial passage in chapter 2 of *Sense of an Ending*, Kermode sets fictions in opposition to myth only to proceed to assert that they are capable of mutating one into the other.

> We have to distinguish between myths and fictions. Fictions can degenerate into myths whenever they are not consciously held to be fictive. In this sense antisemitism is a degenerate fiction, a myth; and *Lear* is a fiction. Myth operates with the diagrams of ritual, which presupposes total and adequate explanations of things as they are and were; it is a sequence of radically unchangeable gestures. Fictions are for finding things out, and they change as the needs of sense-making change. Myths are the agents of stability, fictions the agents of change. Myths call for absolute, fictions for conditional assent. Myths make sense in terms of a lost order of time, *illud tempus*; fictions, if successful, make sense of the here and now, *hoc tempus*.[24]

Thus, although they would appear to be mutually exclusive concepts, myth and fiction might also seem on this description to constitute the poles of a continuum or the isotopes of a chiasmus in which each pole is at once the necessary presupposition, and at the same time the irredeemable negation, of the other. Any interplay between the positive and negative poles of this relationship could be emplotted dialectically or (after the manner of Kenneth Burke) "dramatistically." In any event, Kermode uses this dialectical or chiasmatic structure to generate "places" in a semantic field in which the mixed cases of truth and falsity, real and imaginary, fact and fiction, and so on, can be cleared for occupancy by "history" and "science" respectively.

In the elaboration of his theory, Kermode needed a notion of a dimension of human being that, while "real" in the sense of "really existing," does not wear the mask of "ultimate being." This turns out to be "history," which, so it seems to me, has the virtue of being able to mediate between the chaos of ultimate being and the fictions of literature. But this "history" is not that of the professional historians; rather, it is a hybrid of the raw experience of temporality, on the one hand, and the narrativized versions provided by historians and literary writers, on the other.

Kermode puts it this way: we do not in fact like history to be what Lord Acton said it ought to be, critical and colorless; we accept without much question a measure of mythmaking, the intrusion of personal feeling, or, as it may be, nationalist or class feeling. Of course, there are different kinds of history, each with its own peculiar conditions, but we would expect most of these general provisions to obtain for all. Kermode wanted clothes for Clio:[25] "patterns, causes, events, rather than mere facts, opinions rather than flat chronicles" in his histories, and he wanted these because only a history thus construed could contribute to the "making of a usable past, a past which is not simply past but also always new."[26] This idea of making the past new was central to modernism, Kermode thought, and it was central to the kind of history he hypothesized as a justification for regarding history itself as a kind useful fiction.

But this idea of history was not unique to Kermode. In the very years in which Frank Kermode, on the basis of his distinction between literary fictions and historical fictions, was working out his theory of fictional history, the philosopher Michael Oakeshott was working towards a similar conception. In a collection of essays written in the early 1970s, titled *On History*, Oakeshott distinguished between the *historical* past—the past as it is constructed by historians—and the *practical* past—the past that ordinary people carry around with them in the form of memories, both accessible and repressed, and to which they have recourse when they find themselves in situations in which they must act without fully adequate knowledge of where they are or sufficient certitude of who they are.[27] For Oakeshott, such situations were practical in two senses: first, they are practical in the sense of raising the ethical question "What *should* I do?" (in the sense of Kant's second *Critique*) and, secondly, they are practical in the sense of raising a utilitarian question, "What *can* I do?"

In the absence of any religious, metaphysical, or otherwise transcendental source of authority for answering these questions, our only resource is to our own past experience and/or that of the community to which we belong. It might be thought that in such situations, the past to which we would have recourse would be that past resurrected, reconstructed, or restored by the professional historians of our community. But nothing could be further from the case. First, professional historians are for the most part interested only in that part of the past they can restore to perception on the basis of the kinds of evidence they take to be relevant to a specifically "historical" way of grasping the past. Second, professional historians are, or profess to be, interested in the past in itself, or the past for itself alone and not as an object useful for understanding the present or anticipating the future. Third, the historical past, which is written from the standpoint of someone who knows how events of a specific present turned out, is a past that no one living in the past could ever have experienced. The historical past exists and can only have existed in the books and articles in which historians have distilled it. Thus, the historical past has no ethical or utilitarian importance. If anything, the historicity of the historical past consists of its distance, difference, and irrelevance to the existential present. Such a past, it could be said, is of only *theoretical* interest. Oakeshott wanted to justify another kind of past, a past that could serve the "practical" purpose of suggesting possible ways that human beings in an aporetic present could imagine a kind of sea anchor to give them provisional orientation in the ocean of time.

From his first work until his last, Frank Kermode demonstrated an "appetite" for history.[28] For Kermode, history is a kind of degree zero of human actuality against which all of the grand narratives of human development and the myths of ultimate meaning can be measured, their ideological content identified, and their authority as guides to the future definitively dispelled. Although short-range historical narratives provided history with a provisional meaningfulness, which is to say, evidence of a potentiality for meaning, their overriding interest in particular facts saved them from any tendency to holism. Kermode followed Karl Popper in the conviction that history could never become a predictive (nomothetic-deductive) science nor serve as the raw material of a religious or metaphysical vision of human destiny. And, like Popper, Kermode believed that historians did their work or played their game properly only when they told stories about human beings trying to live meaningful lives in specific times and places and under specific conditions of existence.

But stories about sets or series of real events do not possess the truth-value of factuality. This is because stories do not inhere in sets of real events. At best, a given series of real events may provide intimations of elements of stories: extraordinary happenings, grand actions, felicitous outcomes of conflicts, elevations of the humble or humiliations of the great. When historians seize upon these intimations, enfigure them as story-types and cast them as stories with well-marked beginnings, middles, and ends, endow them with plots, peripeties, and pathos, and provide endings that "fulfill" what had appeared to be aporetic beginnings, then historians are engaging in an activity much older than the practice of "historical research" itself. They are, according to Kermode (and this is his radical move), engaging in *fiction*. That is to say, Kermode rejects the idea that historians "find" the stories they tell in the events they study. No set of events occurring in a given time and place, even if arranged in the temporal order of their occurrence, would ever manifest the formal coherence of a story. They could at best take on the meaning of a "chronicle." In order for a history to be made out of a chronicle, the events of the latter must be restructured, rearranged, and represented as having the form (and content) of a story. This is to say that, in order to be turned into a plausible story, the events of a chronicle must be "narrated" or, as I would have it, "narrativized." As thus envisaged, historical stories have a twofold referent: the events of which they speak, on the one hand, and, on the other, the plot-type by reference to which a story is endowed with a generic meaning or paradigm of sense-giving inherent in the culture of which the story-teller is a member. This set of paradigms exists in the myths, religions, ideologies, dogmas, doctrines, and conventions of a culture. They also exist in "literature," but here they exist in a peculiar condition of stable instability. In literature or, as I would prefer, literary writing, the paradigms of meaning-giving of a culture are subjected to a range of uses and experimentations that effectively make manifest their implicit idea that meaning equals (is worth or is equivalent to) form.

It should be stressed that Frank Kermode in no way wished to be taken as an authoritative contributor to the debates over the nature of history, historiography, and philosophy of history that were raging in the 1960s. His thought on these topics appears to have been derived from a reading of Popper, Arthur Danto, and Morton White, and later on, E. H. Gombrich and Thomas Kuhn. What Kermode was trying to do was to save the idea of literary fiction as a mode of cognition, as the essence of literature, and as an antidote to mythical thinking in any form. The notion of literary fiction allows Kermode to argue that history (or, as it is said, historical reality) is the defining referent not only of "literature" but of modernist literature in particular—indeed, it is the pole-star that keeps the great modernists (including Eliot, Pound, Wyndham Lewis, D. H. Lawrence, etc.) from declining into myth.[29] But fiction can have this function because, in Kermode's formulation of the topic, it is also the essence of a specifically historiological way of thinking about the enigmas of being's relation to time.[30]

Notes

1. Frank Kermode, *The Sense of an Ending: Studies in the Theory of Fiction* (Oxford: Oxford University Press, 1967).

2. The aporias (enigmas or "undecidables") of temporality is the subject of Paul Ricoeur's discussion of three kinds of time (chronological, historical, and ontological) in the three volumes of *Time and Narrative*, translated by Kathleen

McLaughlin and David Pellauer (Chicago: University of Chicago Press, 1984–88), a work heavily indebted to Kermode's *Sense of an Ending*.

3. I feel that I must draw attention to the most hostile review of *Sense of an Ending* that I know of, the late Richard Webster's "New Ends for Old: Frank Kermode's *The Sense of an Ending*," *Critical Quarterly* 38, no. 1 (1974): 311–12. Webster seems to think that Kermode wished to convince us that "only by a 'theory of fiction' could the enigmas of the universe be unlocked." There are many other critical reviews of this and other of Kermode's work; its status as a classic is not uncontested.

4. Mieke Bal, *Quoting Caravaggio: Contemporary Art, Preposterous History* (Chicago: University of Chicago Press, 1999). This book argues for the possibility of "reversing" history—or at least the history of art—insofar as the present can change the *historical* past by rewriting it. To be sure, this is to suggest that the only "history" we can have is that found in books and scholarly articles. Bal's book is inspired or at least sustained by the work of Patricia Parker on the rhetorical figure of *hysteron proteron* or the trope of *metalepsis*, by which one can quite plausibly "put the cart before the horse" or the post- before the pre- by the simple device of spatializing a temporal relationship. See Patricia Parker, *Shakespeare from the Margins: Language, Culture, Context* (Chicago: University of Chicago Press, 1996).

5. This is jargonistic, I know. But I needed a way to suggest that for Kermode the "fictive" is produced by *poiesis*. See Kermode, *An Appetite for Poetry* (Cambridge, MA: Harvard University Press, 1989), where the ideas of the fictive, the poetic, and the aesthetic are all run together.

6. Erich Auerbach, *Mimesis: The Representation of Reality in Western Literature*, trans. Willard R. Trask (Princeton, NJ: Princeton University Press, 1968), 19.

7. Kermode, *Sense of an Ending*, 53.

8. I am not clear whether Kermode, when speaking about history, means the thing itself (i.e., a mode of human being, comprised of the whole past, present, future continuum that we take to be completed insofar as it is past, still happening insofar as it is present, or still yet to come insofar as it is future) or the accounts given of the past by modern professional historians. It is obvious that he does not mean those metahistorical or mythical accounts of history of the kind produced by Hegel, Marx, Spengler, or Toynbee. It is from such mythical accounts of history that modern historiography saves us. But Kermode's adoption of Karl Popper's criticism of historicism, of both the scientistic and the philosophicist kind, suggests that he (Kermode) prefers his history in the old-fashioned, narrative mode of presentation. Certainly, Kermode respects the work of analytical historical researchers who produce reports (of archival findings) rather than stories with beginnings, middles, and ends. Kermode expects his historians to respect the research findings of their peers, but prefers them to bring together the facts into a coherent story with a plot that consonates an ending with a beginning. This bringing together of the facts into a coherent story is the work of narrative or, as I would prefer, narrativization (by which I mean the endowment of a series of events with story-meaning). Narration, narrative, and narrativization are the subjects of the semiotic subject of narratology.

9. Here I allude to a fundamental text of modernist philosophy of history, Reinhart Koselleck's *Future's Past: On the Semantics of Historical Time* (Cambridge, MA: MIT Press, 1985), which proposes a "semantics of historical time" focused on the dialectical relation between a society's "space of experience" and its projected "horizon of expectations."

10. Again, I allude to the similar project of E. H. Gombrich in *Art and Illusion*. Gombrich stresses that his book is not a "history of art" (he had already written such a work, entitled, significantly, *The Story of Art*) but rather a consideration of how it is that art can be said to have a history.

11. See Kermode's discussion of Heidegger in *An Appetite for Poetry* (Cambridge, MA: Harvard University Press, 1989).

12. Kermode, *Sense of an Ending*, 56–57.

13. Kermode, 56–57.

14. Frank Kermode, *History and Value* (Oxford: Clarendon, 1988), 111, my emphases.

15. Kermode, *History and Value*, 111.

16. Kermode, *Sense of an Ending*, 36.

17. Roland Barthes, "The Discourse of History," trans. Stephen Bann, *Comparative Criticism* 3 (1981): 7–20.

18. For a discussion of the ethics of using the Holocaust as the subject of a fiction or indeed of any kind of artistic performance, see Saul Friedländer, *Probing the Limits of Representation: Nazism and the "Final Solution"* (Cambridge, MA: Harvard University Press, 1992). The discussion has been carried much further today, especially by Berel Lang and Friedländer himself. [Ed: See the successor volume that commemorates this publication, *Probing the Ethics of Holocaust Culture*, ed. Claudio Fogu, Wulf Kansteiner, and Todd Presner (Cambridge, MA: Harvard University Press, 2016). Both White and Friedländer contributed to this volume.]

19. Kermode, *Sense of an Ending*, 38–41.

20. Kermode, 38.

21. Kermode, 39.

22. Kermode, 39–40.

23. This dependency of "realistic" art on illusion was the thesis advanced by E. H. Gombrich's aforementioned *Art and Illusion: A Study in the Psychology of Pictorial Representation* (London: Phaidon, 1960), which effectively argued that the realism of Western art depended on the discovery of the necessity of illusionary techniques, if objects depicted on a two-dimensional surface were to "appear" as three-dimensional to the viewer. The same thing applied to the production of the effect of proportion in perspective, in which the relative sizes of objects were discernible at different depths in the picture plane.

24. Kermode, *Sense of an Ending*, 39.

25. Kermode, *History and Value*, 112. [Ed: See also Stephen Bann, *The Clothing of Clio: A Study of the Representation of History in Nineteenth-Century Britain and France* (Cambridge: Cambridge University Press, 1984).]

26. Kermode, *History and Value*, 116.

27. Michael Oakeshott, *On History* (Oxford: Basil Blackwell, 1983), chap. 1.

28. I allude to Kermode's *An Appetite for Poetry*.

29. Kermode, *History and Value*, 119.

30. The allusion is to Heidegger's *Being and Time*, which Kermode reflected on in reference to Stevens's interest in the German philosopher. *Sense of an Ending* is, as the title indicates, about how things end and, more specifically, how human beings try to come to terms with the awareness that all things must end, how they might make endings more than mere terminations.

CHAPTER 7

The Substance of the Sixties [2013]

> Being a child and being an adult are two
> inconsistent properties that cannot belong
> to the same being at the same time.
>
> —Anita Kasabona

My title promises a revelation of the "substance" of "the Sixties" in the United States, what that raucous and potentially revolutionary decade was *really* about. But obviously no one believes in "substance" in the old-fashioned, metaphysical or Scholastic sense, as the magma that holds a thing together and constitutes an "essence" without which it would not be what it in fact *is*. By substance, I mean something like the modern chemical idea of the elements of a thing in a (molecular) combination such that if you remove one element, the thing ceases to be what it had formerly been. In other words, what I propose is to identify at least one of the elements of the Sixties that, if removed from its makeup or canceled out in some way by retrospective revision, would deprive the concept, idea, or figure of "the Sixties" of its most prominent identifying traits.

Now, one of the elements of "the Sixties" without which it could not possibly have been what it appears to have been is the sheer *quantity* of persons between the ages of twelve and twenty-one (some seventy million) believed to have been undergoing a process known as "adolescence" in the period between 1960 and 1969.[1] Take away these adolescents or reduce their number by half, and you would have had something quite other than "the Sixties." The period might have been just as raucous, contentious, contested, and so on, but it would not have been whatever it is that we think the Sixties to have been. You cannot think away these seventy million youths and their condition of adolescence without changing our notion of the possibilities of what actually happened during the decade that carries the nick- or proper name of "the Sixties."

This is obviously not an empirically testable idea, but more of an intuition based on my own experience of the Sixties, on quite a bit of reading about it, and on continuous thinking about it since I first began to realize (in the Seventies?) that what I had lived through in the decade preceding had been nothing other than—"the Sixties." And the more I pondered the adequacy of this nickname for that decade, the more it seemed to me that the Sixties had "substantially" been a generational experience of a particular kind—the kind indicated in that locution "adolescence," invented by social scientists in the early twentieth century to name the experience of young persons put "on hold" on the way from puberty to adulthood in a modern urban setting. But more than that: it was the sheer number of persons considered to be adolescent during the Sixties—seventy million persons out of a total population that increased from 123 million to around 193 million—that makes of it a statistically significant decade.[2]

I think now that the name "adolescent" reflected a deep ambiguity about the value or worth of this generation of young persons on the part of their elders, their teachers, and the legal system. In any event, it seems to me that the very term "adolescent" carries with it an ambivalence that has permeated the attitude of Americans towards other processes of development such as economic, legal, educational, and military institutions since World War II, as America has transformed into a society organized for war on a world-wide scale, and a national mode of organization has given way to a global and transnational one. In the half century after World War II, America achieved the status of a fully realized capitalist system, only to discover that the utopia promised by capitalism created as many divisions between the haves and have-nots of society as the God of Calvinism. One of the biggest casualties of this process of division has been the adolescents, who have effectively been expelled from the labor force of every industrialized nation in the world.

America has always celebrated itself for its *youthfulness*, its newness, freshness, prospects for the future, and so on. At the same time, however, due to its Puritanical heritage, it has also been heavily suspicious of youth, for its disorderliness, its passion, its lack of discipline, its delinquency. The party of Puritanism values nothing more than (male) adulthood, the state of maturity, conformity to the Law, devotion to duty, self-discipline, and work "for the greater glory of God," rather than for the enjoyment that material wealth makes possible. At the same time, however, "the Protestant ethic," which had once instilled "the spirit of capitalism" with moral fiber and resistance to material self-indulgence, now gave way to a new "ethic" of narcissistic self-regard and a culture of consumerism necessary to keep the capitalist machine geared to the infinite increase in the rate of profit even at the expense of the health of the Earth itself.

In the immediate postwar period, the older Puritan ethic remained the official doctrine of the religious, legal, and educational institutions, but the practices required by a society increasingly geared to consumption as an end in itself were at direct odds with this way of thinking. The generation of the Sixties was the first to grow up with exposure to new media whose main purpose was to fuel an orgy of consumerism while maintaining illusions of the traditional family, work, and knowledge values of an older preindustrial and even agrarian kind.[3] It is small wonder that "adolescence" loomed in the imaginary of middle-class parents as both an extended age of childlike innocence, on the one hand, and a stage of life providing temptations and dangers to youth formerly unknown, on the other. "Adolescents" are an ideal target group for an advertising industry aimed at creating a huge population of consumers with adult desires and, because they tend to be still dependent on their parents, with the leisure to spend most of their time thinking about or actually indulging the manufactured fantasies of the modern (*noire*) city. At the same time, the American war machine's expanding investment in military adventures, such as those of the Cold War, Cuba, and Vietnam, meant that these adolescents had to be propagandized to die for their country as well.

It was in the Sixties that "adolescence" achieved a legal status that constituted a reason for establishing a host of social, medical, and educational "services" meant to treat adolescence as a kind of illness and the adolescent as a kind of "delinquent" arrestable on suspicion of being inclined to commit a crime even when he or she had not actually committed one. It is little wonder that the kind of crimes committed by American military forces in Vietnam were laid to their contamination by the adolescent culture of "sex, drugs, and rock 'n' roll" promoted by the American "culture industry" since the late 1950s. In 1957 the US Supreme Court ruled in favor of a ban on display of Elvis Presley's hips, and in January 1959 the Mutual Broadcasting Company forbade the playing of "rock 'n' roll" records on its member radio stations. All of this resistance to the new music and recreational practices of the Sixties' generation faded away once the monetary gain from their promotion had been recognized. The original culture of resistance was progressively assimilated to the mainstream (white, corporate, market) by commodification and mediatization, which may account for the increasing violence of exploited minorities for whom assimilation meant dissolution of traditional ethnic, gender, or class identities.[4]

In many respects, the socio-dynamics of the Sixties can be comprehended as a result of a new generation's lived experience of what Marxist historians call "contradiction," social psychologists have labeled as "double bind" and "cognitive dissonance," and others, of a more artistic or literary bent, call enigma, paradox, or irony. And no one lived this experience of contradiction more than that cohort of Sixties' young people—seventy million in number—caught in the web of contradictions called "adolescence." Quite simply, what Gregory Bateson called the "double bind" consisted of that quintessential social situation—explained by Aristotle, Rousseau, Kant, Hegel, Kierkegaard, Marx, Weber, Durkheim, and Marcuse as the very basis of life in society—in which, by trying to live up to one principle of law, morality, or custom, you inevitably and even necessarily violate another. Thus, for example, the double bind of the bourgeois father's order to his son to "be like me" and, at the same time, to "be an individual." Or: the idea that one has to be ruthless in the pursuit of economic gain but, at the same time, "love thy neighbor." "Man is born free, but everywhere he is in chains"—how is this possible, asks Rousseau. To which the Puritan capitalist answers by citing the "Saint Matthew Rule": to him who has, it shall be given; and to him who has not, it shall be taken away even that which he has.

The condition of "adolescence" differed from the notion of childhood by the ambiguity of its moral significance. Presumed to be a stage between childhood and adulthood, a stage "on the way" to adulthood, the "teenager" was supposed to have all the duties of an adult—including the duty of work and military service—but none or only *some* of the rights.[5] The pathos of this condition of contradiction endured by young people in postwar America was the theme of many books and films of the early postwar period, such as the James Dean movie *Rebel without a Cause* (1955), J. D. Salinger's novel *Catcher in the Rye* (1951), and above all Joseph Heller's *Catch-22* (1961). Heller's message is contained in the "catch" built into the rule that allows one to apply for relief from combat on grounds of insanity, but presumes that anyone applying for such relief must be sane, must be therefore faking his condition, and consequently can be denied his request. A whole culture of contradiction—in the form of enigmas, paradoxes, puzzles, and mysteries—is posited as the basis of the plot of Thomas Pynchon's novel *The Crying of Lot 49* (1966), in which one enigmatic situation is "resolved" by being passed over to another situation equally enigmatic, in a kind of (*noire*) detective story—an inquiry into the nature of the "legacy" America provides its citizens—without an identifiable crime, on the one hand, or a solution to this crime, on the other.

The contradictions of adolescent life in America of the Sixties can serve as another instantiation of the paradigmatic contradictions contained in the Constitution of the United States. In the Bill of Rights appended to this document, certain rights (of assembly, conscience, expression, to bear arms, to enjoy "due process" in courts of law, etc.) are extended to *all* citizens, but with the tacit proviso that these rights pertain only to adult, white, male property owners. Women, people of color, children, homosexuals, the poor and homeless, and all of the "Others" in American society were consigned to a subaltern position in the social system. And although there were movements aimed to secure these rights for those denied them, it was not until the Sixties that women, adolescents, people of color, and children took to the streets to militate for these rights and laid the groundwork for later political action that would in fact extend them (at least, in part) to women, people of color, children, etc.

Was it the general weight of adolescent disillusionment that reactivated the various subaltern groups to demand their rights in the 1960s and beyond? Surely it was the experience of young people in the exercise of their rights to assemble, to protest, and to criticize government agencies for their prosecution of a war against the Vietnamese people, and their experience of police and military forces' brutality in opposing them, that dispelled the illusion that "the law" was on the side of the righteous, rather than a force for the defense of the property of the wealthy. By the end of the Sixties, every adolescent knew what every occupant of a ghetto, slum, or *barrio* had long since known: if you report a crime to the police, you are as likely to be accused of a crime as given aid in seeking relief from one.

The white, suburban middle class of America did not know this, but their adolescent children found it out soon enough whenever they tried to exercise their rights of assembly, free speech, and opinion in public protest of policies and programs they deemed unjust. And the sheer weight of numbers—those seventy million persons of different genders, ethnicities, social class membership, languages, etc.—made of adolescents a force that could not be and ultimately was not ignored by the forces of law and order. This is attested by the number of laws and statutes passed in the Sixties and Seventies directed at the repression of adolescent and other "deviant" (or in Nixonian language "hedonistic") activities.

The quotation used as an epigraph for my essay is ironic, being an example of substantialist thinking that presumes that childhood and adulthood are utterly different "properties" and so could not exist in the same "being" without producing a monster, such as a child with adult attributes or an adult with childlike features. But in fact, adolescents have been constituted as a genus of childlike human beings that, according to the *doxa* of a certain modernity, possess many of the physical properties of adults and therefore have to endure the legal status of children. These "adolescents" are treated in law and in fact as being "delinquent" in some way, as "lacking" in the mental and moral virtues that would allow them to assume the rights of a fully gown, American citizen. It is my contention that the onset of a wave of adolescents—the seventy million of them in the decade between 1960 and 1970, added to a population of roughly 150 million souls—so disrupted the social imaginary of American society that it generated a spate of laws and legislation that effectively created a generational divide hitherto unheard of in American history. It was this divide, I think, that accounts for the ambivalence with which historians and other social analysts have typically viewed "the Sixties."[6]

With these remarks in mind, I am prepared to try to follow the instructions for our lecture series,[7] which are: "(1) to take *a closer look* at the 1960s from *different disciplinary perspectives, focusing on important* events, developments, and persons in the cultural, social, political, and economic life; and (2) *discuss the legacy* of the 1960s for *present America*." Since my discipline is history, this means that I should try to deal with "the Sixties" historically, which is to say, "contextualize" the Sixties, set this moment of American social-cultural history into its original spatial and temporal context, and determine what if anything of it remains alive and active as a component of America's "present." But there is a "catch" attached to any attempt to execute these instructions. As I have argued elsewhere,[8] "context" is an ambiguous concept: how extended in space and time would this context be? Moreover, where does the event end and the context begin? Finally, what is the nature of the relationship between the event and its context? Is it causal, mutually implicative, structural, expressive, or what?

Beyond all this, what are we to do with the term "legacy"? Is it to be construed in its legal, its biological, or its historical meaning? Which is to say: is "the Sixties" to be treated as a part of the genetic endowment of "America" that subsequent generations must live with, or is it to be thought of as a cultural matrix that can be accepted or rejected as an element of American character, as one chooses an ethics or a career, or a new hair style, an automobile, or a religion? In other words, does "the Sixties" belong to the (economic, technological, physical) Base of American life in the twenty-first century, or does it belong to the (social and cultural) Superstructure? Is it something we cannot not deny as an element of our current makeup, or is it something we can take or leave according to whatever uses we can make of it in "present America"?

The "catch" is that much of this depends on how we construe the "science" of historical studies. Or rather, what *kind* of science do we think historical studies to be? These questions are especially relevant to the way we think about "the Sixties," because it was during the 1960s that, in America especially, "history" lost its status as an authoritative *story* of how the national identity was formed, and historians ceased to be accepted as *custodians* of the genealogical record of the nation.

Already by the end of the nineteenth century, history had lost its capacity to distinguish adequately between scientific and mythical accounts of the past and to serve as an antidote to every kind of ideology—as its earliest "historicist" apologists had promised. In the first half of the twentieth century, (positivist) philosophers had deprived history of its status as a science of general laws of causality, experimental control of data, and ability to predict the future. Then, the ease with which professional historians all over the world adapted to the ideological requirements of the totalitarian states of the interwar period undermined history's status as the enlightened or progressive discipline it was thought to be during the liberal nineteenth century.

History's failure to adapt to the criteria of the "behavioral" social sciences emerging from World War II resulted in its derogation in the 1960s and 1970s to the status of a justifier of the social status quo, a story told by (white, upper class, European) men, about men, to other men—which explained how whatever happened to be the case in any given disposition of power, wealth, and privilege had its good reasons and could be questioned only at the risk of disrupting the cosmic order. In short, by the end of the Sixties, straight history—bourgeois history, professional historiography—had become the conservative science *par excellence.* Whence the sudden revival in the 1960s and into the 1970s of interest in new or older, alternative modes of historical inquiry: Marxist, Maoist, history from below, everyday life history, *longue durée* (or what might be thought of as an anticipation of ecological) history, people's history, women's history, gay history, postcolonial (and, later, "subaltern") history, and the like.[9]

History—understood as at once a distinctive mode of human being in the world, a reserve of knowledge or at least information about the human past, a basis for an a-religious and non-metaphysical but nonetheless *foundational* science of humanity—now appeared to be as "mythical," or at least as arbitrary, as the ideologies and fables it had once claimed to have displaced. History now seemed to be whatever one wished to make of it, a kind of fiction or myth in its own right. All of which succored that strain of Existentialist thought (especially of Sartre, de Beauvoir, and Camus, but also of Nietzsche, Kierkegaard, and Dostoyevsky) that flourished in the immediate postwar period and that had already achieved a popular currency in novels and films. Indeed, existentialism was intrinsically a-historical inasmuch as it presupposed a past made up of discrete *actes gratuites* (or random events) that bore no substantive relationship to one another and were to be considered "real" only in the extent to which they had been retrospectively chosen as a subject's own. Any custom or practice distilled into institutional procedures was held to be "inauthentic" insofar as it had only its age to commend it.

These attitudes towards the past and (establishmentarian) history color any possible thought we might advance regarding "the legacy of the 1960s for present America"—because the dominant attitude of "the Sixties" towards the past rendered the very idea of a "legacy" suspect. Inherited institutions, values, and authority were suspect precisely *because* they had been handed down from the past.[10] The youth, and especially the middle-class youth of America who were on their way to maturity during the Sixties, not only did not feel particularly grateful for their inheritance from the past, they had more than enough reason *not* to regard their future with optimism and hope. Beneficiaries of an extraordinary postwar economic boom, targets of advertising blitzes designed to confuse identity with commodity consumption, products of childcare theories and psychological/pedagogical ideas designed to reinforce ego and link growth to "happiness," the youth of the Sixties—along with the rest of the population but especially women—were encouraged to pursue "youthfulness" as an aim good in itself rather than think of it as a stage of life on the way to maturity. The triumph of what psychoanalysis called the pleasure principle over the reality principle, coupled with the idea that society itself and especially the institution of the nuclear family were the principal causes of mental illness—celebrated in books like Norman O. Brown's *Life against Death* and R. D. Laing's *The Divided Self*—along with a general turn to mood-altering or "recreational" drug use, created an atmosphere of anti-repressiveness that increased in direct proportion to the attempts of the law to control it.[11]

But then the Sixties revealed the illusionary nature of these anodyne visions of the future. First, there was the string of the assassinations of esteemed leaders: President John F. Kennedy, Martin Luther King Jr., and Malcolm X. Next, a succession of events that revealed the extent to which America was becoming a war society: the Cuban Missile Crisis of 1962; the escalation in 1965 of what had been a virtually secret war in Vietnam; a sharp increase in the Draft along with American troop casualties in Vietnam (14,000 in 1965 alone). Then, a chain of race riots that had begun during World War II but continued in Detroit, Los Angeles, and a number of smaller cities into the Sixties bared the truth about America's chronic racism. Events like these showed the extent to which the roseate life of the American middle class, increasingly suburbanized and dedicated to consumerism as a way of life, had been purchased at the expense of groups—women, people of color, young persons, children, homeless, etc.—that had been routinely excluded and exploited by a system designed to serve the white, wealthy, and ensconced upper class. The disparity between the golden "promises" contained in the myths of America and the realities of a capitalist system devoted to the increase of the rate of profit at any cost constituted the "substance" of the Sixties in America and accounts in large part, I wish to argue, for both the political activism of many of its adolescents and the harshness of the system's reaction to their demands for reform.

The Woodstock Music Festival of August 15-18, 1969, in rural New York State, with its manifest disregard for the values, customs, and laws of "straight" society, was for the establishment a fulfillment of all of its worst fantasies about "flaming youth." Woodstock was an event that was for, by, and in praise of youth, sexual license, drug use, and a pastiche of other "alternative" cultural practices. Again, the sheer size of the event—with some 500,000 participants, thirty-four musical acts, public nudity, sexuality, and casual profanity—made of it a politically rebellious, not to say, revolutionary event. The popularity of the event and its rapidly achieved status as a symbol of a new consciousness among the youth, combined with its celebration of a new kind of music, new kinds of media, and a whole new semiotic, gave it a political heft and weightiness that immediately resulted in legislation (the Nixon war on drugs of 1971 and years following) that could only be interpreted as being *against* youth, *against* pleasure, and *for* the military-police state that many citizens saw emerging with the Vietnam War, the resistance to the war, and the response to this resistance mounted by the military-industrial complex that would effectively replace the state as the governing agency of the nation.

Obviously, there are many similarities to the protests, riots, and demonstrations of the 1960s in America and earlier internal and fratricidal social conflicts. But one difference remains between the Sixties and earlier periods of discontent, and this is the element of youth that remains both an inextinguishable content of Sixties' social protest, the image of a utopian ideal of a community of love and sexual freedom, and a symbol for the political Right of everything wrong with a "permissible" society that had lost touch with its Puritan and agrarian moral roots. Many of the themes of reaction to the youthfulness-*cum*-licentiousness of the Sixties have returned in the oratory and legislation advanced by advocates of "Tea Party" politics in the current American scene. But already at the beginning of the 1970s, the forces of conservatism had cast criticism of the Vietnam War, the use of drugs, and the sexual revolution as a veritable "plot against America," driven by a kind of "moral poverty" (Secretary of Education William Bennett) that could best be countered by harsh new laws, mandatory sentences for offenders who used drugs for "recreation," and prosecution of those who had sought to evade military service by flight abroad.

The irony of the "war on drugs" launched in the Seventies by Nixon and Company lay in the fact that the Sixties generation had grown up witnessing the promotion by the medical profession and the advertising industry of a whole new array of mood-altering drugs (Librium, Valium, Xanax), guaranteed to make those who could afford them "normal" once more and free of the kind of anxieties that a modern way of life inevitably fomented. Increasingly harsh measures were used against users of "illegal" drugs such as marijuana, cocaine, and heroin. Indeed, by 2005, more than half of the seven million American adults jailed or on parole were serving sentences much more severe than anything laid upon "white collar" criminals in high finance and the professions. It is hardly accidental that of the total number of convicts, most are poor and some 80 percent are people of color.

But there is one event that can serve as a symbol of the substance of the Sixties and as a fitting symbolic end to the decade: I mean the Stonewall riots that followed upon a police raid on a Mafia-owned homosexual bar in Greenwich Village, in Manhattan, on the night of June 25, 1969. This event may be thought of as the rebellion of the most abject fraction of that wide constituency of "adolescents," of those members of American society defined by their presumed "lack" of what it took to grow into a law-abiding and law-enforcing, manly, adult male, patriarch, gun-owner, and parent. The Stonewall Inn was known to attract a young, poor, and marginalized homosexual, transvestite, and transgendered clientele; it was also known to be a bar that regularly paid off the police for the right to illegally host homosexuals and that connived with the police to stage regular raids of the premises in which homosexuals would be beaten, arrested, and jailed as a matter of routine. This double exploitation of homosexuals by organized crime, on the one hand, and by the police, on the other, was emblematic (in my opinion) of the treatment of all marginalized groups in US society, of which, as I have argued, the millions of adolescents forced to defer the full exercise of their rights as adult citizens constituted the largest group.

On the night of June 28, 1969, however, under sustained intimidation and brutalization, the patrons of Stonewall not only fought back; they forced the retreat of the police and sustained their rioting, with growing crowds of sympathizers and news media willing to document the injustice with which the rioters had been treated. The event inaugurated the Gay Pride movement and promoted the demand for not only full rights of citizenship for gays but also for the recognition of a humanity that had been denied them for time immemorial. This event, coming at the end of the chronological Sixties, along with the Woodstock Festival following in August of the same year, really marked the beginning of the last phase of the symbolic Sixties. It would take another five years before the Vietnam War would end, the Draft would be eliminated, and the first of a series of economic crises (1973–1975 recession) would succeed in pulling the teeth of the political and social movements unleashed in the Sixties by young people who had lived the "double bind" of adolescence.[12]

The Sixties is nothing if not a time when youth, or more specifically adolescents, entered the public scene as a political, social, economic, and *physical* force. Between 1960 and 1970, in a population of roughly 125 million, more than 70 million people passed through the travails of that ambiguous status of a life *after* puberty but *before* admission to adulthood that had only recently come to be called "adolescence." By legal definition, adolescence is a period in which persons both male and female have the physical capacities but neither the intellectual nor the emotional capacities of adults. The so-called "baby boom" of the 1940s–1950s resulted in the production of an enormous number of adolescents who entered the public scene—as consumers, as agents, as interpellants of the law—in the 1960s. Fear of these adolescents was manifested in the passage of a large number of laws, at both the state and national level, for the education, disciplinization, and incarceration of "delinquent" youth—youth whose only danger to society was contained in the fact that they were lacking in some way (*delinquere* = to lack, or to want); and more specifically, lacking in the virtues presumed to come with "adulthood."

The category of the "delinquent" is a late-nineteenth-century invention, the purpose of which is to justify the surveillance and disciplinization of members of society deemed likely to commit a crime of some sort, less because of overt criminal intent than because of a "lack" of the qualities presumed to be possessed by "adults." Laws were passed, such as, for example, against smoking tobacco by persons under the age of sixteen. Of course, at the same time, advertising and the media in general (the movies, television, popular literature) presented smoking cigarettes as a highly desirable activity, sexy, indicative of sophistication and cosmopolitanism, upper class, etc. So, too, for the consumption of alcohol and other recreational drugs, such as marijuana.

Needless to say, it is not as though the events that occurred in the Sixties and which are presumed to have constituted the substance of its historicity have themselves changed. What has changed is the substance of American society as a result of certain post-Sixties experiences: defeat in a series of wars (Vietnam, Iraq, Afghanistan); the dissolution of the USSR, America's principal "enemy" in the Cold War; a series of economic and social crises caused by the advent of a new kind of (global, corporate, consumer) capitalism; the transition of the US from a hemispheric to a world hegemon; and commitment to an endless war on "terrorism" that has changed the legal no less than the spiritual basis of American society. As each of these experiences has occurred, American ideologues, scholars, and intellectuals have felt the need to reassess the significance of the Sixties as the event, or congeries of events, that first manifested the symptoms of an epochal structural change in American society. Although there has been disagreement over the nature of this change and whether it was progressive or retrogressive for the nation at large, successive reassessments of the nature of the Sixties have themselves depended in large part on what investigators conceive the state of American society to be at the time of their investigations, whether they believe the nation is in relatively good shape or is suffering from the effects of structural changes first manifested in the period immediately following World War II, or not. All of which is to suggest that historical reassessments of the meaning or significance of earlier periods in a community's past, however "objective," will be more ideological than scientific in kind and instead of resolving earlier disputes over the nature of the period in question will only add to the number of equally plausible but conflicting interpretations thereof. This is to suggest that any given period's interest in the Sixties will itself have to be assessed in the light of current preconceptions about the nature of its current situation and the extent to which it considers this situation to be a consequence or an effect of causes that first appeared in or around the 1960s.

Now, it is hazardous to attempt to characterize "the current situation"—political, economic, social, and cultural—of the American Republic as of the last decade, but it is certainly easy enough to list the changes that have occurred in American society since the end of World War II. First, the transformation of American capitalism from a national, industrial to a transnational and predominantly finance mode. Next, changes in the nature of work, employment, and the workforce, the debilitation of labor unions, and the internationalization of corporations. Next, privatization of the military establishment along with the militarization of American society: the US has been at war (open and covert) continuously since 1948 (the advent of the Cold War), has been defeated in three major conflicts (Vietnam, Iraq, and Afghanistan),[13] and is currently maintaining between 750 and 1,000 military bases and outposts around the world. Then, expansion of the prison system, militarization of police forces, and politicization of the judicial system. In 2010, of a population of 300 million, 7 million adults were in prison, jail, on parole, or under supervision of legal authorities (2.7 percent of the adult population, one-half for victimless—drug-related—crimes). In large part, this process of militarization, on the one hand, and domestic disciplinarization, on the other, can be seen as beginning in response to social changes first articulated as utopian dreams in the Sixties.

And this is because the Sixties—a chronological term now extended to name a complex amalgam of images and concepts indicative of hopes and dreams as well as of projects and practices—brought under criticism both the fundamental structures of society—such as the family, the military, the police, educational institutions, and the political system—and the myths that sustained the authority of these institutions. Thus, the protests that marked the symbolic decade of the Sixties—from roughly 1956 to about 1976—were launched less in the interest of recalling the country to its traditional values and vision (as in the American Revolution of 1776, which, as Edmund Burke argued, was a revolution on behalf of tradition and against the new practices and regimens of a British Empire) than against the very institutions, social practices, and legal apparatus that had defined an "American way of life" in the first place.

This allows us to finesse the question of what "the Sixties" *really* was or consisted of and concentrate on what later periods or moments in the history of American society made out of the Sixties. Why does America feel compelled every so many years or decades to reassess the legacy of "the Sixties" and to treat it as either "the best of times" or an incubus that will not go away, as if it were a genetic endowment in some way determinative of who or what "we" are? Historical reassessments of earlier periods of a given history tend to attenuate ideas and especially images of them as the period in question recedes in time and documentation replaces memory as the principal source of information.

A given moment in the history of a society is not a thing passively lying before us or behind us, like a landscape to be surveyed and mapped according to an agreed-upon legend or code. Nor is it a force field emitting electromagnetic charges expanding out of a center and exerting "influences" on later times and other spaces. On the contrary, a historical period or moment is not "alive" in any sense at all until it is summoned up to memory or "fixed" as an object of study, submitted to analysis, and given a proper name (like "the Sixties") endowing it with a substance around which its attributes can be ordered and ranked according to some criterion of valuation that gives it meaning. If "the Sixties" seems worthy of a kind of attention that other decades of our recent past do not, it is because it has a social-genealogical value rather than a genetic connection to "America."

There have been many evocations of "the Sixties" since the thing that this term supposedly names has supposedly come to an end and passed into history. What these evocations indicate, however, is not so much the influence exerted by the Sixties on the different presents that succeed it as, rather, some need or desire on the part of successive presents to come to terms with the meanings deposited in "the Sixties."

So, we might approach our problem by asking in what way we (we Americans), in the present moment and in our present situation (our condition of economic stagnation, political stasis, and state of "war on Terror") feel a need to look back upon the Sixties, to identify its substance, meaning, or value (for us), and determine the weight we wish to assign to it as a part of our identity and lodestar for charting our future.

Obviously, there are as many Sixties as there are communities who believe that this period of their past represented crucial moments in their subsequent political and social development. Italy, Germany, France, the UK each has its own Sixties, none of which corresponds in detail to any of the others. Fredric Jameson, in one of the first attempts by an American scholar to put the Sixties within the context of the process of globalization that will define the socio-economic basis of post–World War II history, sees the Sixties as a moment in the process of decolonization-recolonization, marking the transition from high (industrial) to late (financial) capitalism on a world scale. This process of decolonization-recolonization takes place also, according to Jameson, *within* the advanced capitalist social formations as well as between these and the so-called third world or Southern Hemisphere in general from the mid-1950s on. Thus, the *protest mode* of political expression—civil rights, antiwar, women's rights, gay militancy, Black and Brown militancy, etc.—characteristic of the Sixties can be seen as movement against the *internal* colonization of different constituencies in the US that mirror the process of recolonization by economic and other forms of disciplinization similar to those that took place in Africa, the Middle East, Southeast Asia, Latin America, and the South Pacific contemporaneously.

For Jameson, then, the Sixties in America constituted an upsurge of utopian hope and desire for liberation in a general sense, rather than in terms conformable to the economic and social powers prevailing at the time. Over the long run, for Jameson, the Sixties—in both its positive and negative aspects—must be seen as the first phase of a process that leads, on the economic plane, from high capitalism to late or advanced capitalism and, on the cultural plane, from the moment of high modernism to late or post modernism. Whence Jameson's famous synthesis of post–World War II American culture, *Postmodernism, or, The Cultural Logic of Late Capitalism*,[14] in which the Sixties have to be grasped as out of sync with history: as being both desirous of overturning capitalism and blind to the realities of capitalism's power to not only defeat but also expropriate, commodify, and turn to its own purposes the most idealistic impulses of the Sixties' militants.

Indeed, according to Jameson, postmodernism turns rebellion and resistance into kinds of play, fad, or fashion, so that henceforth one has no need actually to rebel against the alienating effects of commodity capitalism but only feign to do so—in the clothes one wears, the automobile one drives, the "lifestyle" one affects on the weekend, or the movies one watches; all surface, no depth; and, as for history, it is all an endless present, devoid of future and past.

Any effort to reassess the historical significance of "the Sixties" in US society must entail a reassessment of what is meant by a specifically "historical" assessment in the first place. Because it was during the Sixties in America that the idea of "history as past politics" inherited from the nineteenth century was brought under question, "deconstructed," and effectively reconstituted in a distinctly postmodernist form. First, in the Fifties and Sixties, American historiography underwent changes in the direction of scientification along with the other social sciences emerging from World War II in a distinctively quantitative and behaviorist mode. A new kind of capitalism, the Cold War, and Stalinism fomented the birth of a "New Left" and the cultivation of versions of Marxist historical theory (Sartre and Althusser, Frankfurt School—Adorno, Marcuse, and Habermas—and Maoist) at once populist (E. P. Thompson and "history from below") and discursive rather than "scientific." Academic historians remained for the most part resistant to the upsurge of "theories of history and historiography"; but by the end of the Sixties, the putatively scientific status of historical inquiry had been destroyed, its death chronicled in the pages of the journal *History and Theory*, whose popularity was itself a symptom of history's fall from its earlier position as "Queen of the Social Sciences" and *magistra vitae*. For the next forty years (1970–2010), the prestige of history declined step by step with the authority of the classical humanities in general.

Thus, the current call for a historical reassessment of the Sixties raises as many questions about the kind of history one has in mind as it does about the nature of the thing we are being asked to study. Do we want to study the Sixties "historically," in the sense of setting the Sixties within the context of its original constitution? Or do we want to compose "the history of the Sixties," i.e., tell the story of how the Sixties came to be what it was, achieved a "substance" that distinguished it from all other similarly defined periods, such as "the Twenties" of modern American history? And although each of these possible projects presupposes the other, each also presupposes its own mode of grasping the essence of its object of interest: in the first, emphasis falls on a structure of social and cultural being within a specific temporal duration; in the second, the emphasis will be on the development, the fate, and the significance of the Sixties over the succeeding decades of American history.

As observed above, one of the features distinguishing the Sixties from the decades preceding and following it was the way this period expressed its own epochal self-consciousness.[15] "The Sixties" was self-consciously "utopian," driven by a desire to turn history in a new direction. It was this "utopian," almost millenarian, arguably apocalyptical aspect of "the Sixties" that distinguished it from the various "utopias" of the decades that preceded (the Thirties and Forties) and followed it (the Seventies, Eighties, and Nineties). It was the onset over the decades following the Sixties of distinctively different utopianisms that required, or seemed to require, the various historical revisions of the Sixties that have occurred since then.[16] In each of the periods following the Sixties, it has seemed necessary to return to the Sixties and to reassess it for the light it might cast on the path followed by American society after the dreams of the Sixties had been realized or, alternatively, dispersed as illusions and dispelled from consciousness.

Notes

I should note here that, although the term "the Sixties" indicates a plurality, it has become conventional to treat it as a collective singular—as if the congeries of phenomena it references were united by a single substance or shared a single essence. Needless to say, the "substance" alluded to has more in common with the modern chemical idea of substance than with the older, Aristotelian and metaphysical notion thereof.

1. World Health Organization: "Adolescents are different both from young children and from adults. Specifically, adolescents are not fully capable of understanding complex concepts, or the relationship between behavior and consequences, or the degree of control they have or can have over health decision making including that related to sexual behaviour. This inability may make them particularly vulnerable to sexual exploitation and high-risk behaviours. Laws, customs, and practices may also affect adolescents differently than adults. For example, laws and policies often restrict access by adolescents to reproductive health information and services, especially when they are unmarried. In addition, even when services do exist, provider attitudes about adolescents having sex often pose a significant barrier to use of those services" (http://www.who.int/maternal_child_adolescent/topics/adolescence/dev/en/).

2. "Advances in neuropsychological research have produced a new body of knowledge showing that teen brains remain immature through early adulthood. These new studies have zeroed in on the areas of the brain where impulsivity, risk taking, and poor social judgment are regulated. Because adolescent brains are not fully developed, they do not achieve critical mechanisms

of impulsivity and behavioral control until perhaps age 20 or beyond" (Jeffrey Fagan, "Adolescents, Maturity, and the Law," *American Prospect* [2005], http://prospect.org/article/adolescents-maturity-and-law).

3. *The Andy Griffith Show*—presenting a world of sunny, rural, and preindustrial village life—was the most-watched TV program of the Sixties.

4. "More importantly, the 1950s themselves were not entirely a golden age, despite the gains. The infant and child mortality rate at the end of the decade was still four times as high as it is today. In 1955, two-thirds of black children and more than one-fifth of their white counterparts lived in poverty. Nearly a million children with disabilities were denied public schooling as uneducable, and 40 percent of kids dropped out of school before graduating high school. Happy sitcom reruns to the contrary, the parents of 50 years ago were not insulated from fears about youth violence or children's poor academic achievement. *In 1955 alone, Congress considered nearly 200 bills aimed at combating what was seen as an epidemic of juvenile delinquency.* Rudolph Flesch's 1955 bestseller, *Why Johnny Can't Read*, announced that '3,500 years of civilization' were being lost to bad schools and incompetent teachers. It is neither feasible nor desirable to return to the patterns of mid-20th century childhood" (Steven Mintz, "The Evolution of Childhood," *Conscience: The News Journal of Catholic Opinion* [2006], http://www.catholicsforchoice.org/conscience/current/MintzArticle.asp#top, emphasis added).

5. It was generally thought that the Vietnam War was fought by young men of color under twenty years of age, but fact sheets issued under the name of "The Westmoreland Papers" had it that the average age of the military serving in Vietnam was twenty-two, with 80 percent "Caucasians." Nonetheless, the number of casualties and wounded in this war was unacceptable precisely to the white, middle-class parents who wanted to protect their children from military service. The Draft was discontinued in 1973, and the military services embarked on a path of "professionalization," which would effectively remove military service from the concerns of middle-class parents by the time of the wars of the Persian Gulf, Afghanistan, and Iraq.

6. Thus, in one of the most recent overviews of the late twentieth century in America, Daniel T. Rodgers, *The Age of Fracture* (Princeton, NJ: Princeton University Press, 2011), the Sixties is treated as a period of transition between postwar and postmodern US culture and society. Most of the assessments by writers who participated in the events of the Sixties tend to give it a positive valuation. See, for example, *The Sixties without Apology*, ed. Sonya Sayres et al. (Minneapolis: University of Minnesota Press, 1981), especially Fredric Jameson's contribution to this volume, "Periodizing the Sixties"; and Rick Perlstein, "Who Owns the Sixties? The Opening of a Scholarly Generation Gap," *Lingua Franca* 6, no. 4 (1996): 30–37.

7. [Ed. This essay was originally given as part of a lecture series organized by Laura Bieger and Christian Lammert at the John F. Kennedy Institute for North American Studies at the Freie Universität Berlin.]

8. [Ed. See Hayden White, "Formalist and Contextualist Strategies in Historical Explanations," in *Figural Realism: Studies in the Mimesis Effect* (Baltimore: Johns Hopkins University Press, 1999), 58–59; and Hayden White, "The

Historical Event," in *The Practical Past* (Evanston, IL: Northwestern University Press, 2014), 41–62.]

9. It was this dispersal and ambiguation of the very idea of history that led members of the academic and intellectual establishment to accuse "the Sixties" of a want of historical consciousness. Members of the Old Left—intellectuals still linked to one or another versions of the older Communist International—were similarly critical of the lack of a proper historical consciousness among the utopian visionaries of "the Sixties." But by "proper" historical consciousness they meant "Marxist" historical consciousness—condemned by Michel Foucault as irredeemably *of* and therefore limited in relevance *to* the nineteenth century only.

10. "Never trust anyone over thirty" and "Question authority" were popular mottoes and widespread graffiti (another artistic genre popular in the period) of the Sixties.

11. Norman O. Brown, *Life against Death: The Psychoanalytical Meaning of History* (Middletown, CT: Wesleyan University Press, 1959); R. D. Laing, *The Divided Self: An Existential Study in Sanity and Madness* (Harmondsworth, UK: Penguin Books, 1960).

12. [Ed. This is where the published version of this essay ends. The manuscript continues below.]

13. [Ed. White is referring to the Iraq War of 2003–11, which ended in a voluntary US withdrawal (although US troops did return in 2014–17 to fight the Islamic State), not the Gulf War of 1991, which was successful in dislodging Iraqi forces from neighboring Kuwait. And White is of course writing this several years before the US's role in the conflict in Afghanistan would come to an end with the chaotic withdrawal of all US troops in August 2021; this led to the Taliban retaking control of the country, thus marking the end of the twenty-year war as a definitive loss.]

14. Fredric Jameson, *Postmodernism, or, The Cultural Logic of Late Capitalism* (Durham, NC: Duke University Press, 1991).

15. By "epochal self-consciousness" I mean a certain awareness—manifested in the art, science, and/or dominant ideologies of a given chronotopical social formation—of living in some kind of "modernity," which is to say, an age, era, or period that is qualitatively different from anything in the past. The archetype or paradigm of modernity (like the term *modernus* itself) is to be found in the early Christian belief that the Incarnation of the Christ inaugurates a new age utterly different from both the preceding Hebrew and the Pagan pasts, not least in the opportunities it affords for transcending the limits of the earthly body, redemption of the flesh, and life after death.

16. See Rodgers, *Age of Fracture*.

CHAPTER 8

The History-Fiction Divide in Holocaust Studies [2014]

> In a historical representation of the Holocaust the authenticity of the diarist's identity and the veracity of the description or comment as perceived within its contemporary context give full support to the testimony. Even a hint of fiction cancels it.
>
> —Saul Friedländer

In this essay I use two pieces of writing about the Holocaust to dispel two misconceptions about the relation between history and literature or, as I prefer to call it, literary writing. The first misconception is that "literature" stands to "history" as "fiction" stands to "fact" and that, therefore, any literary treatment of such morally charged events as the Holocaust entails a fall from historical realism into fictionalization. The second misconception has to do with the idea that since "literature" is an art and since art is aesthetical, then any artistic treatment of such a morally charged event as the Holocaust must aestheticize this event, making the evil manifestly present in it in some way attractive and thereby justifying sado-masochistic fantasies about it rather than appropriately ethical reflection on it.

As opposed to the misconceptions noted above, I argue that modernist conceptions of literature as writing provide ways of seeing how art can complement, rather than undermine, science. This is especially important when it is a matter of "coming to terms with" real historical events like the Holocaust, which resist encodation by traditional humanistic disciplines such as historiography, law, and philosophy.[1] To indicate how this happens I use passages from Primo Levi's *Se questo è un uomo*, a recognized classic of Holocaust literature, which was unfittingly translated into English as *Survival in Auschwitz*, and from Otto

Dov Kulka's *Landscapes of the Metropolis of Death*, subtitled *Reflections on Memory and Imagination*.

Primo Levi's *Se questo è un uomo*

There is a moment in Primo Levi's *Se questo è un uomo* when, on a soup detail, Levi recounts his efforts to teach a bit of Italian to his French comrade Jean, known in the camp as Pikolo. He decides to use a passage from Dante's *Commedia* ("Chissà," he says, "come e perché mi è venuto in mente: . . .") and then proceeds to try—unsuccessfully—to call up from his memory the whole "canto di Ulisse" from Dante's *Inferno*. He recalls some lines, a phrase here and there, and uses them to explain— rather pedantically—some fine points of Italian grammar and prosody, but when he comes to Ulysses' "temerario viaggio al di là delle colonne d'Ercole," he is forced to summarize it in prose—"un sacrileggio," he says.[2] But then, all of a sudden, three lines come to him:

> Considerate la vostra semenza:
> Fatti non foste a viver come bruti,
> Ma per seguir virtute e conoscenza.
> (Consider your origins:
> you were not made to live as brutes,
> but to follow virtue and knowledge.)[3]

This passage, Levi says, hit him "like a trumpet-blast, like the voice of God. . . . It was as if I . . . had heard [*sentissi*] it [the passage] for the first time."

But heard *what*?

A message, a message that "had to do with [Pikolo], that . . . had to do with all suffering human beings, and had to do with us in particular, and . . . had to do with the two of us, who dared to think of these matters with the buckets of soup hanging from our shoulders."[4]

But what was the message? Levi the narrator does not have Levi his protagonist spell it out. Instead, he has him call up a famous tercet from Dante's poem that describes the foundering and sinking of Ulysses' vessel:

> Tre volte il fé girar con tutte l'acque
> Alla quarta levar la poppa in suso
> E la prora ire in giù, come altrui piacque.

(Three times it made her whirl with all the waters,
At the fourth time it made the stern uplift,
And the prow downward go, as pleased Another.)

It was "absolutely necessary and urgent," Levi says, that Pikolo comprehend the phrase "come altrui piacque," "before it is too late, tomorrow
he and I might be dead and never see each other again, I have to tell him,
explain to him about the Middle Ages, about the so human and necessary and indeed strange anachronism, and beyond that, something
monstrous that I myself had seen only now" ("qualcosa di gigantesco
che io stesso ho visto ora soltanto"), namely, "perhaps the why of our
fate [destino], the why of our being here today" ("forse il perché del nostro destino, del nostro essere oggi qui").[5]

But what this "qualcosa di gigantesco" might be, the what that, or the
"altrui" who, destroyed Ulysses, all of this is suddenly broken off and we
are returned by a change of register to the mundane world of the camp
where the same old soup ("Kraut und Rüben")[6] is served up day after
day: "infin che 'l mar fu sovra noi richiuso."[7]

This passage attracts the eye of the critic because it relates a scene of
recall, of reconstruction of an early memory, of reading, and of interpretation (in the face of imminent death), which can be taken to instruct us
readers of the text how to read it. The passage has "literature" or "art" or
what the Formalists call "literarity" written all over it. Not only because
Levi has summoned up a literary classic to figure forth a message of
universal import, but also because of the literariness of Levi's writing
itself. There is nothing of the spontaneity and parapraxis characteristic
of the kind of oral testimony in the witness archives now available all
over the world. This is a crafted text, obviously revised, edited, polished,
and consciously shaped to give it the aura of an artwork.

Moreover, at the level of code, the use of the passage from Dante's
Commedia to gloss the situation in which Levi and his friend Pikolo find
themselves ("nostro essere oggi qui"), the citation (without quotes) of
Hamlet's last words ("il resto è silenzio" [the rest is silence]), the occa-
sional schoolmasterly pedantries ("cosa è il contrapasso"), and the effort
at what might be called "archetypal" criticism (of which Dante himself
was a supreme exponent)—all this allows us to ask to what end or purpose Primo Levi adverts to Dante's great Christian epic and specifically
to the passages dealing with the "sin" of Ulysses and his punishment
by drowning, to approach the meaning of this world of the here and
now (the there and then) of Auschwitz. Dante scholars agree that, for

Dante, God drowns Ulysses for daring to try to cross over into a realm of knowledge reserved for God alone. It is as if to say: that journey is not allowed to us.

What happens to the referent—the real world of Auschwitz—as a result of this artistic treatment of a moment of reading and interpretation in the face of death? Is Auschwitz "fictionalized"? "aestheticized"?

From a textological point of view, this move by Levi from an account of a work project in the camp to a report of an attempt to recall and interpret a passage from Dante's *Commedia* is a trope, a "swerve" in the discourse that has nothing of logical determination in it but presupposes a relation between two situations, a scene of manual labor, on the one hand, and a scene of reading/writing/interpretation, on the other. The transition is not marked by any announcement of a shift from *rapportage* to exegesis. The first scene ends with the sentence: "Frenkel, the spy, goes by. Pick up the pace, you never know, he commits evil for evil's sake."

Then there are two line-spaces. And then the scene of reading/writing, etc. commences. "Il canto di Ulisse. Chissà come e perché me è venuto in mente" (The Canto of Ulysses. Who knows how and why it came to mind).[8]

In sum, a disjunctive conjunction, a displacement, a turn, trope, or swerve in the discourse "without rhyme or reason" and joined more by contiguity than similarity. But, the attribute given to Frenkel ("he commits evil for evil's sake") can legitimately be treated as a prolepsis of the scene from Dante's *Commedia* telling of Ulysses' fate. Doing evil for evil's sake.

Recall that the idea that Ulysses made another voyage after the return to Ithaca is Dante's invention; it does not belong to the classical tradition. And recall that when Dante meets Ulysses in Hell, the hero is wrapped in a tongue of flames, symbolic of the punishment for the sin of fraudulent counsel, a *contrapasso* or repetition, as punishment of the act for which the punishment has been given. This sin, the commentators speculate, may have been the very advice that Ulysses gave to his aged companions that led them to set out once more on a voyage of discovery "for its own sake" that would lead to their destruction. Did Dante think, perhaps, that his own poetic journey into Hell and beyond of which he tells in the *Commedia* was similarly hubristic and that, perhaps, his own effort to probe the mysteries of God's justice was itself fraught with danger? Is this what we are supposed to conclude from our own reading of this passage about Primo Levi's "journey" ("Il viaggio" is the title of chapter 1 of Levi's book) to Auschwitz, "metropolis of death," in *Se questo è un uomo?*

We do not need to pursue these questions for the moment, because what interests us is the function of this "turn" in Levi's text from a description of a "reality" to a scene in which he is explicating a literary work, a turn from the world of Auschwitz to that of Dante's *Inferno*. What is going on here? Is Levi aestheticizing his own discourse, inserting a moment of fiction into what he has promised would be nothing but the facts?[9]

In a word, is the Dantean world not quite recalled by Levi meant to *interpret* the world of the camps, or, more precisely, does it interpret the effort of its inmates to discern the "why" of their having ended up there?

Dante's text is full of meanings—Aristotelian, Thomist, Christian, Classical, Virgilian, humanistic, and so on; Levi's text is full of unanswered questions ("Why?" "There is no why here"). To insert (a fragmentary version of) Dante's text into an account of a mundane task assigned to the Häftlinge of the camps provides a model or paradigm for comprehending the meaning of the camps, but in what terms? Classical? Christian? Aristotelian? Certainly not "scientific." The trope seems to allow us to interpret the life of the camps in Dante's terms: a journey into Hell to pose questions to the damned, to find out why they are there and why what they have become in the afterlife was a fitting end to what they had been in process of becoming all along during their lifetimes. But the anticipated "perché del nostro destino, del nostro essere oggi qui" is never spelled out, neither to Levi or Pikolo, nor to us. We are simply, suddenly, "re-turned" to a dull wait for a meal of watery soup, tasteless and insubstantial, without learning who or what found "pleasure" in the destruction of those who would have ventured beyond "the pillars of Hercules" or what the significance of that act of destruction might be for Levi, Pikolo—or us.

But if we turn to the quoted text, the passage has a "content"; the anecdote figures a message about "il perché del nostro destino, del nostro essere oggi qui." Scholars of Dante agree that the gist of the passage in question is that there is a limit to the kind of knowledge vouchsafed to human beings, that there are some things (known only to God?) that not only cannot, but should not ever be inquired into.[10]

In Dante's version of Ulysses' life, the aged hero has learned nothing from his twenty years of journey to Troy and back. In the Dantean myth of Ulysses' old age, we see the trickster tricking his former (and now aged) comrades into a final voyage to penetrate another barrier, the

Gates of Hercules, unsuccessfully and in such a way as to suggest that human knowledge has a limit and that to aspire to total knowledge of God's Creation is to court destruction. Levi says that, for a moment, in the recall of those lines from Dante, he grasped not exactly the "why" of our being there, that day, in the city of death, but maybe the why of his inability to grasp the why of the city of death itself. In this instance, what art teaches is that curiosity or inquiry as an end in itself is not only impossible but sinful as well and that science of whatever kind is not enough but must be augmented by an awareness of human limits and the price that must be paid for any kind of overreaching—of thought, action, or belief.

Kulka's *Landscapes of the Metropolis of Death*

I have repeated the phrase "city of death" in order to trope (or turn) my own discourse to a consideration of another treatment of the relation between art and history, also by a survivor of the camps, but a survivor who became not a chemist like Levi but a distinguished "scientific" historian of Nazi Germany and who, like Levi, found in midlife that his scientific inquiry into the "why" of Auschwitz required augmentation by another kind of knowledge, a knowledge he calls "mythical," but that I think I can justify calling "artistic" in kind.

I cannot do full justice to Otto Dov Kulka's *Landscapes of the Metropolis of Death: Reflections on Memory and Imagination*, written in Hebrew and now translated into English by Ralph Mandel. But from the moment we open this book, we recognize that we are in the presence of some kind of literary treatment of that real historical event called the Holocaust. Not only the title tells us this—"Landscapes of the Metropolis of Death"—but also the epigraph, the table of contents, the acknowledgments (these are "extra-scientific writings," we are told), the introduction ("a choice I made to sever the biographical from the historical past"), and the title of the first chapter ("A Prologue that Could Also Be an Epilogue") make clear that we are in the presence of some effort to mediate what the author takes to be an abyssal gap between "history" and "personal" memory.[11]

Kulka insists that his account of his memories of the camps is purely personal, not historical, and that the image of "the immutable law of the Great Death" that rules that place is purely "mythical" (rather than rational?) in kind. However, although Kulka tells us again and again that he is introducing us to a purely personal world (he calls it, at one point,

"Kulkaesque"),[12] at the same time he continually invokes a number of literary masterpieces as paradigms of the kind of *knowledge* he wishes to impart by way of his "reflections on memory and imagination": Kleist (*Michael Kohlhaas*), Kafka (*The Castle*), Sebald (*Austerlitz*), and so on.

Recalling the last days of Auschwitz, when it felt as if "the overriding law and order that governs all these realms was about to be realized . . . in a kind of terrible justice crushing small wrongs in the grinder of all-surpassing wrong that lies beyond," Kulka suddenly recalls that "many years later, here in Jerusalem . . . it seemed to me that I understood cognitively what I had then [only?] intuited." But this sudden *cognitive* recognition had come, Kulka tells us, not by way of science but by way of his reading of two literary works: Kleist's *Michael Kohlhaas* and *The Earthquake in Chile*. A similar scene of recognition is related in chapter 5 of Kulka's book, in a section titled: "In the Penal Colony."

The allusion is of course to Kafka's famous story of a mode of executing prisoners in a mythical prison in some remote "colony," where a machine has been invented that will kill the condemned by progressively inscribing the words of the crime for which he has been sentenced on his body—a Dantean trope if there ever was one.

In Kafka's story the machine, which works, as it were, autonomously, ends by executing the officer who is supposed to administer it. Kafka's story is alluded to by Kulka in order to gloss and provide a possible "meaning" for a scene of punishment (witnessed by Kulka as a boy) that took place in Auschwitz in autumn 1944. What was the "meaning" of the "ceremony" of the beating of the prisoner by Kapos armed with sticks or cudgels and followed by the use of a "special whipping device" to finally beat the prisoner to death? Kulka gives an interpretation of his remembered "feeling" about this scene;[13] but what I want to highlight is a remark he makes about his later "recall" of the incident and the place this recalled scene came to occupy in his memory: "I probably would not have recalled this incident, would not have engraved the scene and its import on my memory, had it not loomed before me again much later when I read Kafka's story 'In der Strafkolonie'—'In the Penal Colony.'"[14] And what follows is a "reading" of this scene of punishment so interwoven with the themes and imagery of Kafka's story that it is impossible to tell which story is glossing which. The passage ends with an image of Auschwitz

> under the dominion of a shadow of its "glory,"—one aspect of this
> ghost town that still continued to exist, like the penal colony in

the Kafka story . . . Something which has seemingly already passed from the world but still exists, and the order exists, the punishment exists, and the victim plays his part with seeming willingness, and the traveler is puzzled and records the events as he sees them. So they are recorded here by me.[15]

In this last passage the mood, tone or mode of presentation is decidedly passive and dependent upon the putatively more artistic technique of Kafka's story for its force and effectiveness. Indeed, the affect we might have expected is borrowed from Kafka's story and is mixed in with the memory retrieved in middle age.

The chapter in which this scene of "violence" is depicted is entitled "Observations and Perplexities about Scenes in the Memory." The perplexities in question have to do—among other things—with the author's failure of memory when it comes to the kind of "cruelty . . . violence . . . torture . . . and individual killings" that, "as far as I can make out, are portrayed [in witness testimony] as everyday routine of that world of the camps."[16] And the chapter concentrates on two scenes of cruelty and violence he can remember, which seem to defy interpretation—except by recourse to some structure of meaning drawn from literature.

I have indicated how literary works (Kleist's *Michael Kohlhaas* and *The Earthquake in Chile*) serve as both *aides-mémoires* and *interprétantes* of a scene of punishment. The second scene was of the execution of four Russian prisoners of war who had been caught trying to escape and the way they resisted even on the scaffold with shouts of "For Stalin! For the homeland!"—"cries of heroism, of resistance" that inspired the boy who forced himself to look, to remember, and to vow "revenge at the time of justice and retaliation." Commenting on the scene, Kulka says: "The thought about justice being done transcends the immutable law which prevailed in that place. As though those cries ripped through the present of that time and revealed another dimension, utopian, but at least for a moment a concrete reality, because everyone heard, everyone listened, because everyone contemplated the revenge which was there called by its name."[17]

Now, I want to stress that, in my comment on this text, I am following the order or disorder of the genre of *collage* that marks it as an example of modernist *literary* expression. And it is this quality of literariness that distinguishes it from the hundreds of thousands of testimonials by survivors marked by the spontaneity, artlessness, and anarchy of their speech. By literariness I mean the reflexivity, intertextuality, the self-conscious anti-narrativity of the discourse, the dramatism, the display of a complex cultural code, the resistance to any kind of bathos, the use of devices like the historical present and free indirect style, and beyond that, the particular use of images, photographs, drawings, engravings and the like, scattered through the text, used less as documents than as *interprétantes* of the verbal matter (for example, the photo of a ghostly-lit railroad station on page 32, taken from W. G. Sebald's *Austerlitz*, a kind of anti-novel that uses the novel *form* to convey the hopelessness of ever making sense of what happened to the Jews of Europe in that event called the Holocaust).

As indicated, Kulka insists that he is writing neither history nor literature but something like myth, which is what T. S. Eliot, in his famous review of Joyce's *Ulysses*, said distinguished modernist writing from its realist predecessors. ("Instead of narrative method, we may now use the mythical method. It is, I seriously believe, a step toward making the modern world possible for art.")[18] This was all foreshadowed in the epigraph Kulka placed at the entrance to his account of his descent, not into history, but to something more primary or primal than history, "the metropolis of death" where the "immutable law of the Great Death" will be shown to be resistible only by art. The epigraph is described as being "after a parable by Kafka":

> There remained the inexplicable landscape of ruins.—
> History tries to explain the inexplicable. As it comes
> Out of a truth-ground it must in turn end in the inexplicable.[19]

Which, it must be admitted, makes very little sense if read literally:[20] the dash after "ruins" hardly signals a logical link between premises of a syllogism, and does the "it" of line 2 refer to "history" or to "the inexplicable"?

I confess that after having studied (and even researched) this epigraph, I both do not know and know exactly what it means—in the way that I both do not know and know precisely what any Kafka parable is getting at. Yet it is puzzling that a professional historian, well known for the objectivity and impersonality of his accounts of modern German history, should introduce his book with an epigraph that speaks of the "inexplicability" of history and, indeed, of history's inexplicability arising from its "ground" in "truth." Kulka says that, even though "these texts . . . [are] anchored in concrete historical events," they, or they are intended to, "transcend the sphere of history" and to give insight into . . . what? A "private mythology" having nothing to do with the historical reality of Terezin and Auschwitz? Is the moral of the story of Kulka's journeys to the camps, first as a young boy and then as a mature professional historian, that "memory and history" must remain forever severed one from the other? This is asserted many times throughout the text, but since we are dealing in parables—a literary genre if there ever was one—we would do well to look out for the kinds of reversals, inversions, and displacements that distinguish literary or poetic discourse from its literal(ist) counterpart in science.

Before showing how such an approach to a testimonial text like this works to produce a third meaning alongside of, beneath or behind the surface utterance, let me very briefly try to characterize the form of the text we have before us. Although it is narrated and contains a number of different narratives, the text as a whole resists anything like narrativistic or plot-like coherence. Indeed, the text as a whole approaches closer to the structure of a collage, pastiche, *satura* or, not to put too fine a point on it, a dream-like rebus of the kind Freud posits as the object of his *The Interpretation of Dreams*. And indeed, dreams are an object of presentation and analysis in Kulka's book (cf. page 11), but along with these dreams, recordings of "reflections," forty-two images (drawings, photographs of more or less indeterminate scenes, persons, and sites, as well as engravings, paintings, and musical scores), three poems written "from the brink of the Gas Chambers," three chapters from diaries, and, finally, an appendix in which the author provides us with a model of scientific inquiry into the "reality" of the camps. All this within the space of a modest 127 printed pages in the English-language edition.

If I were not afraid of offending the author, I would say that this is a perfect example of what many of us mean by the term "postmodernist." Which is to say that it is a work that has the structure, or rather the anti-structure, of what the Greeks called *sorites* (a heap, a pile, a congeries of items), which by accretion or subtraction undergoes a change of genre: for example, from being a "couple" to being a "pile" to being a "heap," such as a haystack—or a modernist novel. The point is to ask, of the couple, pile, heap, haystack, or novel, at what point does an aggregation transform into a recognizable genre.

I have suggested that Kulka's book can be profitably considered as an instance of the artistic genre "collage." He calls it a "personal myth" and suggests that it belongs to him alone or at least that he lays no claim to its generality as a *mythos* for anyone who made the journey into the "metropolis of death" and returned to a world deaf and blind to what it tells of "history"—and its transcendence.

I leave it to others to assess these claims. I want to turn now to what I regard as a crucial anecdote related by Kulka about an experience in the children's choir at Auschwitz, where a Potemkin's village of Jewish family life had been set up in case of an inspection by the International Red Cross. The children's choir was directed by a man called Imre (his real name was Emmerich Acs) who delighted, we are told, in teaching the naïve children the classics of German music, and specifically Beethoven's setting of Schiller's "Ode to Joy." Kulka recalls the pure pleasure he felt while learning and singing the "Ode to Joy," even though, he now recalls, they were singing this specimen of German high culture within 200 meters of the Auschwitz crematoria: "and we are singing like little angels, our voices providing an accompaniment to the processions of the people in black who are slowly swallowed up by the crematoria."[21]

Then, switching from "then" to "today," Kulka asks: "what drove Imre . . . What was his intention in choosing to perform that particular text, a text that is considered a universal manifesto of everyone who believes in human dignity, in humanistic values, in the future—facing these crematoria, in the place where the future was perhaps the only definite thing that did not exist?"[22] Was it a kind of "protest demonstration"? A reminder that "as long as man breathes, he breathes freedom," something like that?

That was one possibility, Kulka says, a possibility that he would like to have believed in. But a second possibility, he says, seems more likely: "that this was an act of extreme sarcasm . . . a kind of almost demonic self-amusement of playing melodies to accompany those flames that burned quietly day and night and those processions being swallowed into the insatiable crematoria."[23] What was Imre doing?

It is here that Kulka draws a scene of rebellion by, in, and through art: "I often come back to all that," writes Kulka,

> and it also occupies me professionally, even though I never mention the episode directly. But when I come to interpret the continuity of the existence of social norms, of cultural and moral values in the conditions that were created immediately upon the Nazis' ascent to power and all the way to the brink of the mass-murder pits and the crematoria, here I am also inclined, perhaps unconsciously, to choose the belief in that demonstration, a hopeless demonstration but the only possible one in that situation, though

I think, as I said, that the illusion here is sometimes far greater than the fierceness of the sarcasm or the cynical amusement of one who was still able to toy with it in the face of that mass death. That approach was perhaps more—I will not say more realistic—but more authentic.[24]

The History-Fiction Divide

For a long time, it was thought that historians of such extreme events as the Holocaust not only betrayed their discipline but in some way betrayed the event itself in any deviation from a strictly objective presentation of the facts of its matter in the direction of overt ethical concern or stylistic invention. Literature, or, more precisely, "literary" writing, was thought to be inherently "fictionalizing" in the extent to which literature in general was understood to be synonymous with "fiction." The difference between a historical treatment of an event of the past and a literary treatment of it was considered to be analogous to the difference between fact and fiction. And inasmuch as fiction was a product of literary art, fictionalization could be considered to be a means to aestheticization.

But both of these identifications—of literature with fiction and of literary art with aesthetics—are fictitious or, what amounts to the same thing, historical conjunctions that have been surpassed or transcended in the evolution of both literature and the theory of art in modernism. In modernism, literature devolves into "writing" (of which literary writing would be only one species, historical writing another), and literary art is disjoined from aesthetics or the science of the beautiful and assimilated to writing understood as a mode of cognition as well as an expression of affect and emotion. And one result of these de-identifications and re-identifications is to license a re-examination of the relation between what used to be regarded as an opposition between literature and history under the aspect of a comparison of two kinds of writing that share a large number of attributes (devices, figures, tropes, topoi, and the like), without lapsing into "fiction" or "aestheticization" at all.

The division between literature and history properly belongs to the nineteenth century, when the arts, the theory of aesthetic, and what had formerly been called *belles lettres* were split between two possible paths of development: romanticist, on the one hand, realist, on the other. In the battles fought over this divide, history, historical studies, and historiography (historical writing) occupied a central place as paradigm of the kind of truth, "factual" in kind, that one could legitimately hope for in any science focused on the sublunar world of human affairs (Paul Veyne's term for the kind of Aristotelian "science" history had remained even after the Copernican and Newtonian Revolutions). Unable to comprehend human affairs under the terms required for admittance to the status of an experimental science of causal laws and prediction, history—consisting of discrete facts based on educated commonsense and provisional generalizations limited to discrete domains of time and space—served for better than a century and a half as an exemplar of a "realistic" discipline for the human sciences.

Now, all of this changed with the advent of modernization, modernity, and modernism. Modernism I take to be a congeries of *responses* in Western cultural practices to the changes wrought in society and our ideas about nature by modernization. For history and the place it occupied among the human sciences, the principal threat of modernism seemed to have come from the new social sciences conceived in the late nineteenth century to deal with the effects of industrialization, urbanization, and population growth. But more important, in my opinion, than this threat was another that occurred in the arts in general and in literature in particular from around 1910 or thereabouts and that cut the ground from under the theoretical opposition of history to literature on which the claims by history to a modern kind of "realism" had been based.

To very quickly summarize this much more complicated process, I want to mention—without being able to discuss comprehensively—the most important developments:

(1) The substitution of "writing" for "literature": henceforth, literary writing will be one among many different kinds of writing, the aim of which is less to "represent" or "imitate" reality than to "perform" it.

(2) This will entail a revision of the very idea of "narration, narrative, and narrativization (emplotment)" to stress the paradigmatic (diachronic) axis of elaboration as against the older syntagmatic (synchronic) axis.

(3) The substitution of "psychoanalytic" for an "aesthetic" conception of the relation between the senses, the mind, and the body: art will cease to be "about" the beautiful in order to pursue knowledge of the psychosomatically "real," and it will

cease to designate objects in reality presumed to be more noble or higher than others—the end of aesthetic hierarchy.

(4) The transformation of the idea of "fiction" from an ontological to an epistemological concept: henceforth, "fiction" is no longer identified with "lie," falsehood, or "imaginary," but is treated as a cognitive instrument, specifically of the (productive) imagination (poietic); it is a mode of literary writing featuring certain "devices" rather than a discourse about imaginary beings; along with all this goes the collapse of the hierarchy of literary genres, which dictates a certain "content" for particular "forms" of literature.

Now, these changes in the idea of "literature" were products, we cultural historians would say, of a sensed necessity to deal "realistically" with the new historical phenomena produced by modernity and the processes of modernization that had invaded every corner of traditional society and threatened their stability as supports of bourgeois life. The change of scale and the pace both of change and of the awareness of such change (the modalities of their elaboration) gave to both agents and patients of these processes an air of phantasmagoria that required radical transformations in both the means of representation and description, on the one hand, and the kinds of questions one might pose in the face of these changes, on the other. In my opinion—and, again, as much a hunch as a hypothesis—nothing has been more radically disturbing of these changes to inherited ideas of both (social) science and art than the event known by the different names of Holocaust, *Shoah*, the Destruction, the Extermination, and so on.

This event, as much if not more than any other in our modernity, brought under question traditional ways of construing the past, the ways past and present were related, and the mode of presenting them as objects of presentation for both science and art. The older oppositions— between history and literature, past and present (anachronism), and fact and fiction—fall by the wayside, to be replaced by relationships better construed as those of a spectrum or, better, a Venn diagram. The meanings attached to terms like "fiction," "literature," "realism," "art," "aesthetics" and even "fact" have undergone radical change, even as the terms themselves continue to be used without any indication that they no longer carry the signifieds they once did. This means that the stakes in the game that set historical fact over against literary fiction have changed as well.

Notes

[Ed: An abstract by Hayden White appears at the head of this essay. It reads: "We study the past for many different reasons and in many different ways, of which the historical way or rather the historians' way is only one. The police and the courts, psychoanalysts and ethnographers, archaeologists and antiquarians confront pasts different from that (or those) posited by historians and use different methods for studying them. In this essay I raise some differences and similarities between a historical and a literary way of dealing with the communal past. This has special relevance for anyone working in the field of Holocaust studies, because it was thought for a long time that an artistic or literary treatment of this event posed two dangers: fictionalization (or endowing real events an imaginary or fantastic air or aspect) and aestheticization (or making the evil of this event fascinating and even perversely attractive)."]

1. On this subject see Karyn Ball, *Disciplining the Holocaust* (Albany: State University of New York Press, 2008).

2. Primo Levi, *Se questo è un uomo* (Turin: Einaudi, 1989 [1958]). English translation: *Survival in Auschwitz*, trans. Stuart Woolf (New York: Collier, 1960), 108–9.

3. *Oxford Essential Quotations*, 5th ed., ed. Susan Ratcliffe (Oxford University Press, published online, 2017), https://www.oxfordreference.com/view/10.1093/acref/9780191843730.001.0001/q-oro-ed5-00003433).

4. Levi, *Survival in Auschwitz*, 110.

5. Levi, 110–11.

6. Literally, "cabbage and beets," and metaphorically, a mishmash, crap.

7. Levi, *Survival in Auschwitz*, 111.

8. Levi, 108.

9. "Mi pare superfluo aggiungere che nessuno dei fatti è inventato" (It seems superfluous for me to add that none of the facts are invented) (Levi, "Prefazione," *Se questo è un uomo*, 6).

10. Whence the story of the Greeks' effort to penetrate the walls of Troy, their use of a "Trojan horse" to do so, and the role of "wily Ulysses" in tricking the Trojans into accepting this "gift horse" without looking inside it to see what it contained. In Virgil, the story of the penetration of the gates of Troy by the horse, itself a figure of "art" rather than of "force," prefigures the exit *from* Troy of Aeneas, the founder of Rome, who also prevails as much by trickery and fraud as by virtue. In Virgil's account, Aeneas's voyage is a success; Rome does get founded. But Dante writes a thousand years after Virgil and knows that Rome, too, had to pass away, leaving nothing but ruins and a knowledge blind to the "why" of human existence, aspiration, and failure.

11. Otto Dov Kulka, *Landscapes of the Metropolis of Death: Reflections on Memory and Imagination*, trans. Ralph Mandel (Cambridge, MA: Harvard University Press, 2013).

12. Kulka, *Landscapes*, 40.

13. "What I retain from this scene comes down to a feeling of a peculiar 'justice' that resided in all this; a feeling that it was some sort of actualization of a perplexing 'order' that overlay the camp's everyday life. Victim and

perpetrators, or the floggers and the lashes of justice to which the prisoner was sentenced, were as though one system, in which it was impossible to distinguish, to separate the victim from the deliverer of the punishment" (Kulka, 44).

14. Kulka, 44.

15. Kulka, 44–45.

16. Kulka, 41.

17. Kulka, 47.

18. T. S. Eliot, "Ulysses, Order, and Myth," *Dial* 75 (1923): 480–83. Thanks to Gerald Lucas's blog, *Eliot and the Mythic Method*, which you can read at https://grlucas.wordpress.com/2004/07/19/eliot-and-the-mythic-method/. Eliot credits W. B. Yeats with having first perceived the necessity of myth for the comprehension of the modern condition. Eliot writes: "In manipulating a continuous parallel between contemporaneity and antiquity, Mr. Joyce is pursuing a method which others must pursue after him. . . . It is simply a way of controlling, of ordering, of giving shape and significance to the immense panorama of futility and anarchy which is contemporary history."

19. I could not find the German. I presume that it is in Hebrew in Kulka's book. Was the epigraph translated into English from the Hebrew or from the German? Needless to say, such questions would hardly arise in a reading of an oral statement made ad hoc and without the kind of editing, revision, and rewriting I presume this text has undergone.

20. Needless to say, Professor Kulka uses the idea of myth in a purely personal way; but it seems to be a metaphor for an alternative way of grasping the aporias of human life outside the bounds of history, religion, and science. My own understanding of "myth" is closer to that of Northrop Frye: as sublimated in a postclassical and post-Christian world, myth(s) provide(s) plot-types, imagery, structures of meaning, and symbolizations by which "art" (and especially "literature") can try to mediate the conflicts of human life in an "imaginary" register. I mean "imaginary" in a Lacanian sense.

21. Kulka, *Landscapes*, 27.

22. Kulka, 27.

23. Kulka, 27.

24. Kulka, 28.

CHAPTER 9

The Limits of Enlightenment

Enlightenment as Metaphor and Concept [2014]

> God is the sun and the light of souls, "the light which lighteth every man that cometh into this World." [John 1:9]
>
> —G. W. Leibniz

> The light of the spirit and therewith of world history arises out of Asia.
>
> —G. W. F. Hegel

In this paper,[1] I take the eighteenth-century "age of Enlightenment" as a synecdoche of a distinctively modernist idea of enlightenment considered as a practical project of casting "light" onto areas of (ontological, natural, social, cultural) darkness to elevate, edify, awaken or otherwise educate mankind to the responsible uses of a freedom or autonomy that has been withheld by the forces in whose interest it is to keep the mass of humankind subjected to ignorance, superstition, and despotism. Obviously, the "light" at the heart of the enlightenment project is the same light traditionally identified with the sun, with fire, with majesty, and with the Godhead in Christianity and the various religions based on a dualism of light versus darkness. It is the light identified with good in its conflict with evil, with spirit in its conflict with matter, and with life in its struggle against death, but now secularized, materialized, at once brought down to earth and elevated to the status of a symbol figuring forth the substance of all that is good and pure in human life.

Eighteenth-century notions of light and therefore of enlightenment differ significantly, then, from earlier notions thereof, specifically in the ambiguity with which they are conceived to be related to light's other: darkness, impurity, mixture, and matter.

This modernist project of enlightenment differs from earlier counterparts by virtue of the muddying of the distinction between lightness and darkness deriving from the modern scientific conception of matter. Whereas older conceptions of enlightenment had presupposed a simple opposition *between* light and darkness that equated with an opposition between spirit and matter, heaven and earth, the "two cities" of Saint Augustine, and the like, the modern scientific conception of matter elaborated by Newton in his *Opticks* (1704) was so much more elastic, so much more attenuated that, instead of being seen as light's opposite, matter could be just as easily conceived as light's foundation, basis, a primary form. In other words, in modern scientific materialism, light could be accommodated as a mode or species of matter. The older Neoplatonic conception of the relation between spirit and matter connected them by emanation: matter was spirit at the further remove from the source from which it emanated. Matter was *not* non-spirit, and everything appearing in the space between spirit and matter was either quasi-matter or quasi-spirit, a mixture of the two. The Newtonian concept of matter makes everything secondary to it, including light.

In a certain sense, the Enlightenment—that period of Western cultural history in which the *literati*, or a significant portion of it, named itself as the champions of light and their program as the triumph of enlightenment—can well be seen as obsessed more with darkness than with light. The enlighteners considered light to be benign even in its excess, and darkness was the problem they tried to solve with the aid of light. Kant's great philosophical project begins with the attempt to answer the question, "Given a world in which mind must be considered to be adequate to its objects of interest, how is error possible?" This project is only another form of the question that impels the *philosophes* in the service of Enlightenment: "Given the fact that light is in every way superior to darkness, how is darkness possible?" In his theory of colors, Goethe solved the problem by placing white and black at the poles of a spectrum, with all the colors consisting of shades of "gray," different mixtures of black and white ("Yellow is a light which has been dampened by darkness; Blue is a darkness weakened by light").

Kant solved the problem by making darkness primary and defining light as derivative. Speaking of the relation of understanding to reality, Kant writes: "Reality is . . . logically first, and from this I conclude that it is also metaphysically and objectively first. But because the objects of the senses are not given by the understanding (and are not given *a priori* at all), negation, and the darkness from which the light of experience develops its figures, are what is first."[2] With the advent of modern science, no one had need of the spirit-hypothesis any more than they had for the god-hypothesis. For science, everything that existed possessed extension, weight, mass, and measurement. Some things might be lighter than others, and some things might be brighter than others, but however light and bright they might be, they had to be considered as matter only. On this view, light, far from standing over against and "illuminating" matter, could be conceived as only a mode of matter's different kinds of manifestations. In fact, the triumph of Newtonian materialism in the eighteenth century threatened the authority of light's traditional position atop of the hierarchy of being and, as a consequence, the power of the Enlightenment's claim to produce the conditions of possibility for mankind's liberation from its "self-incurred tutelage" (Kant).[3]

So that "light," which in "enlightenment" is considered to be both the means and the end or result of a process, has anything but a fixed meaning during the period in which "The Enlightenment" (*Aufklärung, Éclaircissement, l'Illuminismo, la Illustraciòn*) is supposed to have occurred. And indeed, during this same period, everything conspires to dissolve the oppositional structure in which light is accorded ontological superiority over darkness.

The weakness of that light celebrated by the enlighteners (*les lumières*) was perceived early on by their critics, of whom Giambattista Vico has recently been identified as among the most perspicuous. Vico knew from his study of history that knowledge, and especially knowledge of things human, was never a matter of the triumph of unalloyed truth over error, of mind over body, of reason over passion, or of light over darkness. In fact, Vico solves the (Hobbesian) problem of how civilization could emerge from savagery without the aid of divine intervention by positing a dialectical relation between error and truth, desire and need, the emotions and thought, darkness and light. This kind of insight will serve later on as the basis of devastating critiques of *the* Enlightenment by Hegel, Nietzsche, Heidegger, and Adorno and Horkheimer, based on the charge of the enlighteners' failure of self-criticism. Thus, Adorno: "Ruthless toward itself, the Enlightenment has eradicated the last remnants of its own self-awareness."[4] The enlighteners wanted to "disenchant" the world but succeeded only in extirpating "animism."[5] The enlighteners wanted to de-mythify the world, but "with every step enlightenment entangles itself more deeply in mythology."[6] In fact, the enlighteners'

efforts to elevate light to the status of supreme symbol of scientific reason and human cultural achievement ended in much the same way that
Kant's effort to overcome dualism ended: with the phenomena of light
blocking access to its noumenal ground. The Enlighteners could just
not see for looking.

In my title I speak of enlightenment as metaphor and concept. The
difference between a metaphor and a concept is crucial for understanding the different ways in which a sign such as "enlightenment" can function in discourses purporting to relate the features and the substance
of the process to which the sign refers. The heart, soul, or meaning of
a term like "enlightenment" is given in the figure of "light" that functions as agent, act, and effect of the process of "enlightening," or the
condition of "becoming enlightened" that "enlightenment" wishes to
promote. If light is considered as a *metaphor*, then its analysis will tend
to take the form of a list of the members of the class of phenomena of
which light itself is a paradigm and to which other members of the class
are related by resemblance, contiguity, or substantive identification. If
light is considered as a *concept*, its analysis will tend to take the form of
a set of contraries, contradictories, and negations of negativity. In this
case, light would be identified by whatever it is that is taken to be its
opposite (darkness), its contradictory (anything that is not light), and
the negative of its contradictory (non-darkness or, what amounts to the
same thing, *not* non-light).

This way of putting the matter before us allows us to see that a worldview based on an *opposition* of light to darkness generates an intermediate
ground of the un- or partially illuminated, the "darkened" or obscure,
what the poet Giacomo Leopardi will call *il vago* and identify as the very
principal of poetic or aesthetic insight. *Il vago* (which can be translated as
either "unclear" *or* as "vagrant, wandering, approximative," etc.) would
refer to that range of experiences in which things are or appear to be
either imperfectly illuminated or partially hidden, manifest but reces-
sive, not-dark or not-not light and not-not dark, in any event, neither
perfectly light nor perfectly dark but, as with all feelings, too much and
not enough.[7] The *concept* of light directs attention to the pure states of
lightness and darkness and away from the mixed cases, the hybrids, or
crossbreeds, mongrel, impure, and so on, whereas metaphors of light
direct attention precisely to such mixed kinds, since members of the
class of which light is a paradigm only resemble one another, or typically reside next to one another, or as a unit-in-difference find common
occupancy under, the aegis of a symbol.

Light is or has a substance in the scientific sense of the term *substance*: electromagnetic rays—whatever those are—and can therefore be spoken about with minimal ambiguity in conceptual terms. But experienced light—the light of the fire, of the candle, of the sun and moon, of the lightning flash—is or can be used as a metaphor; indeed, light has been in many cultures, including our own, a paradigmatic metaphor, a metaphor of metaphor when considered to be an effect (illumination) of metaphoricity itself.[8] I am or can feel to be illuminated by figures of expression such as "Jesus, light of the world" or "Lead, kindly Light" or "Let there be Light." The metaphor *carries* (< Greek: *pherein*, Latin: *ferre*) an attribute of one genus (light) over to (*meta-*) the substance of another (Godhead), or vice versa. "The light of reason" tells us something about thinking that could not be derived from either the observation of thought processes or experiments carried out on the brain. It does not tell us that reason is like light or has the qualities of light, but that reason is, has, or uses light to do its work. And if one is or was a *philosophe*, it followed that the work of reason is to penetrate darkness (ignorance and superstition), illuminate the world, make observation possible, identify what was inherently illuminated and what needed illuminating, and contribute thereby to the maturation of humankind, its "awakening" to the truth of its condition.

And "enlightenment," too, has or is supposed to have a substance, a substance that, according to Hegel at least, consists of "insight" (*Einsicht*), indeed, insight in and for itself, insight into insight itself, which allows it a clarity of proprio-consciousness opposed to all forms of simple *belief*, which is pseudo-insight, a "thought, not a notion, and hence something absolutely opposed to self-consciousness, while the reality in the case of pure insight is the self—they are such that *inter se* the one is the absolute negative of the other."[9]

According to Hegel, this absolute opposition between enlightenment and belief—shared by both believers and enlighteners alike—constituted the error at the heart of the eighteenth-century enlightenment's program or project. Hegel—product and stern critic of the dogma of "enlightenment"—was obsessed by the ambiguity of the light-image. "As light," Hegel says in the *Phenomenology*, "being . . . is, then, the shape of spirit in relation simply to itself—the form of having no special shape at all."[10] Hegel ends up castigating enlightenment for its self-absorption, its failure to comprehend simple belief, and likens it to an "infection" of consciousness, as destructive of community as it is of authority.

Does it matter that Hegel thought and wrote before the discovery that light was composed of electromagnetic rays? Although this discovery undermines the Enlightenment concept of light, does it eliminate the need for the light metaphor to characterize all that is high, present, here, early, and whole, in contrast to all that is low, absent, there, late, and fragmentary? Does it make sense to speak of "the electromagnetic rays" of reason or of "the electromagnetic ray of the world"? Or of enlightenment as the bringing to bear of electromagnetic rays upon the darkness? But none of this matters. What matters is that *the* Enlightenment and whatever *project* of "enlightenment" derives from it, either as a new program or an extension of that distilled into the *Encyclopédie*, have to do *not* with any science of optics or electricity but with desire, more specifically, the desire to know and to know by seeing, to know by shining a light into hitherto closed, darkened, or hidden places, to bring forth to vision what had before been hidden, to make the invisible, visible; to see "where the sun don't shine" and to destroy (*écraser*) whatever "infamous" thing is found there (Voltaire).

The conceptualization of light will require it to be *opposed* to darkness, and if darkness is seen as the principal attribute of matter, light will be viewed as opposed to matter as well. This last analogy—in which light is to darkness as light is to matter—generates the quest for a way of dissociating matter from darkness and transforming it into a kind of light ("darkness visible").

Thus, the Enlightenment of the eighteenth century must conceive light-spirit as both the absolute antithesis of darkness-matter and as matter's hidden substance. And it is here that the historical specificity of the Enlightenment of the eighteenth century can be stipulated: it is contained in the identification of matter as the substance of being effected by the scientific revolution of the seventeenth century. Whereas, in all previous instances of enlightenment, light was conceived to stand in opposition to darkness (and therefore to base matter) or occupied the top position in a hierarchy that extended through different degrees of obscurity into the basest of matter, by the time of Newton matter had prevailed in "enlightened" circles, and everything previously regarded as nonmaterial had now to be reconceptualized as matter. This process of reconceptualization was the *agon* through which light had to pass over the course of the eighteenth century. And as light went, so went enlightenment. The physics of the age was tending towards the dissolution of mechanic matter into energy—Newton knows that light was both particle and wave—but that would not occur until the late nineteenth century. Meanwhile, light remained an anomaly, at once particle and wave—which only repeated the matter-spirit dichotomy that light, re-conceptualized as matter, was supposed to resolve.

The connection between enlightenment and the sense of sight, the privileging of the sense of sight and of observation as the principal mode of knowledge production deflected the attention of the Enlightenment from the other senses and the kinds of knowledge of reality they could provide. The article on "sense" in the *Encyclopédie* insists that we are right to believe only what can be seen and that what is only heard must be suspect, coming as it might from sources of authority (despots and priests) in whose interest it is to keep the masses in a condition of ignorance and superstition.[11] But the idea that darkness could precede and, as it were, generate light as one of its effects, was difficult to swallow. It resembled the Christian idea of *generatio ex nihilo*, the generation of something out of nothing.

It turned out that the dualism of light versus darkness could be overcome only in some version of ontological monism in which light would appear as a mode of darkness or the reverse, in the same way that, in Spinoza's *Deus sive natura*, nature is presented as a mode of God's being in the world and the reverse. And indeed, Newton's *Opticks* (1704) can be seen as an effort to *raise* light to the status of matter by conceiving light as matter convertible into "body" and vice versa. Thus Newton:

> *Quest.* 30. Are not gross Bodies and Light convertible into one another, and may not Bodies receive much of their Activity from the Particles of Light which enter their Composition? For all fix'd Bodies being heated emit Light so long as they continue sufficiently hot, and Light mutually stops in Bodies as often as its Rays strike upon their Parts, as we shew'd above. I know no Body less apt to shine than Water; and yet Water by frequent Distillations changes into fix'd Earth, as Mr. Boyle has try'd; and then this Earth being enabled to endure a sufficient Heat, shines by Heat like other Bodies.[12]

Just as black and white were ultimately shown to be modes of refraction of light rays, so too the relation between darkness and light, or matter and mind, could be so construed. But then the question was: Could ignorance be regarded as a mode of knowledge, superstition a mode of reason, magic a mode of science, and beyond that, to finish out the list, what Kant offered as impediments to Enlightenment, obedience as a mode of autonomy, slavery as a mode of freedom?

Isaiah Berlin has popularized the idea of the counter-enlightenment, an ideology that, although interested in enlightenment, does not accept the materialist and observationalist prejudices of the mainstream enlighteners. Johann Georg Hamann (1730–1788), the self-styled "Magus of the North," is generally recognized as the theorist of this counter- (but *not* anti-) enlightenment frame of mind. First of all, Hamann pointed out that the kind of knowledge the Enlighteners commended to the masses was a gnostic kind of knowledge, a knowledge of, by, and for the *literati*, and therefore a knowledge without any redemptive force for the masses. Secondly, Hamann rejected the "dialectical" method of Kant and the *philosophes*, a method that favored logic as its organon and prose as its medium of communication. This method had no understanding of the cognitive power of the emotions or passions, no interest in the poetic and the wisdom distilled into language itself and, moreover, was blind to what may exist and still be hidden to sight. Knowledge comes less from the visual image than from the (divine) word, of which poetic utterance is a human manifestation. Hamann seeks to redeem those senses—hearing, smell, taste, and touch—that have been neglected in the celebration of sight, light, and brightness. In the process he finds the Enlightenment's failure to consist in its anaestheticism. So, against what he called Kant's "dialectical" method, Hamann posits a method he calls "aesthetical." The quest for clarity, Hamann asserted, was a delusion; we live in a "twilight" zone, a land of shadows, in which reality is veiled and truth is seen "through a glass darkly."[13] The brilliance of the noonday sun is itself an illusion; looked at directly, it blinds. There is a reason that the God of the Hebrew Bible manifests himself in a light that blinds rather than illuminates: the Lord is to be heard, attended to, and heeded, not viewed or observed. Hamann wanted to redeem the word over the concept, the figure over the letter, poetry over prose, and this meant, for him as for Vico, a plunge into the dark sides of *both* matter and spirit.

It is this willingness to accept life as a "midden" that allows the counter-enlighteners to conceptualize an idea of history much more richly textured, more nuanced, and more "believable" than the history presented in Voltaire's *Le siècle de Louis XIV*, a paean to Louis XIV and his "siècle" (a word more properly translated as "season" than "century"). It was this counter-enlightenment tradition that spawned the "historicism" of the nineteenth century. And it is historicism that will destroy the idea of enlightenment as the criterion for measuring mankind's achievement, its progress in history. What historicism does is to locate the proper zone of human life neither in the empyrean achieved by the few children of light who rose above bodily determination to gain the rank of hero, nor in the muck, mire, and darkness in which the masses toiled and drowned unknown and unlamented. Historicism locates history in the gray zone where events appear in chiaroscuro rather than silhouette. Recall that Voltaire begins his *Siècle de Louis XIV* by asserting that history properly consists of distinct periods (*âges, siècles*) but that only "les *âges heureux*" really count as parts of the "histoire du monde." These "happy ages" are those in which the arts were perfected and that, "servant d'époque à la grandeur de l'esprit humain, sont l'exemple de la postérité" (by serving as the epoch of the greatness of the human mind, are examples for posterity). After identifying the first three of these periods of happiness as the times of Athens, Rome, and Renaissance Florence, Voltaire then proceeds to characterize "le siècle de Louis XIV" as the age that "comes closest to perfection." Admittedly, Voltaire concedes, the arts had not been pushed beyond the point they had arrived at under the Medici of Florence, "mais la raison humaine en général s'est perfectionnée. La saine philosophie n'a été connue que dans ce temps" (but human reason in general was perfected. It was only in this age that we became acquainted with sound philosophy). All of which adds up to the judgment that "le siècle de Louis XIV . . . [a été] le siècle le plus éclairé qui fût jamais" (The age of Louis XIV . . . [was] the most enlightened of all ages).[14]

Now, it is obvious that, in this passage, Voltaire is using the idea of *éclaircissement*, understood as "human reason perfected," as a criterion not only for assessing the relative value of different ages of history but also as a criterion for determining the *content*—the historicity—of history as well. In principle, one cannot object to this procedure because the distinction between that part of the past that is "historical" and the part of it that is not requires some such criterion of determination. But from the standpoint of the later "historicist" idea of history, which judges the value or worth of any given phenomenon in the past as a function of the time and place of its appearance, Voltaire's use of his own age's idea of enlightenment as the criterion for determining the "historicity" of all other ages, is worse than a mistake; it is a violation of the principle of empirical method and of sympathetic *Einfühlung* informing a properly "historical" kind of historical inquiry.

From the perspective of modern theory of history, Voltaire's procedure is anything but "properly" historical; it is, rather, characteristic of that "philosophy of history" intended to extract the meaning, aim, purpose, or laws governing historical processes, to predict the future or indicate the path forward that the present should follow.[15] And all this, from the standpoint of historicism, runs counter to a respectful study of the past that ought properly be oriented to the consideration of the individuality of events, persons, institutions, processes, and periods of past human life. And from this perspective, one can comprehend how Voltaire's use of "enlightenment" as a criterion for determining both the content of history and the relative value of its various ages, periods, or epochs indicates a blind spot in the eighteenth-century idea of enlightenment in general.

But does the *opposition* presumed to exist between Voltaire's kind of philosophy of history and history properly so-called—between the Enlightenment philosophy of history, on the one hand, and the kind of "proper" historiography developed by Ranke and his epigones in the nineteenth century—not also conceal more than it reveals about the modern opposition to both philosophy of history and "enlightenment"? So much is presumed in Hegel's famous defense of the complementarity of "Philosophical History" to the kind of "Reflective History" in which "each period . . . involved in such peculiar circumstances, exhibits a condition of things so strictly idiosyncratic, that its conduct must be regulated by considerations connected with itself and itself alone."[16]

Reflective historiography, Hegel argued, cannot be brought under consideration of some general principle that would allow the kind of judgment on the past that a *free* life in the present requires. This is why Hegel recommends a different kind of philosophy of history from that of Voltaire, based on a different notion of "enlightenment" as a model for discerning the general shape of history's development and its import. For Hegel, history displays a spectacle of the immersion of spirit in matter, its identification with matter, its self-conflict with that matter that is an aspect of its existence in time.[17]

That this process can be metaphorized as a process of enlightenment is demonstrated in the opening paragraph of the "Classification of Historic Data" from Hegel's *Lectures on Philosophy of History*:

In the geographical survey, the course of the World's History has been marked out in its general features. The *Sun*—the Light—rises in the East. Light is a simply self-involved existence; but though possessing thus in itself universality, it exists at the same time as an individuality in the Sun. Imagination has often pictured to itself the emotions of a blind man suddenly becoming possessed of sight, beholding the bright glimmering of the dawn, the growing light, and the flaming glory of the ascending Sun. The boundless forgetfulness of his individuality in this pure splendor, is his first feeling—utter astonishment. But when the Sun is risen, this astonishment is diminished; objects around are perceived, and from them the individual proceeds to the contemplation of his own inner being, and thereby the advance is made to the perception of the relation between the two. Then inactive contemplation is quitted for activity; by the close of day man has erected a building constructed from his own inner Sun; and when in the evening he contemplates this, he esteems it more highly than the original external Sun. For now he stands in a *conscious relation* to his Spirit, and therefore a *free* relation. If we hold this image fast in mind, we shall find it symbolizing the course of History, the great Day's work of Spirit.

The History of the World travels from East to West, for Europe is absolutely the end of History, Asia the beginning. The History of the World has an East *kat xochn* (the term East in itself is entirely relative); for although the Earth forms a sphere, History performs no circle round it, but has on the contrary a determinate East, viz., Asia. Here rises the outward physical Sun, and in the West it sinks down: here consentaneously rises the Sun of self-consciousness, which diffuses a nobler brilliance. The History of the World is the discipline of the uncontrolled natural will, bringing it into obedience to a Universal principle and conferring subjective freedom. The East knew and to the present day knows only that *One* is Free; the Greek and Roman world, that *some* are free; the German World knows that *All* are free. The first political form therefore which we observe in History, is *Despotism*, the second *Democracy* and *Aristocracy*, the third *Monarchy*.[18]

This enlightenment and this history of it have little in common with that of Voltaire or the other *illuminati* of his *âge*. And although this Hegelian elaboration of the idea of enlightenment exerted profound influence on Western conceptions of history throughout the nineteenth century, it was not this idea but another one—an aesthetic or rather aestheticist one—that prevailed among those historians for whom Voltaire's philosophy of history was too metaphorical and Hegel's too conceptual. Whatever else it may be, historicism takes as the proper object of historical inquiry neither the particular nor the universal, but the individual in which the two are fused in an image more aesthetic than cognitive in kind. The articulation of this aesthetic idea of individuality was the work of Johann Joachim Winckelmann (1717–1768), who used it as a basis of a new conception of the history of art.

I do not have the time in this presentation to do justice to Winckelmann's "enlightened" notions of the work of art, the place of art in the cognitive disciplines, and the history of art as a history of enlightened views on the nature and function of light itself in art. Prior to Winckelmann, art was considered an area of general history—in the way Voltaire considered it. The dominant mode of art history itself was that of the "lives of the artists" tradition inherited from Giorgio Vasari and discussion, not so much of art objects as, rather, of *writing about* art and works of art. Winckelmann, however, conceived the idea of a history of works of art themselves and, moreover, a history based on the personal inspection of individual works of art. He considered the artwork as a paradigm of cultural work in general. And this equation of culture with art rather than with religion, philosophy, or science provided the basis for a conception of the enlightenment project quite different from that based on the equation of light with reason or thought alone.

Winckelmann's idea of personally inspecting the various works of art to serve as the subject matter of his history of ancient Greek art allowed historians to entertain the fantasy of viewing the past directly, rather than simply reading about the past in documents. For a work of art from the past could be said to be related to the agent and act of its creation differently from the way historical documents were related to the agents, agencies, actions, and effects of other kinds of historical events. The work of art could be seen *by its form alone* to be a product of an intention concreted in a material medium that made it directly accessible to sensory and not merely intellectual inspection. Whereas the historical *events* spoken about or attested by historical documents could never be empirically perceived, the work of art, however worn down or fragmented, manifested a formal coherency of a kind quite different from anything produced by nature or by the various utilitarian activities of human beings in the course of their daily lives.[19] This coherency could not only be described but could also be measured, weighed, copied, reproduced, and imitated in practice. As a product of human agency, the work of art permitted access to the kind of knowledge Vico called "maker's knowledge,"[20] the kind of knowledge the artisan can demonstrate he possesses by reproducing the artifact again and again if called upon to do so. Such knowledge was not only *not* abstract, but eminently practical inasmuch as it permitted insight into the process of *human self-making* that could be taken as the subject-matter of human history. In other words, for Winckelmann, the history of art objects or works of art is, or could be considered to be, a synecdoche for human history in general. Other kinds of historical objects can be known only indirectly and as objects of intellectual perception, whereas the art object lives on in the present and is indexically rather than only iconically or symbolically related to the event of its creation.

If the work of art permits direct sensory inspection in a way that other historical artifacts do not, what is to be looked for in such inspection? It is here that Winckelmann makes his most original contribution to the idea of enlightenment, what might be called artistic or aesthetic enlightenment, insofar as it has to do with the recognition that in itself light can both reveal and conceal, and that it is only in its relation to darkness or matter and in its production of different kinds of grayness, different shades of gray, that light can aid in the production of enlightenment.

Thus, when Winckelmann undertakes to reveal the secret of the pleasure given in the contemplation of a Greek sculpture, he does not deal with the form-content distinction in the conventional way of his time. He does not see the content of the sculpture as matter endowed with form, as if the form were "inside" the matter of which the sculpture was made, in the way that light might be thought to be inside a material medium but "shining through" it like a flare dropped in water. On the contrary, he insists that the form of the whole can be liberated from the dissociation of the discernible parts of the piece only by the imitation of the action by which the great sculptors of ancient Greece revealed the form of the whole, *by veiling or covering with drapery* the parts of the model so as to cover the transitional zones between the parts.[21] Light, like magnification, has to be attenuated to figurate the whole of the object as against its several and all too discernible parts.

What this all boils down to is the idea that the artwork, precisely insofar as it manages to attenuate the form and shape of the model (the human body of which it is a representation), can be thought of as producing the *substance of the form* of the original. This substance of form is to be thought of as the form of the shape of the original; it is neither a copy nor even a symbol of the original model. Consistently with Hegel's later notion that light is pure relation, the form of relationality itself, Winckelmann sees light and shadow as a totality, within which the parts of the model are related as transitional moments, graduations that produce a vague sense of the wholeness of the whole. Such a relationship Winckelmann posits as existing between the artwork and its original milieu, in which the work is to be conceived as being at once a product and a producer of its milieu, at once original and utterly one with its environment. And this organic relationship is conceived to apply to time as well as to space. The substance of the form of light in an ancient Greek statue shines through and fuses with the substance of the form of later art objects, produced in different milieux and different time zones.

Thus, Winckelmann provides at least one answer to the problem that puzzled so many nineteenth-century philosophers of history: how could the art object be both completely one with its own time and place, and still living and illuminating for later times and other places? Winckelmann's answer to that question provides a way of answering a similar question about history: how can an event, person, or institution that once existed but has now passed away still appear present and relevant to the solution of current problems long after they have ceased to exist? The way we answer that question might allow an approach to the answer to the related question: how can we compare different concepts of enlightenment and the traditions thereof without falling into abstraction, on the one hand, or the fallacy of misplaced concreteness, on the other? It would not be by seeking some middle ground between abstraction and concretion that a synthesis would be sought. It is rather by moving away from, beyond, or to some point before the distinction between abstract and concrete has been posited. Like the idea of the right distance for viewing things in order to discern their relations with their milieu,[22] Winckelmann's notion of light requires that it be brightened or dampened according to whether we wish to concentrate on the parts of things or on the totality of which the parts are component.

Notes

[Ed: This essay was published posthumously in the Italian journal *Storiographia* in 2018. The editor of this journal, Massimo Mastrogregori, included the following explanatory note (in Italian, my English translation) on the first page of the article: "A few years ago, upon returning to Rome after one of his intercontinental trips for lectures and conferences—I believe this trip was for an interview in China on tradition and enlightenment—Hayden White gave this article to me to read, promising to fine tune it as soon as possible for publication in *Storiographia*. After his death in March 2018, I found these pages among my papers, and I decided to publish the article—a reflection on enlightenment, which turns into a reflection on history—as is. Readers of our journal will thus be happy to be able to hear his voice once more in this luminous, previously unpublished piece."

An abstract by Hayden White that appears at the head of the article reads: "The Enlightenment and whatever *project* of 'enlightenment' derives from it, either as a new program or an extension of that distilled into *L'Encyclopédie*, have to do *not* with any science of optics or electricity but with desire, more specifically, the desire to know and to know by seeing, to know by shining a light into hitherto closed, darkened, or hidden places, to bring forth to vision what had before been hidden, to make the invisible, visible; to see 'where the sun don't shine' and to destroy (*écraser*) whatever 'infamous' thing is found there (Voltaire)."]

1. This paper was originally delivered as a lecture at Wellesley College on April 16, 2014.

2. Quoted in Beatrice Longuenesse, *Kant and the Capacity to Judge: Sensibility and Discursivity in the Transcendental Analytic of the "Critique of Pure Reason"* (Princeton, NJ: Princeton University Press, 1998), 309.

3. "Enlightenment is man's release from his self-incurred tutelage" (Immanuel Kant, "What Is Enlightenment?," trans. Lewis White Beck, in Immanuel Kant, *On History* [Indianapolis: Bobbs-Merrill, 1963], 3). It has to be said that the Enlightenment, for Kant, was more a matter of will and volition than of knowledge and reason. The great portion of mankind, Kant maintained, was lazy and cowardly and averse to "growing up," inclined to lean on authorities for direction in every aspect of life. Freed from authority, however, the masses could become enlightened to their own individual worth and value and inclined to take responsibility for their actions. Enlightenment, for Kant, was more of a result of freedom than its precondition. It remained nonetheless a kind of knowledge—self-knowledge as a species of knowledge.

4. Max Horkheimer and Theodor W. Adorno, *Dialectic of Enlightenment: Philosophical Fragments* (Stanford, CA: Stanford University Press, 2002), 2.

5. Horkheimer and Adorno, *Dialectic of Enlightenment*, 2.

6. Horkheimer and Adorno, 8.

7. "The more vague and imprecise language is, the more poetic it becomes . . . Italian is the only language in which the word *vago* (vague) also means 'lovely, attractive.' Starting out from the original meaning of 'wandering,' the word *vago* still carries an idea of movement and mutability, which in Italian is associated both with uncertainty and indefiniteness, and with gracefulness and pleasure" (Italo Calvino, *Exactitude*, in *Six Memos for the Next Millennium* [Cambridge, MA: Harvard University Press, 1988], 57). Cf. Margaret Brose, "Il potere del suono: Leopardi, Valéry, Wordsworth," in *Leopardi sublime* (Bologna: Re Enzo, 1998), 119–75.

8. Cf. Jacques Derrida, "La mythologie blanche," in *Marges de la philosophie* (Paris: Éditions de Minuit, 1972), 207–72. [Ed: Jacques Derrida, "White Mythology," in *Margins of Philosophy*, trans. Alan Bass (Chicago: University of Chicago Press, 1982), 207–71.]

9. G. W. F. Hegel, *The Phenomenology of Mind*, vol. 2 (New York: Cosimo Classics, 2005), 561.

10. Hegel, *Phenomenology of Mind*, 700.

11. "Observation and experiment are the only paths that we have to knowledge, if one recognizes the truth of the axiom: we have nothing in our minds that did not originally come from the senses. At least these are the only means by which one can attain knowledge of objects that fall within the province of the senses. It is only through them that we can cultivate physics, and it is not doubtful that observation, even in the physics of inorganic bodies, infinitely surpasses experimentation in certainty and usefulness, although inanimate bodies, without life and almost without action, only offer the observer a certain number of phenomena that are relatively uniform and in appearance easy to recognize and combine. Although one cannot overlook the fact that experiments, especially those in chemistry, have shed a great light on that science, we see that the parts of physics, which are entirely within the province of observation, are the best known and perfected. It is by observation that the laws of motion have been determined, that the general properties of bodies have been known. It is to observation that we owe the discovery of gravity, attraction, acceleration of heavy bodies, and the system of Newton; on the other hand, Descartes's system was based on experience. Finally, it is observation that created astronomy and carried it to this point of perfection in which we see it today, and which is such that it surpasses in certainty all the other sciences" ("Observation," in *The Encyclopedia of Diderot & d'Alembert Collaborative Translation Project*, trans. Stephen J. Gendzier [Ann Arbor: University of Michigan Library, 2009], http://hdl.handle.net/2027/spo.did2222.0001.314).

12. "The changing of Bodies into Light, and Light into Bodies, is very conformable to the Course of Nature, which seems delighted with Transmutations. Water, which is a very fluid tasteless Salt, she changes by Heat into Vapour, which is a sort of Air, and by Cold into Ice, which is a hard, pellucid, brittle, fusible Stone; and this Stone returns into Water by Heat, and Vapour returns into Water by Cold. Earth by Heat becomes Fire, and by Cold returns into Earth. Dense Bodies by Fermentation rarify into several sorts of Air, and this Air by Fermentation, and sometimes without it, returns into dense Bodies. Mercury appears sometimes in the form of a fluid Metal, sometimes in the form of a hard brittle Metal, sometimes in the form of a corrosive pellucid Salt call'd Sublimate, sometimes in the form of a tasteless, pellucid, volatile white Earth, call'd *Mercurius Dulcis*; or in that of a red opake volatile Earth, call'd Cinnaber; or in that of a red or white Precipitate, or in that of a fluid Salt; and in Distillation it turns into Vapour, and being agitated *in Vacuo*, it shines like Fire. And after all these Changes it returns again into its first form of Mercury. Eggs grow from insensible Magnitudes, and change into Animals; Tadpoles into Frogs; and Worms into Flies. All Birds, Beasts and Fishes, Insects, Trees, and other Vegetables, with their several Parts, grow out of Water and watry Tinctures and Salts, and by Putrefaction return again into watry Substances. And Water standing a few Days in the open Air, yields a Tincture, which (like that of Malt) by standing longer yields a Sediment and a Spirit, but before Putrefaction is fit Nourishment for Animals and Vegetables. And among such various and strange Transmutations, why may not Nature change Bodies into Light, and Light into Bodies?" (Isaac Newton, *Opticks: Or A Treatise of the Reflections, Refractions, Inflections and Colors or Light*, 4th ed. [London: William Innys, 1730], 374–75).

13. J. R. Betz, *After Enlightenment: The Post-secular Vision of J. G. Hamann* (New York: John Wiley, 2009), 304ff.

14. Voltaire, *Le siècle de Louis XIV*, vol. 1 (Paris: Garnier-Flammarion, 1966), 35–36.

15. Jerome Rosenthal, "Voltaire's Philosophy of History," *Journal of the History of Ideas* 16, no. 2 (1955): 151–78.

16. G. W. F. Hegel, *Lectures on the Philosophy of History*, trans. John Sibree (London: Henry G. Bohn, 1861), 6.

17. Hegel, *Lectures*, 75: "History in general is therefore the development of spirit in time, as nature is the development of the idea in space."

18. Hegel, 109–10 (italics in the original).

19. It is true that one kind of implement produced for use in daily life has many of the properties of the work of art, and this is the tool, especially the tool invented for the purpose of making other tools, which is often cited as a uniquely human kind of product. But Winckelmann was interested in the work of art as a product of the desire to produce a pleasing form rather than a useful one.

20. [Ed: White is referring to Vico's dictum "the true is precisely what is made" (*verum esse ipsum factum*).]

21. For this brief discussion of light in Winckelmann's work, I am very grateful to the essay by Donovan Miyasaki, "Art as Self-Origination in Winckelmann and Hegel," *Graduate Faculty Philosophy Journal* 27, no. 1 (2006): 1–22.

22. Here I refer to recent works in historical theory that suggest that the "microhistorical" approach is superior to a macrohistorical approach to the study of the past. This newly minted "microhistory" would seem to be product of a reaction to the so-called "grand narratives" or philosophies of history that purport to provide a key to the understanding of history writ big.

CHAPTER 10

Outcasts, Monsters, and Simulacra of History [2015]

The nice thing about this kind of occasion is that it gives one an opportunity—at an advanced age—to offer excuses for one's sins, both of commission and omission committed over the course of a career.[1]

So here goes. I began my career as a scholar of medieval history and enjoyed the antiquarian experience of years in Rome and Florence imbibing the melancholic atmosphere of days spent dreaming in ancient churches and monasteries, ruined castles and fortified cities of days gone by. And although I thought of myself as a *Wissenschaftler* in the mode of Max Weber and a scholar in the mode of Gerd Tellenbach, I was always aware that my interest in the past was more philosophical than scientific. My work on the history of the Church, Roman and Canon law, and the Gregorian Reform (*Investiturstreit*) was always done with an awareness of the extent to which "the past," this past, this medieval past, was utterly alien to both my perception of reality and the values I tried to impart to my students in the classroom.[2] Increasingly over the years my interest shifted from this past to those historians who had devoted their lives to its study.

My interest shifted from history to historiography and the modes of presentation (of *Darstellung*) that the great writers of history—Michelet, Ranke, Burckhardt, Mommsen, and, yes, Marx, Guizot, Gebhart, Spengler, and Egon Friedell—employed in bringing this past to life, endowing it with vivacity and color, making it real, in the manner of Johan Huizinga, the great Dutch scholar who lured me into medieval history in the first place.

So, in the first ten years of my career, I lived a double life, writing and teaching "history," on the one side, and pondering the *mystery* of historiography, the writing of history, how persons could be made into characters, events into drama, facts into reality, on the other. Ultimately, I came to think that historiography was, as its very name implied, a species of the genus *writing* and that the secret of its fascination since Herodotus and Thucydides on down to Huizinga, Mommsen, Tawney, Croce, and Beard lay, first of all and fundamentally, in its status as a kind of writing.

By the time I turned to composing a history of historical writing, I found myself in an academic atmosphere being revolutionized by new theories of writing, inscription, figuration, textuality, linguistics, semiotics, and an idea of "literature" revolutionized by attention to the great masters of literary modernism, an idea of literature as "writing": Henry James, Joseph Conrad, Virginia Woolf, James Joyce, Marcel Proust, Gertrude Stein, Thomas Mann, T. S. Eliot, Ezra Pound, and a host of others. For these writers, the older distinctions between poetry and prose, literal and figurative, rhetoric and logic, *Sinn und Bedeutung*, and even fiction and fact, did not line up easily with Aristotle's idea of the relation between poetry and history, the *doxa* that had reigned as dogma in thought about history until very recently.

So, I came to think, if one were going to compose a history of historical *writing* (or writing about history), one had to begin by conceptualizing it in terms consonant with current thought about writing. And this resulted in a book, *Metahistory: The Historical Imagination in Nineteenth-Century Europe*, which was generally received by professional historians as wanting in a proper *content* (the research dimension of historical inquiry) and a proper *form* (abstract ideas, etc.).

What was not perceived, even by me at the time, was the simple idea that in historical writing, as in writing in general, the *form* of the presentation was an element of the *content* as well. It was not quite a matter of the medium being the message but rather that the medium was certainly part of the message, if not the most important part, even in scholarly or scientific discourse. Indeed, the implication was—and I think still is—that the modernist notion of writing permits an understanding of *ideology* more as a matter of the *form* of the presentation (*die Darstellung*) than of the so-called content or referent thereof. And this is what got me involved in the then emerging question of the epistemic and ontological status of narrative (narration, storytelling) as a form, genus, or mode of writing adequate to the representation of that way of being-in-the-world called historistic, historiological, historiosophic, or simply "history."

As thus envisaged, any written presentation of a past reality in the manner of a narrative had to be viewed as a product of an imposition upon "data" of a form more mythological or mythologizing, poetic or literary, than scientific or mimetic. Any putatively realistic representation of past reality—the actual existence of which was attested by "evidence" of a particular kind—had to be grasped as a construction rather than as an image or congeries of propositions that was true by virtue of its correspondence to "the facts" of that reality. A theoretically justified defense of narrativity as a mode or genus of representation of a putatively "given" set of real events had to take account of modernist notions of "writing" (écriture, Schriften, scrittura, and so on) if one wanted to maintain that historical writing was anything other than a fictionalization (or aestheticization) of a world truthfully presentable only in scientific metalanguage or educated common sense.

I have recently been struck—more than normal—by the number of colleagues and friends who utilize various kinds of historical knowledge (or "history") in their research and never imagine that "history" might be problematic as a basis or foundation of the other kinds of knowledges (sociological, political, economic, anthropological, literary, linguistic, and so on). Of course, most of them have been educated to think of history as a domain of established factual information, which, if not properly scientific, is at least "objective" and established by "ground up," empirical, or commonsensical methods. I have a colleague who believes that when we invoke "historical reality" or "history" or "the past" for the understanding of some present situation or problem, there is nothing very "philosophical" involved, nothing that might require us to stop first and reflect on the epistemological and/or ontological status of historical knowledge in general. History, for him, is just there, like a landscape or geographical terrain that we can map by informed commonsensical means and without a lot of fancy philosophical reflection. Thus, when I suggest that the very history of historical writing raises questions about the status of history considered as a scientific discipline, I am typically told that such epistemological speculations are ultimately not very useful for the doing of history.

In the brief time I have on this occasion I would like to take issue with this commonsensical view and offer some thoughts that, I believe, provide good grounds for revising what we think to be the kind of knowledge history provides us with and some justification for regarding literature, and particularly the modern novel, as useful supplements for the kind of knowledge of the past that history gives us.

Let me begin by suggesting that histories or discourses purporting to be representations (or descriptions) of past events are third-order, rather than first- or second-order, accounts of "the way things were in the past." First-order evidence of the occurrence of events in the past would consist of what historians call "primary sources"—documents and monuments. These are *indices* of the occurrence of events (contracts, legal documents, medals struck for occasions, remains of material objects, such as weapons found on a battlefield, ruined buildings, and such like). Second-order evidence would consist of eyewitness portrayals of aspects of events, testimonies more or less contiguous in time and space to the occurrences themselves. Third-order evidence would then consist of the historian's accounts of events of the past based on the critical analysis of first- and second-order evidence.

Giles Deleuze has suggested that these different kinds of evidence can be profitably thought of as analogous to what in art history is sometimes treated as the differences among an original, a copy, and a simulacrum (a copy of a copy that "estranges" by distortion to draw attention to the copy's problematic nature) or *eine Scheinbild*. Deleuze's argument implies that the historian's account of events long past and no longer accessible by direct observation or experience could be likened less to a *copy* of such events (the mimetic thesis of realistic representation) than to a *simulacrum*.

As I understand these orders of observation, the first-order referent for a painting such as Da Vinci's *La Gioconda* would be the *person* (Mona Lisa) who posed for it, the (second-order) copy would be Leonardo's famous *portrait*, and the third-order referent (a simulacrum) might be Salvador Dali's *copy of Leonardo's painting* but with a mustache drawn onto the upper lip of the figure.

Simulacrum might be one way of speaking about what historians have typically objected to in the infamous "philosophy of history" à la Hegel, Marx, Spengler, Toynbee, and so on, what they view as the "distortions" of history, as mythical or mythologizing of historical reality. So, too, from this perspective, a historical novel such as Tolstoy's *War and Peace* produces a simulacrum by adding fictional materials to the known facts established by historians.[3] But to view philosophy of history—however messianic or apocalyptical, teleological or chaotic it might be—as a distortion *of history* instead of a distortion of mainstream historiographical accounts of the past, is to eschew the opportunity provided by the concept of simulacrum to account for the ineluctably artistic (or poietic) element, not only in every philosophy of history, but also in every narrativistic (or storytelling) account of the past. And although philosophies of history are manifestly more constructed than "found" in the "data" of the past, these very data are constructed by simulacral processes of thematization and nominalization that are more "artistic" or "poietic" than nomological and deductive in kind, as properly scientific accounts of the past are supposed to be.

To be sure, this idea of historiography requires a conception of art or poetic utterance more devoted to "truth" than to beauty or goodness, which is to say, to the kind of realism aspired to by the modern and the modernist novel, than to, say, the traditional genres of literature before modernism. But it would allow us to accept the intuition that the modern novel and hybrid genres such as the historical novel have as their referents a real rather than a fantasmatic past and that this realism consists precisely of a desire to provide something like a simulacrum of the historiographical past, rather than only an "aestheticized" or "fictionalized "version of past events, persons, processes, and institutions.

Moreover, on this view, we would be able to credit the belief that the modernist novel provides a *supplement* to, rather than a non- or antihistorical account of, the past. We could then see that those versions of the past found in the great modern and modernist novels—from Balzac, Marcel Proust, and Virginia Woolf to Günter Grass, Don DeLillo, Ian McEwan, David Grossman, and W. G. Sebald—like Dali's "deformation" of Leonardo's great portrait, are themselves simulacra of the histories written in a different register by the great, or at least canonical, historians of a given time and place. Such an idea would allow us to entertain the "distortions" found in modern myth, literature, and philosophy of history less as betrayers of "truth" than as treatments of the ethical and aesthetic implications of the truths found in proper histories. Presentations of the historical past in novels such as Virginia Woolf's *Between the Acts*, H. G. Adler's *Eine Reise*, William Faulkner's *Absalom, Absalom*, Hilary Mantel's *Wolf Hall*, Philip Roth's *American Pastoral*, David Grossman's *See Under: Love*, Thomas Mann's *Doktor Faustus*, Günter Grass's *Tin Drum*, and so on, should be seen less as "fictionalizations" of a real world than as critiques of the modes of representation used in proper historiography as a uniquely proper way of presenting it. Moreover, it would allow us to understand how any understanding of any reality must utilize figurative as well as literalist language (or code) for the comprehension of what lies below, above, or beyond a literalist and quantitative conception of material reality. And it would allow us to recognize that a literary work such as Primo Levi's *Se questo è un uomo* comprehends the world of Auschwitz not so much because of the putatively "scientific" precision and accuracy of its propositional content (on the presumption that Levi's training as a chemist had given him an inordinately "clear" eye) as, rather, because of its "literariness," its poetic and rhetorical manner of presentation, its "style."[4]

Primo Levi's work provides us with a way of discriminating between (and thereby resolving a problem in Holocaust studies concerning) two kinds of testimony: that of survivors and perpetrators in general; and that of witnesses who use their experience as content of an artistic or literary performance. It is the difference between those thousands of survivors who have bravely recounted their subjective experiences of the camps, to add to the record of "what happened" therein, and the few, like Levi, Charlotte Delbo, Tadeusz Borowsky, Jorge Sempron, Saul Friedländer, Otto Dov Kulka, and Jean Améry, whose testimony rises to the high ground of literary art. These artistic treatments do not aestheticize or fictionalize, prettify or perversely fetishize the camps, but on the contrary render the experience of them more concrete, more personal, more terrifying and compelling precisely inasmuch as they filter them through sensibilities attuned to the enigmas, ironies, paradoxes, and ambivalences of the feelings aroused by them.

A couple of years ago, during a visit to the University of Konstanz, a young instructor of history spoke to me about the confusion he felt when teaching Levi's book about Auschwitz. He was never certain, he said, or how much of it was truth and how much of it was "made up" or invented. I pointed out to him that, in his Preface, Levi has written: "It seems superfluous to add that none of the facts was invented." I also added that this straightforward statement could be taken two ways. Does it mean: "none of the *facts* was invented." Or does it mean: "none of the facts was *invented*." In this statement Levi implies two different notions of the content of his text: facts experienced, as it were, from outside himself and other kinds of materials—opinions, considerations, beliefs, and judgment—which are not fictions so much as simulacra, because they are not given to sense and must be invented on the basis of inner experiences (*Erlebnisse*). These latter kinds of materials can be thought of as products of what Immanuel Kant called the *productive* (as against the *reproductive*) imagination, the basis of a *poiesis* that is cognitive, even if not a product of "pure reason." Facts are found, not invented, or facts are not invented—a tautology if one believes that facts are hard and solid like rocks or stones and are found in research, not inventible. And, on the other hand, some facts—even facts of nature—have to be made by the "productive imagination," because science does not yet possess the categories and concepts to grasp them in pure thought.

We are only lately emerging from a long debate over the true nature of the Shoah and whether this event is a genuine novelty or only a reprise in different guise of a long series of events substantially similar to it. A historical approach to this event seeks its meaning in its origin, provides a genetic or genealogical explanation of its occurrence, on the presumption that nothing under the sun is really new, that continuity trumps discontinuity in history in a way that it may not in nature (where chaos, big bang, fuzzy sets, and fractals rule the day). But if history is continuous with nature, is made of the same stuff as nature, then history must be as productive of emergent and genuinely novel events as nature is today thought to be.

As a discipline, history tends to be conservative and resistant as much to the idea of novelty in general as it is to *new theories* of the nature of historical reality and new notions of how to study history properly. Lately, there has been a widespread movement to rethink history in terms of what has been ignored, suppressed, or excluded in the process of constructing normative accounts (or paradigms) of national, group, and individual pasts. The discipline of history faces hostile demands for revision of its theory and methods as well as what it takes to be its proper "historical" content or referent. Women's history, feminist history, Queer history, animal history, subaltern history, native history, even the history of things, have been proposed as subjects of history every bit as proper to it as states, laws, societies, peoples, or nations. I remember when labor history and economic history were considered with the same kind of condescension with which Queer history and subaltern history were met only a few decades ago.

Resistance to the inclusion of both new contents and new modes of presentation in history might be relaxed somewhat by the introduction of the idea of the simulacrum into historical studies. Then, in place of a rigid conception of what constitutes real or proper historiography, on the one hand, and what constitutes a pseudo-, fake, or heretical historiography, on the other, we might envision a spectrum of degrees of self-conceptualization of the historiographical project. At one end of the spectrum would be the *event*, that problematical phenomenon for which modern physics has no use. Then, in extending order of self-consciousness, would come the *written and monumental record* of events out of which the traditional kind of Western European historian makes (or discovers) his or her "facts" and writes his or her "histories"— macro or micro as the case might be. After that, would come those *novelistic and poetic treatments* of those histories made by the historians disciplined in those methodologies of understanding and explanation serviceable to the dominant classes of the societies in which they work. And then, after that, would come the literary and poetic accounts of that past that had been distilled into the history books written by licensed historians of the academic kind and producing simulacra of those accounts, in a manner similar those of the "philosophers of history."

Of course, the authority or credibility of these simulacra of history does not derive from their authors' research into the primary sources, any more than the authority or appeal of philosophers of history might so depend. I have always been impressed by how much research goes into the typically serious modernist novels of writers like Conrad, Joyce, Woolf, Proust, Thomas Pynchon, DeLillo, David Grossman, Philip Roth, Hilary Mantel, etc., not research into the sources but into those histories based on the sources. Roth's set piece on the history of the glove industry in Newark, New Jersey, puts many a historian of labor to shame in the precision, detail, and concreteness of its presentation. And—I have to say—I gained more insight into British society by reading Virginia Woolf than I ever did in my reading of the historians of early twentieth-century Great Britain. Woolf's description of a day in London as experienced by her protagonist, Clarissa Dalloway, helped me conjure with the mysteries of the British class system better than any historian's treatment that I can recall.

But it is not that Woolf or Roth possessed a higher historical consciousness than G. M. Trevelyan or A. J. P. Taylor or Hugh Trevor-Roper. They possessed a different consciousness of the discursive potentialities of writing for the representation of reality in historiographical terms. Thus, the modernist literary presentation of historical reality often does much the same thing that Dali did to Leonardo Da Vinci's masterpiece when he painted that mustache on the Mona Lisa. Or the same thing that Marcel Duchamp did when he placed that urinal—labeled "Fountain" and signed by R. Mutt—in a space supposedly reserved only for "works of art." What both of these artists were trying to do was to liberate art itself from the constraints of traditions devoted to an *aesthetic* conception of art itself. And question a conception of art committed to fantasy and fancy rather than engagement with a reality hidden behind images of beauty and sublimity in which the refuse of the world—the outcasts, monsters, and simulacra—had no place.

In many respects, the movements known as "history from below," "subaltern history," Queer history, and postcolonial history augured a new, more intellectually generous and humane consciousness of the past. Such kinds of history do not resemble their canonical Western European counterparts, either in content or, in many cases, in form. Does the future of historiography lie in what Barthes called the "novelesque" or "novelistic" (*romanesque*) mode, rather than in the modes that have typically been used to legitimize European capitalism and empire? Can the unfortunate schism between history and literature be overcome by recognition of the propriety and adequacy of a hybrid genre that takes the simulacrum as a paradigm of a historiography that combines scientific and artistic practices in a distinctively modernist mode? For myself, I do not think that a historiography that is genuinely global has to be imagined before it can be conceptualized and operationalized. And since historiography is a verbal medium dealing as much in images as in concepts, this work of imagination will require as much artistry as it does science, to rise to the challenge of creating polities and economies never thought of before even by our greatest theorists of utopia. Up until only recently, historians had insisted that our reflections on history had to exclude the future from any consideration with the past and the present. Aristotle distinguished between history and literature (poetics) on the basis of the distinction between the actual and the possible. But recall that he ranked literature higher than history precisely because knowledge of the possible was more comprehensive (philosophical) than knowledge of the actual.[5] So it is time to return the project of our philosophers of history to full membership in our profession, to our curricula, and to our sensibilities. But now with full recognition of the poetic nature of their enterprise. György Lukács spoke of the need in his time for a philosophy of composition and the cultivation of a poetic sensibility for philosophers. I think that the same thing is needed not only for historiography but for the humanities in general. We should get over our habit of identifying literature with fiction. Not all literary writing is fictionalizing, just as not all fictional writing is literary. We in the humanities can only profit from breaking down a naïve belief in an opposition between history and literature. The modernist novel teaches us the value of mixed genres, hybridities, and what Mikhail Bakhtin called "*carnival.*"[6]

Notes

1. [Ed: This lecture was given at the Freie Universität Berlin on June 9, 2015, on the occasion of receiving an honorary doctorate from this university.]

2. [Ed: White is referring to his doctoral dissertation, "The Conflict of Papal Leadership Ideals from Gregory VII to St. Bernard of Clairvaux with Special Reference to the Schism of 1130" (University of Michigan, 1955).]

3. [Ed: See chapter 15 of volume 1 of White's *The Ethics of Narrative*, "Against Historical Realism: A Reading of Leo Tolstoy's *War and Peace*."]

4. [Ed: See chapter 9 of volume 1 of White's *The Ethics of Narrative*, "Figural Realism in Witness Literature: On Primo Levi's *Se questo è un uomo*."]

5. [Ed: See Aristotle, *Poetics* 9 (trans. Stephen Halliwell, in *Aristotle "Poetics," Longinus "On the Sublime," Demetrius "On Style"* [Cambridge, MA: Harvard University Press, 1995, Loeb Classical Library], 59): "It is also evident from what has been said that it is not the poet's function to relate actual events, but the *kinds* of things that might occur and are possible in terms of probability or necessity. The difference between the poet and the historian is not that between using verse or prose; Herodotus' work could be versified and would be just as much a kind of history in verse as in prose. No, the difference is this: that one relates actual events, the other the kinds of things that might occur. Consequently, poetry is more philosophical and more elevated [of greater *ethical import* (by philosophical standards)] than history: for poetry tends to express the universal, history the particular" (note in brackets by Halliwell, my emphasis).]

6. [Ed. See Mikhail Bakhtin, "Carnival and Carnivalesque," in *Cultural Theory and Popular Culture: A Reader*, ed. John Storey (New York: Prentice Hall, 1998), 250–60.]

CHAPTER 11

Modernism and the Sense of History [2016]

> The poet . . . is not likely to know what is to be done unless he lives in *what is not merely the present, but the present moment of the past,* unless he is conscious, not of what is dead, but of what is already living.
>
> —T. S. Eliot, "Tradition and the Individual Talent" (emphasis added)

> Whoever has approved this idea of order . . . will not find it preposterous that the past should be altered by the present as much as the present is directed by the past.
>
> —T. S. Eliot, "Tradition and the Individual Talent"

> When, however, one's existence is inauthentically historical, it is loaded down with the legacy of a "past" which has become unrecognizable, and it seeks the modern. (Die uneigentlich geschichtliche Existenz dagegen sucht, beladen mit der ihr selbst unkenntlich gewordenen Hinterlassenschaft der "Vergangenheit," das Moderne.)
>
> —Martin Heidegger, *Being and Time*

Many years ago, my professor of philosophy, Lewis White Beck,[1] told me that when two equally intelligent and sincere philosophers are unable to resolve differences of opinion on some matter of genuinely philosophical concern, it is more likely that it is because they share a common error or false enabling proposition than that they are doing philosophy badly. I want to suggest that this may have been true of many of those modernists and antimodernists I will be considering. Moreover, I want to suggest that one error or false enabling proposition that they may have shared is to be found in the conception of history and the historical or historicality in general that lay at the basis of many of their disagreements over the nature of time, temporality, the past, tradition, heritage, culture, civilization, and just about everything else that is implied in the label "modernist."

As we all know, the term "history" had come, by the beginning of the twentieth century, to be synonymous with "reality," so much so that the phrase "historical reality" had become a pleonasm. Indeed, the relation between "history" and "realism" had become so intimate by the end of the nineteenth century that, insofar as "modernism" appeared to wish to succeed "realism" as the content of "serious" literature, it had come to seem to wish to succeed "history" itself. In any event, any discussion of modernism and its others cannot not take account of its problematization of "history."

I take modernism to be a *cultural* movement that crystallized sometime between 1910 and 1930 as a *response* to (rather than as only an expression of) the process of modernization that sought to rationalize and thereby demystify the world, destroy superstition and religion, demythify politics, and make the world safe for capitalism. I stress that, for me, cultural modern*ism* is a *response* to modernization—positive or negative, as the case may be—in the domain of the symbolic, in which the aim is to set up an alternative "imaginary relation to the real conditions of existence" (Althusser) to those prevailing during the nineteenth century in European society. In this sense, modernism in general can be seen as a vision of reality that presumes the necessity of a radical revision of what is meant by "history."

Modernism has a number of common or similar features that appear in its representative forms, but these are more in the nature of family resemblances than uniform attributes shared by all. In the arts and thought, modernism is characterized in general by belief in the autonomy of the aesthetic vis-à-vis other faculties and domains of cultural production and the breakdown of the distinction between art and nonart. In effect, for a genuine modernist, everything made (or in natural processes, seeming to have been fashioned) can be treated as art or have a place in the art world. In poetry, modernism seems driven by belief in the debility of the subject, the impersonal nature of poetic language, and the possibility of automatism in literary writing. These tendencies can be regarded as pathological only on the basis of a belief in the dogmas of a nineteenth-century conception of art as mimesis. Fredric Jameson suggests that modernity, and indeed modernism as well, can be seen as "tropes" that are "useful for generating alternate historical narratives, despite the charge of ideology [they] necessarily continue to bear." Jameson continues: "As for the ontology of the present, however, it is best to accustom oneself to thinking of 'the modern' as a one-dimensional concept (or pseudo-concept) *that has nothing of historicity or futurity about it.*"[2]

This statement stands in vivid contrast to the view of Clement Greenberg, the virtual inventor of American modernism, who held that

> Contrary to the common notion, Modernism or the avant-garde didn't make its entrance by breaking with the past. Far from it. Nor did it have such a thing as a program, nor has it really ever had one—again, contrary to the common notion. Nor was it an affair of ideas or theories or ideology. It's been in the nature, rather, of an attitude and an orientation: an attitude and orientation to standards and levels: standards and levels of aesthetic quality in the first and also the last place. And where did the Modernists get their standards and levels from? From the past, that is, the best of the past. But not so much from particular models in the past—though from these too—as from a generalized feeling and apprehending, a kind of distilling and extracting of aesthetic quality as shown by the best of the past. And it wasn't a question of imitating but one of emulating—just as it had been for the Renaissance with respect to antiquity. It's true that Baudelaire and Manet talked much more about having to be modern, about reflecting life in their time, than about matching the best of the past. But the need and the ambition to do so show through in what they actually did, and in enough of what they were recorded as saying. Being modern was a means of living up to the past.[3]

Some historians (H. Stuart Hughes in particular) regard modernism as a creation of "the generation of 1890." On the evidence available, it can be stated with relative certainty that the generation of 1890 consisted in large part of progeny of both genders who felt that their fathers had squandered their legacies and who felt that they had been "passed over" (preterited) and deprived of their heritage, left with promises and contracts unfulfilled, and fed on doctrines and ideals that bore little relevance to the world they inhabited. (Yeats writes in "Meditations in Time of Civil War": "We have fed the heart on fantasies, the heart's grown brutal on the fare.") The carnage of World War I confirmed the justice of this sense of loss and betrayal and generated a kind of performative existentialism that emphasized the necessity of a kind of decisionism, but without sufficient guidance from inherited ideals to inspire the kind of "resoluteness" (*Entschlossenheit*) that the postwar years, in Germany, France, Britain, Central and Eastern Europe, and even the Americas, required.[4]

In this essay, I want to reconsider the relationship presumed to have existed between twentieth-century cultural modernism and the modern (sense of) history. It is commonplace of current critical theory that cultural modernism was fixated on the new and the novel, repudiated tradition, valued the present and future at the expense of the past, and therefore rejected "history" and knowledge of the past as essentially worthless.[5] This is a view held on the Left but also on the Right: on the Left, modernism is supposed to be hostile to history; on the Right, it is supposed to be hostile to tradition. Actually, modernist modernism, modernism *an Sich*, as we might say, is opposed to both history and tradition. And that is why, although some modernists attempted to revise received notions of both history and tradition, the more radical modernists of the first generation (Eliot, Pound, Joyce, Proust, Kafka, Woolf in literature, and Martin Heidegger, Walter Benjamin, Giovanni Gentile, Theodor Lessing, Oswald Spengler, R. G. Collingwood in philosophy) sought to dissociate history and tradition from Newtonian conceptions of time and temporality, and to envision a post-historical temporality as a necessary precondition for the renewal of culture against the imperatives of both realism and modernization alike.

And when it comes to modernism's relationship to history, another problem arises: modernism is not only a historiological term in its own right, suggesting a valorization of the new and emergent in the field of historical happening,[6] in its remote origin it suggests an entire philosophy, or at least a vision of history in which each moment appears as a plenum of possibilities—a "now"—for the living being's liberation from time and temporality. The term *modern*, as is it is well known, derives from the ablative-dative case of the Latin *modus* (mode, manner, measure, quantity, interval, etc.)—suggesting an existence consonant with and defined by the moment and yielding the sense of "just now," "right now," "only now," "recently," and the like—so that we can justifiably see, buried within the history of the term, that the "modern" is a series of instants, each qualitatively different from every other but no one of which is prior to or superior to another, rather like Leibniz's conception of the monads.[7] This conception of history will make it appear that modernism rejects history, is hostile to it, or has little use for it. But to think this would be to take the term "history" in its accepted nineteenth-century usage, to assume that this usage is the proper usage, and that once its propriety had been established the concept of history itself will cease to change, will cease to have a history.

On the contrary, however, "history" does have a history, just as does the notion of "the past," and, for that matter, the idea that time is "naturally" parsed everywhere and whenever in the same way, i.e., as past-present-future, and in that order. So when it is a matter of modernism and history, we must specify which version of "history" we have in mind. Is the history being referred to "the past," the relation between past and present, or the *process* by which the present becomes a past or, conversely, a future becomes a present, and so on?

One of the undeniable attributes of history in the twentieth century is its explosion into a starburst of different ideas about what "history" is. Already in Nietzsche, "history" is parsed into three kinds: antiquarian, monumental, and critical, each of which we are supposed to need "for life."[8] But this parsing is not yet, in my estimation, modernist in kind. For Nietzsche's idea is still contaminated by the nineteenth-century belief that temporality can be made sense of, if only by parsing it into a threefold sense, each of which is fixed upon past, present, and future.

As we shall see, however, Heidegger, Benjamin, Joyce, Eliot, Pound, Stein, Yeats, and Woolf, not to mention Henri Bergson and Sartre, have different and, I warrant, post-Nietzschean ideas of time and therefore of history.[9]

Modernism is, of course, first and foremost a time-concept but not a "periodical" one. Or rather, although the term "modern" does name a historical period beginning with the Renaissance and the Age of Exploration, the Reformation, and the Scientific Revolution, it does not catch the anti-historicist and anti-historist nuances of the concept of "modern*ism*."[10] For, as the etymology of the term "modern" indicates, modernism has, since its invention in the fifth century AD, connoted a time that is outside of history, an ahistorical temporality, in which no tradition, dogma, nor secular *scientia* can provide sure guide to action in the moment. It cannot even be said that "modern" indicates "the present" (*praesens*) insofar as the present presupposes a past and a future from which it can be distinguished by what it is *not*.

Insofar, then, as the modern can be distinguished from the historical present, modern is not a historical concept at all. And this difference between the modern and the present may give us some insight into the kinds of obscurities, ambiguities, and ambivalences that are so characteristic of modernism in its various phases (right down to about 1950) and its various representatives in so many different fields of the arts and thought (right down to our own time or rather, to our own "modernity").[11] For James Joyce, history was that "nightmare from which I am trying to awaken." And for T. S. Eliot, another undeniable modernist, far from being a resource, "history" *is* the problem.[12]

In fact, the professionalization of historical studies in the early nineteenth century had effectively left the problem of the meaning of history to novelists and poets, who were allowed to fantasize about history and the past as long as they maintained a strict division between fact and fiction, the failure to do so being vilified as the principal failure of the delusory but nonetheless dazzlingly popular genre of "the historical novel." And yet the realistic novel, from Balzac, Dickens, and Flaubert through Tolstoy and Eliot to Zola and Conrad, increasingly took as evidence of its "realism" its attention to the present social world understood as belonging to "history." In the modernist novel, "history" continued to be the ultimate referent, but this history was now understood to be anything but the workings of a benign "progress" or "reason" leading from savagery to civilization on a global scale. Now history understood as "reality" was increasingly seen as a problem to be overcome rather than a source of wisdom or even knowledge.

We have, right at the beginning of literary modernism, T. S. Eliot's emblematic statement in his poem "Gerontion," which begins with the epigraph:

Thou hast nor youth nor age
But as it were an after dinner sleep
Dreaming of both.

And the first and third stanza, which assert: "My house is a decayed house" and "I have no ghosts." Then, in the fourth stanza, he asks:

After such knowledge, what forgiveness? Think now
History has many cunning passages, contrived corridors
And issues, deceives with whispering ambitions,
Guides us by vanities. Think now
She gives when our attention is distracted
And what she gives, gives with such supple confusions
That the giving famishes the craving. Gives too late
What's not believed in, or if still believed,
In memory only, reconsidered passion. Gives too soon
Into weak hands, what's thought can be dispensed with

Till the refusal propagates a fear. Think
Neither fear nor courage saves us. Unnatural vices
Are fathered by our heroism. Virtues
Are forced upon us by our impudent crimes.
These tears are shaken from the wrath-bearing tree.[13]

This passage, in addition to the feelings against history it displays, also manifests another, a generational attitude towards the fathers I wish to call "preteritional"—the feeling of having been passed over or excluded from inheritance of a legacy wasted by the previous generation. It is "the end of the line" phenomenon, the sense that genealogy no longer serves to establish legitimacy and descent in the paternal line (as in Oscar Wilde's *The Importance of Being Earnest*). And along with this, another theme I will touch on: gender ambiguity and the epistemology of the closet.[14] To be modern is to be depleted, ambiguated, and without any resources, not even "manliness," to call on but art.

But it is important to remember that modernism *is* a time-concept; it names an experience of an epoch that, etymologically, indicates an *interval* in history in which the "now" or more specifically the "just now" of the original Latin *modo* is detached from what came before and what must come after it. It should not be forgotten, moreover, that this "now" (which will later reappear in Walter Benjamin's work as *eine Jetztzeit*) not only erases (*entkräftet*) the linearity of conventional historicality; it bespeaks an opportunity, a kairotic moment in which to break through the ordinary (*vulgäre*) idea of historical time and return to what Heidegger—a representative modernist—will call an "authentic historicality" (*eigentliche Geschichtlichkeit*). This "return" is not, however, most decidedly not, the return to the Classical or Christian past dreamt of by Renaissance and Reformation thinkers like Machiavelli or Luther. It is what Heidegger, in *Sein und Zeit* (*Being and Time*, 1927), will call "the recurrence of the possible" (eine "Wiederkehr" des Möglichen), which knows that "authentic historicality" only returns if "existence is open for it fatefully, in a moment of vision, in resolute repetition" ("die Existenz schicksalhaft-augenblicklich für sie in der entschlossenen Wiederholung offen ist").[15]

It was presumed that in "the modern" (*modo modo*), "history" had been jettisoned for "myth." Myth is understood here either as "eternal return," or as the kind of "philosophy of history" represented by Max Nordau or Alfred Rosenberg,[16] or, most pertinently, by Theodor Lessing (assassinated by Nazis at Marienbad on August 31, 1933), who had published a work with the eponymous title *Geschichte als Sinngebung des Sinnlosen oder, Die Geburt der Geschichte aus dem Mythos* (History as Giving Meaning to the Meaningless, or, The Birth of History from Myth).[17]

But although philosophy of history had had a rebirth with the so-called "crisis of historicism" of the years preceding World War I, it must be understood that philosophy of history during this period was more concerned to justify the methods and procedures of professional historiography—to establish the value of historical knowledge, determine what the various works by specialist historians added up to or signified for the understanding of the whole of history, and above all to defend historical *Wissenschaft* from Marxism and Nietzscheanism—than it was to reinvent or rediscover a basis for historical knowledge of the conventional Rankean kind.

But the more modernist move was to conceive a link between myth and an idea of artistic creativity more poetic than discursive in kind. Thus, for Eliot and Pound and Joyce, it was what Eliot called "the mythical method" rather than a specific corpus of myths, classical or Christian, that was needed. In this view, history itself was a myth, what Lévi-Strauss will later call "the myth of the West." But a given myth is one thing, the "method" of mythmaking (as Eliot called it) is quite another. In his famous review of Joyce's *Ulysses*, he wrote: "In using the myth, in manipulating a continuous parallel between contemporaneity and antiquity, Mr. Joyce is pursuing a method which others must pursue after him. . . . It is simply a way of controlling, of ordering, of giving a shape and a significance to the immense panorama of futility and anarchy which is contemporary history."[18]

Like the early modernists, Heidegger and Gentile regarded conventional historiography—with its belief in a "history" that existed before "historiography"—as bankrupt: their modernity consisted of an effort to rethink the historical from the ground up, as it were, that is to say, from a philosophical position that had more in common with pre-Socratic thought—in which, according to Heidegger, science and philosophy had not yet been separated out from myth, or truth distinguished from being.[19]

During the period of the first (modernist or "modo modo") modernism, that is to say, from roughly 1910 to 1930, thought about history and historicality was pretty much dominated by the figure of Benedetto Croce, who, in his *Filosofia dello spirito* (Philosophy of Spirit/Mind) argued that: (1) philosophy of history à la Hegel, Marx, etc. was a contradiction in terms (philosophy was about concepts, while history was about things); and (2) authentic philosophy *was nothing more* than history or historical thinking (after metaphysics there is only history). But, Croce also maintained, one had to distinguish between history understood as the human mode of being-in-the-world and historiography understood as the record and representation of humankind's coming to consciousness of its own freedom. Thus History (the condition of humanity) preceded history (the story of freedom) as the latter's condition of possibility. Reflection on History and its relation to history was reflection on an eternal present that could never be "filled out" or "schematized." Historical knowledge is all we have, but it is incomplete and partial rather than complete and whole. But this incompleteness and partiality is what makes us able to believe in human freedom and human action, even in its vilest form, as a contribution to the desire and pursuit of the good.

Now, Croce's fall from popularity among philosophers after World War I was precipitous; he was definitely not a modernist, nor was he taken up by modernists as a philosophical spokesman. Indeed, in their repudiation of "history," the literary modernists took the distinction between "History" and history to be little more than a delusion, since the latter was nothing more than an account of the former in a different register. And yet the distinction between "History" and "history" was taken up by Heidegger, who provided in his *Sein und Zeit* a characterization of (primordial) "historicality" that effectively justified literary modernism's favorite "method"—what Eliot called "the mythical method."

In 1927, Heidegger sought to put the idea of "historicality" at the center of a post-metaphysical conception of human particularity (*Dasein*).[20] In the last sections of *Sein und Zeit*, he argued that the principal impediment to a proper understanding of the relationship between temporality and historicality was the commonsensical or "ordinary" understanding (*das vulgäre Verstandis*) of "history." And the first of these was the double paradox contained in the word "history" (*Geschichte*) itself. First, it stood for both an object of study (history) and the science of that object (history); and the idea that although the historical object existed in the past, it was knowable only by evidence of its existence in the present. Second, "history" is understood as both "past" and what has been derived or descended from that past (*Herkunft*), which may be apprehended as sometimes a rise and at others a fall, as standing in a condition of "becoming" and therefore implying that what is in history can also make history, which points it to the future and in which "the past" has "no special priority."[21] Third, the ordinary idea of history presumes "the totality of those entities that change 'in time,'" which, ironically, includes "Nature" as well as "Culture" and really subsumes the former to the latter (cf. Foucault). And fourth, history is "whatever has been handed down to us" and has been "taken over as self-evident, [even] with its derivation hidden."[22]

Now, this "vulgar" conception of "history" and the "historical" raises the question: "why is it that the historical is determined predominantly by the 'past,' or, to speak more appropriately [*angemessener*], by the character of having-been, when that character is one that temporalizes itself equiprimordially with the Present and the future?"[23] Heidegger's contention is that "what is *primarily* historical is Dasein. That which is *secondarily* historical, however, is what we encounter within-the-world—not only equipment ready-to-hand, in the widest sense, but also the environing *Nature* as the 'very soil of history.'" The "vulgar" form of history thus derives from "that which is secondarily historical" rather than from that "Dasein . . . which is primarily historical." Which raises the question: "to what extent and on the basis of what ontological conditions, does historicality belong, as an essential constitutive state, to the subjectivity of the 'historical' subject?"[24]

This question is answered in §74 of II, 5 "The Basic Constitution of Historicality":

> Thus, the interpretation of Dasein's historicality will prove to be, at bottom, just a more concrete working out of temporality. [. . .] The resoluteness in which Dasein comes back to itself, discloses current factical possibilities of authentic existing, and discloses them *in terms of the heritage* which that resoluteness, as thrown, *takes over.* In one's coming back resolutely to one's throwness, there is hidden a handing down to oneself of the possibilities that have come down to one, but not necessarily as having thus come down . . . Dasein *hands* itself *down* to itself, free for death, in a possibility which it has inherited and yet has chosen.[25]

Then that famous paragraph set in italics and typographically emphasized:

> *Only an entity which, in its Being, is essentially* **futural** *so that it is free for its death and can let itself be thrown back upon its factical "there" by shattering itself against death—that is to say, only an entity which, as futural, is equiprimordially in the process of* **having-been**, *can, by handing down to itself the possibility it has inherited, take over its own throwness and be* **in the moment of vision** *for "its time." Only authentic temporality*

which is at the same time finite, makes possible something like fate—that is to say, authentic historicality.[26]

. . . The authentic repetition of a possibility of existence that has been—the possibility that Dasein may choose its hero—is grounded existentially in anticipatory resoluteness [*vorlaufige Entschlossenheit*]; for it is in resoluteness that one first chooses the choice which makes one free for the struggle of loyally following in the footsteps of that which can be repeated. But when one has, by repetition, handed down to oneself a possibility that has been, the Dasein that has-been-there is not disclosed in order to be actualized over again. The repeating of that which is possible does not bring again [*Wiederbringen*] something that is "past," nor does it bind the "Present" back to that which has already been "outstripped." Arising as it does from a resolute projection of oneself, repetition does not let itself be persuaded of something by what is "past," just in order that this, as something which was formerly actual, may recur. Rather, the repetition makes a *reciprocative rejoinder* to the possibility of that existence which has-been-there. But when such a rejoinder is made to this possibility of resolution, it is made *in a moment of vision*; *and as such* it is at the same time a *disavowal* of that which in the "today," is working itself out as the "past." Repetition does not abandon itself to that which is past, nor does it aim at progress. In the moment of vision, authentic existence is indifferent to both these alternatives.

We [therefore] characterize repetition as a mode of that resoluteness which hands itself down—the mode by which *Dasein* exists implicitly as fate [*Schickal*].[27] . . . *Authentic Being-towards-death— that is to say, the finitude of temporality—is the hidden basis of Dasein's historicality. Dasein* does not first become historical in repetition; but because it is historical as temporal, it can be taken over in its history by repeating. For this, no historiology is as yet needed.[28]

The history that people think they live is what contributes to the dispersal and alienation of *Dasein*, and it is from this history that *Dasein* must awaken in order to grasp the primordial historicality of *Dasein's* experience of temporality: "In inauthentic historicality . . . the way in which fate has been primordially stretched along has been hidden . . . Lost in the making present of the 'today,' it understands the 'Past' in terms of the 'Present.' "[29] "When, however, one's existence is inauthentically historical, it is loaded down with the legacy of a 'past' which has become unrecognizable, and it seeks the modern."[30]

On such a view, Heidegger provides us (as Paul Ricoeur constantly reminded us) with an insight into the relation between historicality and temporality that comes along with modernism and also shows us how to understand that peculiar rebellion against narrative and narrativity that distinguishes the "realism" of modernism from its earlier historist prototypes (Balzac, Flaubert, Dickens, Tolstoy, Conrad, and so on).[31] The "historicality" of *Dasein*—the primordial historicality—resides in its understanding that it exists "in time," that its existence is finite, and that its "fate" (or "vicissitude") will be authentic only in the extent to which it makes its choices or lives its life in care (*Sorge*). Ricoeur thought that narrative form was a proper way of retailing such a life, because "narrative" constituted the form in which temporality reached consciousness in language. Narrative form mediated, Ricoeur thought, between "primordial" temporality and the chronological temporality of hours, days, weeks, months, and years. And it is indeed interesting to note that Fredric Jameson, whom we might call "the Ricoeur of the Left," shares belief in the intimate, indeed necessary, connection between narrative form and historical consciousness, to the extent to which he can indict modernism for a lack of historical consciousness because of its abandonment or want of "narrative" capability. Indeed, at the level of form, narrative is the mode of expression adequate to the substance of the content of "history." Here he follows the Lukács of the *Studies in Realism* and "Franz Kafka or Thomas Mann?"—the Lukács who indicts literary modernism for its failure to develop further the plot novel of the great nineteenth-century realists.

Lukács's criticism of modernism is apt enough because what Eliot celebrated as Joyce's "mythical method" (and contrasted with the "narrative method") effectively *disemplots* the novel and the modernist long poem (as in *The Waste Land*).[32] Thus Eliot says of the mythical method:

> It is a method already adumbrated by Mr. Yeats, and of the need for which I believe that Mr. Yeats to have been the first contemporary to be conscious. Psychology (such as it is, and whether our reaction to it be comic or serious), ethnology, and *The Golden Bough* have concurred to make possible what was impossible even a few years ago. Instead of narrative method, we may now use the *mythical method*. It is, I seriously believe, a step toward making the *modern* world possible for art.[33]

Although many critics and scholars thought that this signaled a return to mythology, it is evident that Eliot meant something quite different from that. The "mythical method," insofar as it is set over against the "narrative method," refuses the organicism, coherence, and closure of the earlier genres of "realism" as being untruthful to "reality," on the one hand, and as being constraining of the freedom of art, on the other. Actually, Eliot's idea of "the mythical method" comes close to early avant-garde "collage," Duchamp's use of *objets trouvés* in his assemblages, and Lévi-Strauss's notion of *bricolage* as the method of mythic invention (one is reminded, too, of that "rubble" of history espied by Benjamin's "Angelus Novus" as it surveys the ruins of past history).

Writing much later, Ricoeur tried to salvage narrative (or what, after Eliot, we might call "the narrative method") by suggesting that narrative was the most "realistic" of the modes available for depicting "historical reality," because the lives and projects of historical agents actually took the form of narratives. This allowed Ricoeur to salvage a correspondence theory of historical truth.

But here again there is an ambiguity in the referent of the term "history," even if by "history" one means only "the past." Indeed, *especially* if by "history" one means only "the past." For, as Michael Oakeshott noted, there are not only many different kinds of past; there are many different modes of contemplating the past or of drawing upon it for different purposes. Among these Oakeshott distinguished between "the historical past" and "the practical past," the former of which was to be studied "for its own sake" or "for itself alone," as an object of scientific interest only and without any attempt to draw lessons from study of it for use in the present or to derive principles for predicting the future.[34] By contrast, Oakeshott argued, the "practical past" is recalled only for its relevance to discussions about the present and future.[35]

This distinction between "the historical past" and "the practical past" stands in for the older distinction between a "historical" or "scientific" study of the past and all versions of the past intended for ideological or political uses. But to take this tack is to overlook a fundamental difference between Oakeshott's distinction and that of anyone who would assimilate the practical past to ideology. First, Oakeshott, like Collingwood and Croce (as well as Michel de Certeau, later on), presumes that *all* inquiry into the past is motivated by "present" concerns and problems, however "scientific" the method of analysis may purport to be. So what is at issue for Oakeshott is not the difference between the study of "the past" for its own sake or for itself alone *versus* a study of the past out of *present* concerns and interests. In fact, Oakeshott does not identify study of "the practical past" with *presentism* (as many psychologists who have taken up the term would have it) and the study of "the historical past" with "pastism" or antiquarianism. He distinguishes the two kinds of past on the basis of an analogy with Kant's distinction between "theoretical" and "practical" philosophy: the historical past is theoretical (constructed by an exercise of pure reason), while the practical past is constructed for use by "practical reason," which is to say, ethical consciousness, choice, decision, and judgment. So the difference is not between pastism and presentism but between two different construals of the past, the one as an object for scientific study, the other as an object of ethical or aesthetic reflection.

Of course, once we have reached this point, we are on the verge of the charge raised by Adorno against modernism, namely, its aestheticization of what had formerly been construed as epistemological issues. Which in turn constitutes the basis for the differences between Left-wing and Right-wing criticisms of Modernism. What Eliot and his generation of modernists had done in appealing to "the mythical method" was construe the imagination as a cognitive faculty and posit it as a basis for criticism of both the "vulgar ideas of history" (professional and amateur) and the metaphysical ideas about history promoted by the "philosophers of history." In seeking to return to the *archē* or origins, to the time before history began, the first cultural modernists abandoned all of the various "plots" (macro- and micro-) that had been imposed upon temporality in modernity.

Notes

1. [Ed: Lewis White Beck was professor of philosophy and White's colleague at the University of Rochester, where White was a member of the History Department faculty from 1958 to 1968.]

2. Fredric Jameson, *A Singular Modernity: Essay on the Ontology of the Present* (London: Verso, 2002), 214–15. Jameson distinguishes between "modern," "modernity," and "modernism" as "tropes," useful for generating different narratives of the past and the same terms considered as names of "ideologies" aimed to discourage "utopian" expectations about the future.

3. Clement Greenberg, "Modern and Postmodern," in *Clement Greenberg: Late Writings*, ed. Robert C. Morgan (Minneapolis: University of Minnesota Press, 2003), 27.

4. Clement Greenberg ("Modern and Postmodern," 26), wrote: "What can be safely called Modernism emerged in the middle of the last century. And rather locally, in France, with Baudelaire in literature and Manet in painting, and maybe with Flaubert, too, in prose fiction. (It was a while later, and not so locally, that Modernism appeared in music and architecture, but it was in

France again that it appeared first in sculpture. Outside France later still, it entered the dance.) The 'avant-garde' was what Modernism was called at first, but this term has become a good deal compromised by now as well as remaining misleading."

5. This begins with Nietzsche of course, but modernism takes the "critical" idea of history much further than Nietzsche did. This development is typically considered to be indicative of a rebellion against history itself. Thus, Jürgen Habermas asserts that "modernity" begins with the idea that creativity must be utterly originary and original and cannot depend upon prior models. The rejection of prior models is tantamount to a rejection of the past altogether. He cites Koselleck's work on "the new age." See Jürgen Habermas, "Modernity's Consciousness of Time and Its Need for Self-Reassurance," in *The Philosophical Discourse of Modernity: Twelve Lectures*, trans. Frederick Lawrence (Cambridge, MA: MIT Press, 1993), 1–22.

6. "Historically, in fact, in the debates over modernism, a far more abstract notion of change has won out over all its rivals; and the victory was so complete as to render the new account commonplace and virtually self-evident. This is that well-known dynamic called innovation; and it is eternalized in Pound's great dictum 'Make it new': and in the supreme value of the New that seems to preside over any specific or local modernism worth its salt. How the new can be eternal, however, is another question, and perhaps accounts for the equally eternal enigma of Baudelaire's inaugural definition: 'le transitoire, le fugitif, le contingent, la moitié de l'art, dont l'autre moitié est l'éternel et l'immuable'" (Jameson, *Singular Modernity*, 121). One solution to the enigma lies in Heidegger's idea that the eternal return of the Same is not a thing, event, or action, but rather, a "possibility."

7. See Mieke Bal, *Quoting Caravaggio: Contemporary Art, Preposterous History* (Chicago: University of Chicago Press, 1999).

8. [Ed: White is referring to Nietzsche's second *Untimely Meditation*, "On the Use and Abuse of History for Life."]

9. An attitude towards history is not, of course, the sole determining feature of a modernist, but I would say it is a necessary—necessary but not sufficient—condition. Other features might be mentioned. I want in this essay to concentrate on three more: first, preterition; second, gender ambiguity; and third, phagocitation.

10. See Fredric Jameson, "Transitional Modes," in *A Singular Modernity*, 97–138. Jameson thinks that modernism cannot be a period concept because it is a purely aesthetic phenomenon rather than an epistemological one. This means that, for him, modernism is a "narrative" or a way of giving form to a synchronic structure.

11. Note Paul de Man's and Hans Robert Jauss's idea that modernism is a phase or moment in every era's sense of its own uniqueness vis-à-vis other and especially earlier periods. Thus, we might be speaking more properly of "modernisms" than of a single substantive "modernism." But I want to argue that our modernism is different from earlier ones in that it takes its "fallenness" out of history as a distinguishing sign of its originality. Earlier modernisms, such as those of the Patristic period, the various renascences of the medieval period,

the Renaissance, the Reformation, the Jacobins, the Romantics, and so on, still regard history as a resource for *renovatio* or renewal, not so *our* modernists.

12. The problematic nature of "history" in the modern age is indicated by the formation at about the same time that "history" was constituted as a scientific (or at least academic) discipline (by Ranke *et alia*) of the discipline of "philosophy of history." This field has always been regarded by professional historians as an aberration because it appears to aspire to knowledge of history's meaning, aim, or overriding purpose. Moreover, philosophy of history—from Kant, Herder, Hegel, Comte, and Henry Thomas Buckle through Marx and Nietzsche, down to Lessing, Spengler, Toynbee, and Eric Vogelin—has always appealed to "deviant" philosophers, amateur historians, and ideologues in general, rather than to properly domesticated academic scholars. In fact, an interest in philosophy of history has been generally taken to indicate a defective philosophical sense and/or fundamental misunderstanding of what "proper" historiography can legitimately aspire to. After World War II, Anglophone philosophy dealt with this problem by distinguishing between a metaphysical and speculative "material philosophy of history," on the one side, and an "analytical philosophy of history" (devoted to the exposure of the errors of the former), on the other. In general, professional historians were inclined to condemn philosophy of history on the basis of a distinction between a legitimate quest for knowledge, on the one side, and an illegitimate quest for meaning, on the other.

13. T. S. Eliot, "Gerontion," in *The Complete Poems and Plays of T. S. Eliot* (London: Faber & Faber, 1969), 37–39.

14. See Eve Kosofsky Sedgwick, *Epistemology of the Closet* (Berkeley: University of California Press, 1990).

15. Martin Heidegger, *Sein und Zeit* (Tubingen: Max Niemeyer, 1953), 391–92; *Being and Time*, trans. John Macquarrie and Edward Robinson (Oxford: Blackwell, 1962), 444.

16. See Ernst Cassirer, *The Myth of the State* (New Haven, CT: Yale University Press, 1961).

17. Theodor Lessing, *Geschichte als Sinngebung des Sinnlosen oder, Die Geburt der Geschichte aus dem Mythos* (Munich: Verlag C. H. Beck, 1919).

18. See Eliot's review of Joyce in T. S. Eliot, "*Ulysses*, Order, and Myth," in *Selected Prose of T. S. Eliot*, ed. Frank Kermode (New York: Harcourt, 1975), 177. See also Joyce Wexler, "Realism and Modernists' Bad Reputation," *Studies in the Novel* 31, no. 1 (1999): 60:

> One of the principles guiding the formation of the high modernist canon was T. S. Eliot's definition of the "mythical method" as "a way of controlling, of ordering, of giving a shape and a significance to the immense panorama of futility and anarchy which is contemporary history." The control, order, shape, and significance were to come from the author's ability to discern parallels between the chaotic present and the comprehensible past. By coordinating the contingencies of contemporary history with the unchanging patterns of myth, Eliot argued, writers like Yeats and Joyce found a formal principle that made "the modern world possible for art."

As much as Eliot admired this union, it has fallen into disrepute for ethical and political reasons. Critics initially complained that texts employing the mythical method were implausible or incomprehensible. Now the objection is that such texts are immoral. Where Eliot saw an aesthetic solution to a moral crisis, contemporary critics detect an ethical problem. Reading modernist symbolism as if it were realism, they object not only to particular symbols but to the use of extreme acts and foreign cultures as raw material for Western fantasies. When this kind of political interpretation of symbolism prevails, as it does now, the reputation of modernist authors suffers.

19. See Heidegger, *Sein und Zeit*, 213–14; *Being and Time*, 256.

20. *"In analysing the historicality of Dasein we shall try to show that this entity is not 'temporal' because it 'stands in history,' but that, on the contrary, it exists historically and can so exist because it is temporal in the very basis of its Being"* (Heidegger, *Sein und Zeit*, 376; *Being and Time*, 428, italics in the original).

21. Heidegger, *Sein und Zeit*, 379; *Being and Time*, 430.

22. Heidegger, 379; 431.

23. Heidegger, 381; 433 (italics in the original).

24. Heidegger, 382; 434 (italics in the original).

25. Heidegger, 384; 435.

26. Heidegger, 385; 437.

27. Heidegger, 386; 437–38.

28. Heidegger, 386; 438.

29. Heidegger, 391; 433.

30. Heidegger, 391; 444.

31. See Paul Ricoeur, *Time and Narrative*, vol. 1, trans. Kathleen McLaughlin and David Pellauer (Chicago: University of Chicago Press, 1984).

32. Ricoeur thought that the modernist novel—as represented by Woolf, Mann, and Proust at least—had kept "plot" but had shifted the tropology used to connect the beginning with the end of the traditional novel from the syntagmatic to the paradigmatic axis of the discourse. See Paul Ricoeur, *Time and Narrative*, vol. 2, trans. Kathleen McLaughlin and David Pellauer (Chicago: University of Chicago Press, 1985).

33. Eliot, *"Ulysses,* Order, and Myth," 177–78, emphasis added.

34. Recall that this is the basis for Karl Popper's attack on "historicism" and "historism" (in *The Poverty of Historicism*, 1944). Since history is, or aspires to be, a social science, and since social science is interested in deriving laws and predicting the future, "history" lapses into "historicism" when philosophers of history attempt such moves.

35. Michael Oakeshott, *On History and Other Essays* (Indianapolis: Liberty Fund, 1999), 18.

CHAPTER 12

Historical Truth, Estrangement, and Disbelief

On Saul Friedländer's Nazi Germany and the Jews *[2016]*

> Blissful is the nonbeliever who hides the future's
> misfortune beneath the protective covering of the
> present moment, for now everything is obscured
> by darkness. No one seeks protection when hope
> and silence alone mark the passing of time and
> make it believable.
>
> —H. G. Adler

In an earlier essay,[1] I presented Saul Fried-
länder's *Nazi Germany and the Jews* as an example of one way of dealing
with the putative "unrepresentability" of the Holocaust.[2] I suggested
that the Holocaust was not only a novel event in the history of the West
and the history of antisemitism, but also a new kind of event that effectively brought under question the representational practices and
modes of explanation both of modern historiography and the modern human sciences in general.[3] I maintained that the older conventions, which presumed that a factually truthful account of events of the
past constituted the only valid historical interpretation of them (any
other kind of interpretation, such as the meaning of the factualized
events, being considered a questionable addition to a properly historical account), had to go by the board when it came to events like the
Holocaust.[4] This event, I argued, demanded representational modes,
explanatory models, and ethical attitudes that could not be provided
by conventional professional historiography, with its fetishism of "the
facts and nothing but the facts." I went on to consider the possibility
that as a modernist event,[5] the Holocaust might be treatable by the use
of specifically modernist techniques of literary writing, which, in my
view, provided both a perspective on "history" and a mode of presenting

the complex relationships between past and present in modern culture and especially lent themselves to the solution of the kinds of "practical" (by which I meant "ethical") questions that motivated historians searching for the meaning of the Holocaust in history. And I concluded by arguing that in his *Nazi Germany and the Jews: The Years of Persecution, 1933–1939*, and especially in volume 2, *Nazi Germany and the Jews, 1939–1945: The Years of Extermination*, Saul Friedländer had produced something like the kind of modernist historiography particularly required—technically and ethically—by the Holocaust and all other historical events even vaguely resembling it.[6]

This chapter continues my inquiry into the relation between history and literature or, more specifically, historiography and literary writing, to show how Friedländer utilizes literary techniques, devices, tropes, and figures to close the gap between truth and meaning in Holocaust historiography without fictionalizing, aestheticizing, or relativizing anything. It is an exercise in "close reading," the kind of hermeneutic conventionally used in the treatment of sacred, legal, and literary texts rather than historiographical or scientific texts. The aim is to identify the literary devices, tropes, figures, and techniques used in Friedländer's text to generate ways of mediating between the corpus of facts known about the Holocaust and the various meanings that our ethical interests in this event demand of us. In earlier discussions of this issue, I have drawn on Michael Oakeshott's distinction between "the historical past" and "the practical past." The latter kind of past is what we turn to when our interests are as much ethical as they are cognitive. I think that Friedländer's book—like Toni Morrison's *Beloved*—falls into the latter category.[7] It is less interested in adding new information to the "data bank" of the Holocaust than in investigating what of an ethical nature is still "left over" after we have collected all of the factual information contained in the historical record.

Friedländer has long advocated the need for a "stable integrated narrative" of the Holocaust by which to identify and measure deviations from the truth in the directions of fictionalization, on the one hand, and aestheticization, on the other. Fictionalization is regarded as a threat to belief in the *reality* of the Holocaust and aestheticization as a threat to belief in its *moral or ethical significance*. At the same time, he insisted that there was something uncanny about it. In 1992, he spoke of the Holocaust as having some kind of "excess" of the inexpressible left over after all the facts of the matter had been recorded.[8] In volume 1 of *Nazi Germany and the Jews*, this excess would manifest in the feeling of "estrangement" he hoped to effect in his readers. Then, in volume 2, whose topic is the program of extermination launched by the Germans against the Jews, he stated that he wished to produce the effect of "disbelievability." I believe he undertakes to gain these effects—and affects—by the use of literary techniques, devices, figures, and tropes that undermine (perhaps even deconstruct) on a figurative level the stability of the narrative unfolding on the literal or proper level of the text.

Let me begin by trying to characterize the general look or appearance of Friedländer's volume 2, *Years of Extermination*. First, there is a lot of front matter before we get to the narration proper. This alone distinguishes Friedländer's text from the abrupt opening of a conventional narrative history such as Richard Evans's *The Third Reich in Power*.[9] More about this front matter later. Once we make our way through it, the core narrative looks more like a chronicle than a history. It is made up of ten chapters (with dates instead of titles) divided into three parts, each of which has both titles and dates: "Terror (Fall 1939–Summer 1941)," "Mass Murder (Summer 1941–September 1942)," and "Shoah (Summer 1942–Spring 1945)."

If we thought of this as a skeleton of a story of the Holocaust, the three parts might be identified as acts of a classical drama: a central subject (driven by *pathos*) undergoes a trial (*agon*) that results in his destruction (*sparagmos*) on the way to a recognition scene (or *anagnorisis*) in which the mystery motivating the action from the beginning would be cleared up with more or less moral loss or gain to the community to which the hero belongs. But although the events related by Friedländer might be thought of as tragic, there is no central subject undergoing a trial of the spirit, no conception of fate or providence to link the destruction to a cosmic plan, and virtually nothing to suggest the existence of some fundamental nobility of the human spirit in spite of all. The events of the Holocaust are not emplotted to suggest a discernible trajectory from beginning to end that would allow some sense of satisfactory moral or ethical closure for the whole. Friedländer's history of the Holocaust is presented in such a way as to frustrate normal narratological expectations, to produce the effects (and affects) of "estrangement," on the one hand, and "disbelief," on the other. How does all this square with Friedländer's repeated assertions of his desire to create a "stable integrated narrative" of the Holocaust?

The choice by any historian to cast his or her work in the mode of a "narrative" is already to move it out of the discourses of science and into the domain of "literature." Although narrative has long been thought of as a "natural" mode of historiographical presentation, its origin in myth, fable, and allegory has long rendered it suspect as a mode of scientific discourse—ever since *logos* was disjoined from *mythos* in philosophy of science.[10] So, too, to narrativize real events is often thought of as tantamount to "fictionalizing" them, as in the historical romance. But Friedländer narrates his history of the Holocaust without narrativizing, in other words, without using one or another of the classic plot structures by which Western culture has endowed life with meaning in myth, religion, and literature since its beginnings.

But I would suggest that we must distinguish between narration (a mode of speaking) and narrative (story, the product of this mode of speaking). Friedländer launches his narration from within a justified confidence in his knowledge of his subject matter, on the one hand, and his adequacy to the understanding of that subject matter, on the other. But there is nothing stentorian or even very assertive about his delivery. His mode is "middle-voiced"—a manner of speaking or, in this case, writing, in which the speaker deploys neither the active nor the passive voice predominantly but takes up a position from within the act of writing itself, so as to foreclose any possibility of distinguishing between *what* is said or spoken and the *how* of its saying. Thus, in middle-voiced discourse, the gap between the presentation of the referent (the Holocaust) and the meaning being attributed to it is closed, or at least narrowed. In this instance, the meaning of the events depicted and their truth—the fact of their occurrence when, where, and as they did—are fully congruent. But this is because, among other reasons, Friedländer narrates without narrativizing, maps a field, but does not emplot a single course of events, and resists the imposition of stereotypical structures of meaning that would allow any "domestication" of the facts.

It is impossible to forget or ignore the fact that the author of *Years of Extermination* is himself a survivor of that "Holocaust" from within the experience of which he writes. Whence Friedländer's resistance to endowing the Holocaust with the coherence of a conventional story, with a central subject, beginning, middle, and end, and a neat resolution with a clear and unambiguous meaning. Whence the preference for the chronicle form that tends toward parataxis and anecdotage, rather than for the fleshed-out history that explains "what happened" by emplotting it as having the form of a recognizable archetypal structure of meaning (tragic, pastoral, comic, satiric, and so forth). Whence, too, the relatively "weak" line of argument that might seek to explain why the Holocaust happened, to allow its happening to "speak for itself."

Thus, although narrated with the full authority of the one supposed to know and, indeed, of one who has experienced the events of which he writes, Friedländer effectively de-narrativizes and de-storifies the series of events he relates. This process of denarrativization, I submit, puts Friedländer in the category of modernist writers in the tradition of Proust, Woolf, Kafka, Stein, and Joyce. The loose chronological pattern of his elaboration allows him to use the technique of presentation very close to that recommended by Walter Benjamin for modernist historiography: namely, the genre of the "constellation" and the preference for the verbal image over the concept in the depiction of experiences more "modernist" than "realistic" in kind. This puts us in the domain of a specifically artistic writing that is both different from and consonant with the scientific ideal of objective representation.

Let me explain what I mean by citation of a few characteristic passages in Friedländer's work, to show how his distinctive interpretative effects are earned more by literary than by scientific-discursive means.

A literary narration is a verbal whole that asserts more, or says other than, through figuration what is literally asserted in its parts taken distributively. This is the case with all literary devices, genres, figures, and tropes, as against the devices and turns of scientific discourses, which, by the use of technical and quantitative terminology, can hope to avoid the kind of parapractical irruptions that indicate the presence of an "unconscious" in the text that the literal level of expression is intended to cover up and repress. The difference, of course, between artistic parapraxis and the kind found in everyday ordinary speech is that the former is consciously exploited as a way of endowing the discourse with depth as well as extension.

So, how does one *represent* the history of an event that destroyed a wide variety of kinds of Jewish communities (as well as other kinds of communities, races, and groups) more or less unconnected with one another in space, time, and culture, and in different kinds of relationships with the host countries in which they had come to reside, and their reactions and responses to a machine designed primarily for the purpose of exterminating them? Here, Friedländer's problem was to provide a coherent but nonlinear account of the facts and their meaning without emphasizing argument or explanation at the expense of concreteness and particularity of detail. But since a written discourse is necessarily consumed as a linear process, he had to find a way of shifting attention from the "before-and-after" axis of the diegesis to a "surface-depth" axis where "meaning" is deposited at each "turn" of the discourse. Although Friedländer's text comes to us loosely organized on the temporal axis, the temporal units do not have the same function and meaning that they conventionally have when used to parse organic or biological processes (birth, youth, maturity, old age, and so forth). After all, each of the two volumes of *Nazi Germany and the Jews* covers only six years, and, as at least one reviewer noted, does not provide any significant temporal "contextualization" of the events covered in the text. There is a general thematic continuity, produced by repetition, reduction, and nominalization of the notion of "extermination," but a thematization is not an argument. It is a literary (or rhetorical) strategy by which a series of events can, by varied kinds of redescription, be endowed with "substance."

However, thematization requires "discourse-time" and what some critics call "phrasing" or segmentation by which to transform series into sequence,[11] a process of layering in which what appears on a literal (or proper) plane is shown on a figurative or allegorical plane to have meaning that is at once revealed and concealed as such. These effects—disemplotment, middle-voiced narration, thematization, sequentiation, and the like—are produced by identifiable literary or rhetorical devices, techniques, genrification, and tropes.

Thus, *Years of Extermination* opens with a cascade of literary devices. This is the front matter I referred to earlier. It begins with an epigraph that is a quotation from a diary written by a victim of the Holocaust. This is followed by an "Introduction," which itself begins with an ekphrastic analysis of a photograph of a ceremony, David Moffie's graduation from the University of Amsterdam School of Medicine on September 18, 1942. Next, part 1 of *Years of Extermination* begins with an epigraph taken from the diary of Victor Klemperer, while chapter 1 (of part 1) is followed by an anecdote recounting Klemperer's response to the news that Germany had invaded Poland on September 1, 1939. The Klemperer anecdote, which consists of two paragraphs, is followed by three more anecdotes relating the ways in which certain Jews in Warsaw and Lodz responded to the same news. The last of these anecdotes tells of the original enthusiasm of Adam Czerniaków for his new post as chairman of the Jewish Citizens Committee for the defense of Warsaw. It ends with the ironic remark of the narrator: "Four days later Poland surrendered." (I say narrator and not author because, in fact, one does not know who speaks these words.)

I would like to point out that the passages I have cited are all literary genres or devices: epigraph, ekphrasis, anecdote, commentary, and figure. This means, to me at least, that all of these passages by (the substance of) their forms alone and quite apart from any factual "information" they may be thought to contain, emit messages of a particularly poetic, by which I mean symbolizing, kind.

Thus, for example, every epigraph not only has to be written but, by its placement and structure, also refers primarily to the writing it introduces or prefigures, rather than to something outside the text. An epigraph is placed on the border of the text it introduces, but its function is intratextualizing, to link the thematic content of the work to follow with the title of that work.

So, it is not by chance that the first epigraph in Friedländer's book, the epigraph that introduces the whole volume, is explicitly about writing and, moreover, about writing in a state or condition of extremity, in the face of death. It begins: "The struggle to save myself is hopeless . . . But that's not important. Because I am able to bring my account to its end and trust that it will see the light of day when the time is right."

Moreover, the epigraph is not only about writing under conditions of extreme travail; it is about the impossibility of writing "the truth" about the grotesque (*fantastyczna*) event that was happening in Warsaw, as viewed from "the 'Aryan' side of the city," sometime in 1943. The epigraph (which has been edited by Friedländer)[12] ends by saying: "And they will ask, is this the truth? I reply in advance: No, this is not the truth, this is only a small part, a tiny fraction of the truth . . . Even the mightiest pen could not depict the whole, real, essential truth."[13]

The opening words ("The struggle to save myself is hopeless . . . But that's not important")[14] are startling—they are not surrounded by scare quotes—and we might take them for the words of our author, that is, until we recognize that they begin an epigraph, which excuses us from treating this statement as a properly historiographic one. That is, we will not ask whether it is true or false, whether what it says is a matter of fact, or whether it is simply an aid to reading the text to follow. But we might wish to reflect on the theme of the epigraph, since according to the rules of genrification, this passage is supposed to foreshadow or anticipate or enliven us to the theme of the book to follow.

On reflection, I note that this epigraph (at least as it has been edited by Friedländer)[15] consists of a kind of affirmation—of the task the writer has set for himself, which is to "bring my account to its end," and a denial, or more properly, a disavowal: "No, this is not the truth, this is only a small part . . . Even the mightiest pen could not depict the whole, real, essential truth."[16]

In fact, the epigraph can be read as an emblem featuring an image of the writer *in extremis* and wagering everything on the possibility that his "account" will see "the light of day" sometime in the future, so that "people will know what happened" in spite of the fact that what he writes is "only a small part, a tiny fraction of the truth." So if Friedländer used the passage from Ernest's diary to say that his own text is "not even a fragment of a fragment of the truth,"[17] he must also take ownership of the other part of the passage, which is about writing *in extremis*— writing in the face of death, writing on the wager that what one writes is worth the candle, in spite of its inadequacy to the "whole, real, essential truth," that, in some sense, the effort to tell "what happened" will find a kind of redemption "when the time is right" and "people will know what happened." Condensed into this small fragment of text is a whole allegory of the truth of writing as the writing of truth and the impossibility of that charge. And this makes it a comment on the whole book it introduces.

We should note also that the writing in this passage is literary writing, and it has nothing at all to do with either fiction or aesthetics. Friedländer uses it as a literary device to mark the inauguration of an account that will be as much about the travail of writing (his writing) as it is about the kind of truth that can be expected in a narration of the Holocaust.

Did Friedländer consciously intend all this? I do not know, but the fact is that he chose this passage from Ernest's diary as his epigraph. He edited it to say what it says and not something else. And he placed it at the start of his book to do what epigraphs are supposed to do: indicate a theme of the book to follow. This passage is not meant to be a contribution to the "database" of the Holocaust—an epigraph is not a contribution to the factual record. Of course, the book has a rich and varied thematic content, but the thematic content of this epigraph, placed as it is, at the head of this text, has a special function. It tells the reader that the text to follow is as much about the stakes of writing, the difficulty of telling the truth and the necessity of testimony in situations of extremity, as it is about the facts of the matter.[18] This small fragment of text alone would be enough to demonstrate that we are in the presence of "literature" as well as "historiography." The writing in this passage is literary writing, and it has nothing at all to do with either fiction or aesthetics.[19]

In *Years of Extermination*, epigraphs are used to introduce the volume as a whole, as well as each of the three parts ("Terror," "Mass Murder," and "Shoah") into which the narration is divided. There is a kind of "line" of development in the events laid out for our inspection, but the line is only that of the "this happened here or there" of the chronicle. Friedländer calls this "loose" chronological arrangement a "temporal" line, but actually time does not order this text or the events about which it speaks. The turns from "Terror" to "Mass Murder" and from "Mass Murder" to "Shoah" do not mark transitions between different phases of a single process of development. The events are not "emplotted" in such a way as to represent the development of some central subject, such as Nazi Germany, the Jews, or the Holocaust. There is no plot structure informing the whole chain of clusters or constellations of facts, anecdotes, epigraphs, quotations, and theories, or speculations about why the Holocaust occurred. The only relations between one part of the text and another are the "before and after" and "here and there" that allow the clustering of events related only by similarity and contiguity rather than by equivalence and identity. Thus, although "Terror" precedes "Mass Murder," which, in turn, precedes "Shoah," there is no spatial or temporal connection or causal chain posited in this sequence. Nor is any "plan" being implemented. It is a matter of *furor Teutonicus*, on the one side, and descent into a condition of "patiency," on the other, that makes me want to grasp the whole text as a kind of modernist *Walpurgisnacht*, *satura*, or pastiche, rather than as a story.

There are lots of anecdotes or *petits récits* in this book, but they do more to impede the movement of the narration than to help it along. In fact, Friedländer uses the genre of the anecdote to do most of the heavy work of commenting on and interpreting the events he relates.[20] I could make a case, I think, for the idea that Friedländer's is a modal text, that its principal explanatory effect is produced by modalizations, transitions from one structure of deprivation to another. This would imply an interest less in conceptual and categorical characterizations of the referents ("Nazi Germany" and "the Jews") than in figurations of persons, places, and events in terms of feelings of "strength to world," mood, atmospheres, and "humors."

Thus, Friedländer chooses as the epigraph to "Part I: Terror," a statement from Victor Klemperer's diary: "The sadistic machine simply rolls over us." By using Klemperer's figure of Nazi Germany as a "sadistic machine" as an epigraph, Friedländer can at once present an image of oppression, register a judgment on "Nazi Germany," project the feeling of helplessness felt by the oppressed, and indicate the power of the Nazi war machine, but without having to document or establish the adequacy of the judgment. In fact, whatever judgments are rendered in this text are rendered by the voices of those caught up in, and being destroyed by, the "sadistic machine." All reviewers note the evenhandedness, calm, fairness, and objectivity of Friedländer's account of how the "sadistic machine" operated. He leaves the judgments to the victims.

All of this is reinforced by the anecdote that opens chapter 1 of the text proper, another quotation from the diary of Victor Klemperer: "On Friday morning, September 1, the young butcher's lad came and told us . . . the war with Poland was underway, England and France remained neutral . . . I said to Eva [that] a morphine injection or something similar was the best thing for us; our life was over."[21]

Friedländer has been praised, and rightly so, for admitting the "voices" of ordinary people—especially the victims, but also the perpetrators and bystanders—into his account of the Holocaust, thereby injecting a sense of personal experience and humanity into the presentation, but at the same time risking violating the demand for established fact rather than opinion in the historian's text. In his response to my suggestion that artistic images might be more effective than statements or numbers for presenting the shock of events like those of the Holocaust,[22] Friedländer said that "the only solution . . . for keeping to the strictest historical practice and nonetheless giving expression to those moments of shock, amazement, or denial, was to turn to the reactions of the victims as they were confronted by the events as expressed mainly in diaries and letters . . . in memoirs, etc." Here, he says he did not look for " 'statements' by the victims . . . but for their raw 'voices,' for the cries and whispers of the downtrodden and oppressed."

Fair enough, but I would point out that the quotations chosen for use as epigraphs in *Years of Extermination* are rather more "artistic" and "literary" than "raw" and "spontaneous," and that, in fact, it is their fashioned rather than their spontaneous nature that gives them their force and power. After all, they were written after the events of which they speak or the experience of the emotions they wish to express. Moreover, the quotations chosen for epigraphs in Friedländer's text are cast much more in figurative than in literal (or proper) terms. Why would they not be, given the fact that they report reactions to events too monstrous to believe?

My point here is that Friedländer's text is replete with different literary, rhetorical, or discursive genres—epigraph, ekphrasis, anecdote, constellation, irony—that at once punctuate his narration and impede

narrativization and, at the same time, create a level of figurative meaning alongside and modulative of the facts given in the chronological
record; these genres serve perfectly well Friedländer's stated aim to produce the specific effects of "estrangement" and "disbelief" that would
protect his account from "domestication." How else could you create
these effects in writing other than by "literary" means?

But I want to caution against a tendency to confuse all literary writing with fictional writing or to identify poetic utterance with fictionalization. Factual writing (writing about matters of fact) can be just as
literary as fictional writing (writing about imaginary things) without
being necessarily fictionalizing. I would point out that the fiction-
nonfiction distinction is based on the nature of the referent of a discourse, while the literary-nonliterary distinction has to do with the
formal features of an utterance.[23] The same formal features (generic,
modal, tropical) may appear in both fictional and nonfictional (or
factual) texts: real events can be presented as describing trajectories
of tragic or comic stories; real people can be configured as characters
of the kinds met within a novel or play (as heroes or villains, as kings
or beggars); and "contexts" can be described as threatening or benign,
supportive or hostile, as the case may be. By the same token, all of
these effects can be reversed by the same techniques, and instead of the
story one had expected, one can find story parts that refuse to come
together as a whole.

The point is that meaning can be imputed to real events by both
conceptualization and figuration, but pathos and especially the pathos
of suffering is more effectively produced by images than by concepts.
Benjamin believed that "history does not break down into stories, it
breaks down into images."[24] It is a succession of images (rather than
an argument, thesis, or explanation) that sums up, gives meaning to,
and provides the principal "understanding effect" of Saul Friedländer's
great work.

I mentioned that the first chapter of Years of Extermination is introduced with an epigraph that quotes Klemperer's figure of "the sadistic
machine" and that the chapter itself begins with an anecdote that features the figure of Klemperer contemplating suicide. The anecdote ends
with the Klemperers' toasting Eva Klemperer's birthday and the British
entry into the war. This is followed by an anecdote that shows that Chaim
Kaplan of Warsaw had "grasped the peculiar threat that the outbreak of
the war represented for the Jews," and had gained little solace from the
efforts of the Warshavians to fortify their city against the attack to come.

Then the action suddenly switches to Lodz, where Dawid Sierakowiak, "a Jewish youngster, barely fifteen," writes in his diary about the sudden enthusiasm of the Poles for everything German. And back again to Warsaw, where Adam Czerniaków is organizing a Jewish Citizens Committee for the defense of the city.

These four anecdotes about four different "ordinary" people in Dresden, Warsaw, and Lodz on the eve of World War II—together with their lapidary comment—are notable in the way that they stand in for the narrator, the way they permit him to draw back behind his text and let his subjects speak for themselves and for him. It is this authorial retreat that I wished to indicate as middle-voicedness in my earlier remarks on the narrator's seemingly passive objectivity. Even before the "historiography" has begun, Friedländer uses anecdotes to block the impulse to narrativize, to block the emplotment of events, to let in a bit of reality in the form of the feelings of confusion, bewilderment, and, yes, "disbelief" of the patients of "the sadistic machine." Friedländer prefers to hear these voices as "raw" and spontaneous, rather than as "art." But his *use* of these voices is nothing if not artistic. And it takes art to conjure up a world with millions of Jews but no place for them.

Perhaps you may think that I am overreading in a way that only a pedant or a Derridean deconstructor would do, that I am making more than even a critical reading calls for of what is, after all, only a convention, the convention of placing an epigraph at the head of a text or opening a chapter with an anecdote. But I would ask you to consider another anecdote, one that opens the introduction to *Years of Extermination* (we are still in the paratext of the narrative). It begins with a statement of fact: "David Moffie was awarded his degree in medicine at the University of Amsterdam on September 18, 1942."

Then follows a longish description, not of this event but of a photograph of this event, somewhat in the manner of the description I have been giving of the opening epigraph of Friedländer's text.[25] We are not shown the photograph in Friedländer's text; rather—and this is the tropological move—an *ekphrasis* (verbal description or "word picture" of an image) is presented in lieu of the photograph. The referent of the passage (the photograph) is withheld (Friedländer certainly could have had it reproduced),[26] but in its stead we are presented with a description of it. There is factual information about the event recorded in the photograph, who is in the photograph, when it was taken and where, and why the photograph can be interpreted as a record of an "act of defiance" on the part of university authorities against the German occupiers of the Netherlands.[27]

But having interpreted the manifest meaning or information of the photograph, Friedländer adds, "there is more." On the surface, he says, we have "a common enough ceremony, easy to recognize," in a "festive setting, a young man received official confirmation that he was entitled to practice medicine, etc." However, "as we know, the *Jood* pinned to Moffie's coat carried a very different message. Like all members of his 'race' throughout the Continent, the new MD was marked for murder."

This statement is glossed by a look "inside" the photograph, "faintly seen," and in "characters specially designed for this particular purpose ... in a crooked, repulsive, and vaguely threatening way, intended to evoke the Hebrew alphabet and yet remain easily decipherable," are the Jewish star and the word *Jood*. It is "in this inscription and its peculiar design" that Friedländer discerns "the quintessence" of "the situation represented in the photograph" and its sinister meaning: "The Germans were bent on exterminating the Jews as individuals, and in erasing what the star and its inscription represented—'the Jood.'"

I hope it will not be considered inappropriate to point out that what we have here is a kind of *mise-en-abîme* or a representation of a representation of a representation, and so forth. Thus, in his (ekphrastic) representation of a representation (a photograph) that represents an event ("a common enough ceremony"), Friedländer perceives a further representation (a sign) he now interprets as the "quintessence" of that complex of events called the Holocaust. In the inscription of the star and the word "Jood," Friedländer says: "We perceive but the faintest echo of a furious onslaught aimed at eliminating any trace of 'Jewishness,' any sign of the 'Jewish spirit,' any remnant of Jewish presence (real or imaginary) from politics, society, culture, and history."[28]

Friedländer's reading of this photograph is allegorical: the photo seems to represent two things or two or more levels of meaning simultaneously. In fact, however, there is no way that the photograph of Moffie's graduation ceremony can be said to emit the message Friedländer purports to find in it. The allegorical dimension is provided by Friedländer and his own knowledge of the fate that had awaited the Jews of Amsterdam in that time, all unbeknownst to them. Friedländer reads back into the photograph a meaning that could hardly have been known to Moffie and the others at the time the photograph was taken. The result is to produce that effect of "estrangement" that Friedländer had described as his aim in volume 1 of his masterpiece.[29] But the effect is produced not so much by a recitation of the facts as, rather, by their figuration. Thus, in his description of the star and its inscription as "characters specially designed for this particular purpose . . . in a crooked, repulsive, and vaguely threatening way, intended to evoke the Hebrew alphabet and yet remain easily decipherable," Friedländer has already built into his description the interpretation that he sees as "easily decipherable." The decision to substitute an ekphrasis for the photograph is a specifically literary or, as I would prefer, a tropological move: it puts a verbal image in place of a visual image, proceeds to interpret the latter, and thereby substitutes the photograph for the event as the referent of this passage of the discourse.

This is not a criticism because—in my opinion—every historian must do something like this to "work up" past events as objects of possible historical analysis. This kind of move does not diminish but rather heightens the reality effect of the text. Why? For the simple reason that photographs are mute. They do not say, assert, or affirm anything. They need captions or texts of some kind to give them voice. This is the purpose of the ekphrasis, to transform a visual into a verbal image.

But the discussion of the David Moffie image serves another purpose as well: placed as it is, as the opening of the introduction of the body of the text, Friedländer provides his readers with insights into the compositional choices he will make to move from event to description of the event, to interpretation of the event. The narratological function of the whole passage is to reveal the literary tools that will be used to bring to life a panorama of brutality, suffering, and death. The analysis (or description or interpretation) of the Moffie photograph can serve as a paradigm (or what Kenneth Burke called a "representative anecdote" and Charles Sanders Peirce the "interpretant") of how to read historical artifacts symbolically.[30] The Moffie photograph opens the introduction and serves as a figure (schema) of reading (allegorically) that will be "fulfilled" at its end. That is to say, at the end of the introduction.

Thus, the last paragraph of the introduction, which comes eleven pages later, begins: "Let us return to Moffie's photograph, to the star sewed to his coat, with its repulsive inscription, and to its meaning. Once its portent is understood this photograph triggers *disbelief*. Such disbelief is a quasi-visceral reaction, one that occurs before knowledge rushes in to smother it."[31] Although the passage states that "once the portent [of the photograph] is understood," it "triggers" disbelief, it cannot possibly mean this; what it must mean is that, once understood, the photograph should trigger disbelief. Did it trigger disbelief in Friedländer? Disbelief in what? Disbelief in the photograph? In the reality of the event it records? In the "portent" of the star and the word *Jood*? In the situation of which the symbol on Moffie's coat is a synecdoche?

These questions are answered by Friedländer's immediately proffered definition of what he means by "disbelief" in this context: "'Disbelief,' he says, "here means something that arises from the depth of one's immediate perception of the world, of what is ordinary and what remains 'unbelievable.'"[32]

This definition is, to say the least, idiosyncratic: syntactically and semantically. I believe that it is a bit of parapraxis—a moment of confusion and disorientation in the text—over which we must linger and try to identify what is seeking to emerge from the text in addition to what it says. Read syntactically or literally, the definition says: "disbelief . . . means (1) something that arises from the depth of . . . immediate perception of the world, (2) of what is ordinary, and (3) what remains 'unbelievable.'" Disbelief, Friedländer goes on to say, is a "quasi-visceral reaction" by or in which something of what is given in "immediate perception" remains "unbelievable." On this view, unbelief is a quality of some aspect of "immediate perception" that, because it is not unbelievable, can be disbelieved. But why should we wish that the truth—which so many have labored so hard to cover up or deny and others have labored so hard to bring to light—be disbelieved?

The usual definition of "disbelief" is something like a conscious rejection or denial of an idea, assertion, or perception offered not only as "believable" but also as actually "believed." Disbelief differs from unbelief by the element of will or volition motivating it. In unbelief, I simply do not believe what others see or hear or feel to be the case. Friedländer wants his readers to have the "quasi-visceral reaction" of "disbelief" to what he will be telling them about the Holocaust, in order to experience the feelings of very many Jews of Europe, not only when they heard news of the death camps and the Nazi program of extermination, but also while they were experiencing what happened to them in the camps and while they were recounting what had happened in the camps after they had returned home.[33] But disbelief is very close to the psychoanalytical notion

of *disavowal*, which, in Freud's classical formulation, consists of the denial
of an absence or lack where one had expected to see something. In denial,
I can deny what I perceived; in disavowal, I deny what I did not perceive.
Disavowal is a product of a moral repugnance, a "quasi-visceral" feeling
of disgust arising from the perception of what is difficult to believe because it ought not to have happened. "Why did the heavens not darken?"
Arno Mayer's question receives a believable and compelling answer in
Friedländer's account of the Holocaust: because of the disquieting realization that, under the Nazi regime, the last vestige of what had formerly
undergirded any sense of human solidarity had been erased.

All very well, but what is the import of the remark about the feeling
of disbelief being threatened by a "knowledge" rushing in immediately
to swamp it? This question is answered by the "metahistorical" comment, "The goal of historical knowledge is to domesticate disbelief, to
explain it away," and by the explanation of what will be grasped immediately by his critics as his deviation from the normal expectations of
the normal reader of a normal historical narrative: "In this book I wish
to offer a thorough historical study of the extermination of the Jews
of Europe, without eliminating or domesticating that initial sense of
disbelief."[34] Friedländer repeats this characterization of conventional
historical knowledge as domesticating and disarming of a moment of
"disbelief" in the face of events or actions that, although grotesque,
bizarre, or scandalous, are rendered quite believable by historical knowledge and have their moral or ethical import neutralized or canceled out
as a result.

I want to comment on two other devices used by Friedländer to break
up his account into discrete temporal and spatial fragments, and reas-
semble them under relatively underdetermined assemblages that admit
no overarching emplotment, summary, or narrativization. These are the
anecdote and the constellation.

In conventional narrative historical writing, the transformation of
a chronicle of events into an emplotted story is supposed to be the
interpretation of the events. Grasping the series of events as a story,
being able to recognize that the story taking shape before one's eyes is
a story of a particular kind (genre) and that it is cast in a certain register or tone (mode), this *is* the interpretation of events produced by
narrativization. In *Years of Extermination*, Friedländer uses epigraphs
as hinges between one section of his discourse and another. By narrativization, a complex of condensed (imaginal) materials is transferred

from a horizontal (before-after) axis onto an axis of vertical (surface-depth) combination. Condensation on a vertical (or surface-depth) axis can be exemplified in the structure of the epigraph chosen by Friedländer to negotiate the transition from the end of part 2 ("Mass Murder") to the beginning of part 3 ("Shoah") of his text. Thus, we turn the page ending part 2 to find a page (357) that in its entirety looks like this:

Part III

Shoah

Summer 1942–Spring 1945

"It is like being in a great hall where many people are joyful and dancing and also where there are a few people who are not happy and who are not dancing. And from time to time a few people of this latter kind are taken away, led to another room and strangled. The happy dancing people in the hall do not feel this at all. Rather, it seems as if this adds to their joy and doubles their happiness."

—Moshe Flinker (sixteen years old),
Brussels, January 21, 1943

We learn a great deal more about Moshe Flinker later on in the text, but for the moment, I want to fix our attention on this passage from his diary used by Friedländer as an epigraph to part 3 of his text, "Shoah (Summer 1942–Spring 1945)," and try to explain why I wish to characterize it as a literary device that adds "interpretation" to the assemblages of "facts" comprising the two chapters it at once separates and joins.[35]

First, the quoted passage itself contains nothing factual. We are invited to entertain what we would in another context regard as a purely imaginary scene in which some people are happy and dancing and others are not, and from which, "from time to time," some of the latter kind of people are taken away and "strangled," while the "happy dancing people in the hall" do not "feel this" except as an increase in own their joy and happiness. The caption, which tells us it was written by Moshe Flinker at a certain time, can be questioned as to its veracity, but the passage itself posits a scene more fantastic or grotesque ("a great hall") than realistic; it is a simile ("It is like . . .") that analogizes a situation (of Jews in Brussels, which we know from the context only) to a wild dance party where "many people are joyful" and "a few people . . . are not happy," where some are taken away and strangled and some are not, and where, finally, those who are not strangled apparently become happier and more joyful in response to, or as a result of, the murders of the less happy lot.

I say that the epigraph negotiates the transition from part 2 to part 3 and from chapter 6 to chapter 7. How so? And what happens during this process of transition? First, it continues a metaphor that has been used to close chapter 6, which ends with an anecdote about objections to a party planned for Jewish children in the Warsaw Ghetto. The anecdote serves to introduce another metaphor for the characterization of the situation of the Jews of Europe during the years of extermination. Thus, the head of the ghetto, Adam Czerniaków, remarking on objections to certain "play activities" that had been organized for the children of the Warsaw Ghetto, writes: "I am reminded of a film, a ship is sinking and the captain, to raise the spirits of the passengers, orders the orchestra to play a jazz piece. I have made up my mind to emulate the captain."[36] The next page takes us from the image of the jazz orchestra on the sinking ship to the image of a dance party conjured up by Moshe Flinker in which, "from time to time . . . a few people . . . are taken . . . and strangled." The image of the jazz orchestra playing as the ship goes down is (ironically) replicated in the image of the dancers at a wild party where some are murdered while others ignore them and, at the same time, are stimulated by their fate. The second image can be taken as a "fulfillment" of the first, and the two taken together can be seen as an allegorical structure that adds meaning to the account quite in excess to whatever "facts" are reported in the conventional historiographical mode.

Let me now conclude—as I could go on like this throughout the entire book—to show the advantages of "close reading," even of nonliterary texts. My point would be to try to show that the literary devices, tropes, genres, and figures found in Friedländer's book are not just a function of the inevitably "figural" aspect of natural languages but, in fact, in addition to their denotative function, they come laden also with a wide variety of connotative significances. The use of literary devices—such as epigraph, ekphrasis, anecdote, constellation, and commentary—by a writer, whether of factual or fictional prose, is not simply a way of clothing unpalatable "facts" with a glossy veneer to make them more ingestible to a resistant reader. Such devices have the effect of drawing attention to the means and modes of literary production themselves (effecting what Roman Jakobson calls "the poetic function") and of endowing the putatively "plain speech" parts of the text with specific affect (the conative function of the speech event, in Jakobson's terms). They are also parts of the "content" of the text.

Thus, Friedländer's substitution of his description (ekphrasis) of the photograph of Moffie's graduation ceremony for the photograph itself draws our attention—draws my attention, at least—to a fundamental trope of historiography: the creation of the subject of the discourse by the description of the putative referent. A photograph of a historical event is a good illustration of this principle because its substitution by a description shows how any historian's gesture toward a real referent in the past must already presuppose a description of that referent to serve as the referent's discursive stand-in. This does not make the events being described less real or more fictional. It is simply that the description of any historical phenomenon is a way of constituting it as a possible object of historiographical representation.

I have suggested that although the devices, tropes, and figures identified here are those known to traditional criticism, Friedländer uses them to produce the specifically modernist (literary) effects of estrangement and disbelief in—not so much the truth, as instead the "reality" of—the events he recounts. And in the representation of historical reality, this constitutes the principal difference between traditional nineteenth-century realism and its modernist alternative.

Notes

1. Hayden White, "Historical Discourse and Literary Theory," paper presented at the Institut für Zeitgeschichte, Jena, June 2011, in *Den Holocaust erzählen? Historiographie zwischen wissenschaftlicher Empirie und narrative Kreativität*, ed. Norbert Frei and Wulf Kansteiner (Göttingen, Germany: Wallstein, 2013). [Ed: This essay was collected in White, *The Practical Past* (Evanston, IL: Northwestern University Press, 2014), chap. 5.]

2. Saul Friedländer, *Nazi Germany and the Jews: The Years of Persecution, 1933–1939* (New York: Harper Collins, 1998); Saul Friedländer, *Nazi Germany and the Jews, 1939–1945: The Years of Extermination* (New York: Harper Collins, 2007).

3. I had in mind Jean-François Lyotard's metaphor of an earthquake that not only destroys large tracts of land and buildings but also the very instruments by which to measure the source, span, and intensity of the tremor. See Jean-François Lyotard, *The Differend* (Minneapolis: University of Minnesota Press, 1988), 56.

4. See Saul Friedländer, ed., *Probing the Limits of Representation: Nazism and the "Final Solution"* (Cambridge, MA: Harvard University Press, 1992), 7; Friedländer writes: "For most historians a precise description of the unfolding of events is meant to carry its own interpretation, its own truth." This statement is similar to that of R. G. Collingwood, who argued that when you know what happened, you already know why it happened.

5. [Ed: See Hayden White, "The Modernist Event," in *Figural Realism: Studies in the Mimesis Effect* (Baltimore: Johns Hopkins University Press, 1999), 66–86.]

6. I am indebted to two analyses of Friedländer's work: Wulf Kansteiner, "Success, Truth, and Modernism in Holocaust Historiography: Reading Saul Friedländer Thirty-Five Years after the Publication of *Metahistory*," *History and Theory* 47 (2009): 25–53; and Dominick LaCapra, "Historical and Literary Approaches to the 'Final Solution,'" *History and Theory* 50 (2011): 71–97.

7. See the foreword to Toni Morrison's *Beloved* (New York: Vintage International, 2004), xvi–xvii: "The *historical Margaret Garner* is fascinating, but, to a novelist, too confining. Too little imaginative space there for my purposes. *So I would invent her thoughts*, plumb them for a *subtext that was historically true in essence, but not strictly factual* in order to relate her history to contemporary issues about freedom, responsibility, and women's 'place.' The heroine would represent the unapologetic acceptance of shame and terror; *assume the consequences of choosing infanticide; claim her own freedom.* The terrain, slavery, was formidable and pathless. To invite readers (and myself) into the repellent landscape (hidden, but not completely; deliberately buried, but not forgotten) was to pitch a tent in a cemetery inhabited by highly vocal ghosts" (my emphasis).

8. Friedländer, *Probing the Limits*, 19–20: "Whether one considers the Shoah as an exceptional event or as belonging to a wider historical category does not impinge on the possibility of drawing universally valid significance from it. The difficulty appears when this statement is reversed. No universal lesson requires reference to the Shoah to be fully comprehended. The Shoah carries an excess, and this excess cannot be defined except by some sort of general statement about something that must be able to be put into phrases [but] cannot yet be. Each of us tries to find some of the phrases."

9. Richard J. Evans, *The Third Reich in Power* (New York: Penguin, 2007). Evans's text is a perfect example of conventional narrative historiography—Evans tells a story, the story has a plot, and the plot functions to tie the end of the story to its beginnings: it shows how "the Nazis' headlong rush to war contained the seeds of the Third Reich's eventual destruction. How and why this should be so is one of the major questions that runs through this book and binds its separate parts together" (xvi). The mode of presentation of this story is spelled out in the Preface, which states: "This book tells the story of the Third Reich, the regime created by Hitler and his National Socialists, from the moment when it completed its seizure of power in the summer of 1933 to the point when it plunged Europe into the Second World War at the beginning of September 1939. The approach adopted in the present book is necessarily thematic, but within each chapter I have tried . . . to mix narrative, description, and analysis and to chart the rapidly changing situation as it unfolded over time. . . . A narrative thread is provided by the arrangement of the chapters, which move progressively closer to the war as the book moves along. . . . I hope that [the thematizing] decisions about the structure of the book make sense, but their logic will only be clear to those who read the book consecutively, from start to finish" (xv). Evans's statement can be viewed as both an instruction on how to read his book and a promise to the potential reader: the author effectively contracts to deliver a conventional kind of narrativized (or storified) account of the Nazis' consolidation of power in Germany between 1933 and 1939. And what follows are 712 pages of thematized narration, augmented by 113 pages

of notes, 41 illustrations, 22 maps, 73 pages of bibliography, and an index of 41 pages (for "anyone who wants to use [the book] simply as a work of reference"). Professor Evans has certainly fulfilled his contract with his potential readers and in a prose that has been described as "brilliant," "gripping," "vivid," "impressive," "fluent," and "often magisterial."

10. The transformation of the relation between *logos* and *mythos* from a complementary into an oppositional one is a topos of modern philosophy of science. They were not so conceived in Classical Greek. *Logos* had the meaning of "discourse" and *mythos* that of "plot." Their modern meanings are "reason" and "myth," respectively, as if there could be no rationality in myth and no myth in rationality.

11. [Ed: For the narratological category of "discourse-time" see Tzvetan Todorov, "Les catégories du récit littéraire" *Communications* 8 (1966): 125–51; "The Categories of Literary Narrative," trans. Joseph Kestner, *Papers on Language and Literature* 16, no. 1 (1980): 381–424.]

12. Here is another translation of this passage: "I clearly feel how I am losing my strength; how [I feel] more and more sultry . . . Fight for a personal rescue becomes hopeless . . . Here, on this side of the wall . . . But this is not important. Because I am able to complete my report, and I trust that it will see the light of day in a proper time . . . And people will know how it was . . . And [they] will ask if this is true. In advance I will answer: no, it is not true, this is only a small . . . it is like part, a tiny fragment of truth. This essential, absolute, true Truth cannot be represented even by the best pen. Because it is so incredibly cruel, fantastic that it escapes in its totality and fragments the perception of normal human imagination. A normal brain, even exercised in the time of these long months and years to note down all perceived and heard atrocities, would not be able to absorb and to memorize this bottomless evil. Eyes were seeing, ears were hearing, but consciousness could not comprehend, grasp, and heart already did not feel. Because it was not for humans." This translation of Stefan Ernest, *O wojnie wielkich Niemiec z Żydami Warszawy 1939–1943*, ed. Marta Młodkowska (Warsaw, 2003), 354, is by Wlad Godzich. I thank Katrina Stoll, currently doing research in Warsaw, for finding the Polish text for me. Friedländer does not cite the source of the version he used for an epigraph, but I presume that it comes from *The Chronicle of the Lodz Ghetto, 1941–1944*, ed. Lucjan Dobroszycki (New Haven, CT: Yale University Press, 1984), listed in his bibliography.

13. Friedländer, *Years of Extermination*, viii. Friedländer's version of this passage from Ernest's diary differs from another published translation of it by Michal Grynberg: "I am hiding in a pit, lingering on without fresh air, without steady nourishment, without sufficient plumbing, without any prospect of change, and every passing hour is worth its weight in gold. I can feel my strength fading away, feel myself suffocating for want of air. The struggle for my personal survival is becoming hopeless. Here, on this side of the wall— but that doesn't matter, because I will finish my account, and I have faith that in the proper time it will see the light of day and people will know how it was. [no ellipsis] And they will ask if this is the truth. I will answer in advance: No, this is not the truth, it is only a small part, a tiny fraction of the truth.

[no ellipsis] The essential truth, the real truth, cannot be described even with the most powerful pen" (quoted in a review by Tim Cole in *History in Focus: Guide to Historical Sources* 7, The Holocaust [London: Institute of Historical Research, 2004], https://archives.history.ac.uk/history-in-focus/Holocaust/bookrevs.html).

14. An interviewer for the *Daily Jewish Forward* asked Friedländer: "You take your book's epigraph from the diary of one Stefan Ernest, a Jew hiding in 'Aryan' Warsaw in 1943. . . . It seems here that you are trying to sound a note of humility. But am I wrong in sensing a hint of bravado here, too? Do you see yourself as wielding 'the mightiest pen?'" To which Friedländer replied: "I don't want to underestimate my work. It would, in a way, be grotesque to write and then say, 'This is worthless.' *But I meant the epigraph very simply and directly*: Don't let us have any illusions. We try, and we have to try, but this is not even a fragment of a fragment of the truth" (my emphasis). "I meant the epigraph very simply and directly. Don't let us have any illusions, etc.?" If that is what Friedländer meant, he could have simply and directly said that. Instead, he used a trope, the epigraph.

15. The Polish version by Ernest, as edited by Marta Młodkowska, reads: "Walka o osobisty ratunek staje się beznadziejna . . . Tu, po tej stronie muru . . . Ale to nieważne. Bo sprawozdanie moje mogę doprowadzić do końca i ufam, że ujrzy ono światło dzienne we właściwym czasie . . . I ludzie będą wiedzieć, jak to było . . . I zapytają, czy to prawda. Z góry odpowiem: nie, to nie jest prawda, to jest tylko niewielka cząstka, drobny ułamek prawdy. Ta istotna, cała, prawdziwa Prawda nie da się przedstawić najtęższym choćby piórem. Bo jest ona tak nieprawdopodobnie okrutna, fantastyczna, że wymyka się ona w całości i szczegółach postrzeżeniu normalnej wyobraźni ludzkiej. Normalny mózg, choćby w ciągu długich tych miesięcy i lat zaprawiony do notowania wszelkich dostrzeżonych i zasłyszanych okropności, nie mógł być w stanie wchłonąć i spamiętać owego bezdennego zła. Oczy patrzały, uszy słyszały, ale świadomość nie mogła pojąć, ogarnąć, a serce dawno nic czuło. Bo to nie było dla ludzi" (Stefan Ernest, *O wojnie wielkich Niemiec z Żydami Warszawy 1939–1943*, ed. Marta Młodkowska [Warsaw, 2003], 354).

16. Friedländer, *Years of Extermination*, viii.

17. Friedländer, viii.

18. Epigraphs play an important role in Friedländer, *Years of Extermination*. In the preceding volume, *Years of Persecution*, there is only one epigraph. It introduces the whole book and consists of a single, direct statement by one of the architects of the Final Solution: "I would not wish to be a Jew in Germany" (Hermann Göring, November 12, 1938). The difference between this epigraph and the one taken from Ernest's diary indicates the difference between the two volumes of Friedländer's text: the one about "persecution," the other about "extermination."

19. The concept of literary writing as distinguished from the mystifying concept of "literature" is crucial for my thesis. Literary writing is identifiable by the dominance of what Roman Jakobson calls the poetic and metalinguistic functions of the speech event. Prior to the advent of literary modernism, realistic writing was identified with the dominance of the referential function

and the world of fact. Modernist writing no doubt problematizes the notion of referentiality and attenuates it in the degree to which emphasis shifts from the referent to the problem of the modes and means of referring. In modernist literary writing, reality and even "history" are present, but as ambiguated and hidden rather than as given to sight and sound.

20. See Joel Fineman, "The History of the Anecdote: Fiction and Fiction," in Fineman, *The Subjectivity Effect in Western Literature: Essays toward the Release of Shakespeare's Will* (Cambridge, MA: MIT Press, 1991). Against the idea that anecdote and even anecdotage are low genres, Fineman seeks to redeem the anecdote as the basic unit of historiographical writing (the historeme) that gets lost or at least subdued in the process of narrativization. The irreducibility of the anecdote serves to remind the narrativizer of the "reality" of that historical process he or she is trying to incorporate into the "plot."

21. Friedländer, *Years of Extermination*, 3.

22. I had suggested H. G. Adler's *Eine Reise* as a model of what I had in mind, which, in my view, could be considered a veritable lexicon of figures and tropes for representing the Holocaust, with all of the "facts" left out. Friedländer and I disagree over whether Adler's book is to be considered a "fiction." I consider it to be a deconstruction of the fact-fiction dichotomy when it comes to the problem of representing the Holocaust. It is neither factual nor fictional but metafictional, in Linda Hutcheon's and Amy Elias's sense of the term. It shows how the contrast between fictional and factual presentations of an event like the Holocaust cannot do justice to all of the ghostly aspects of that event, the ways in which the facts seem grotesque and the fictions more truthful to them than any simple chronicle or history of them might be. For a survey both of the postmodernist novel in the West and of the theoretical issues raised by the revival of the historical novel as a dominant genre, see Amy Elias, *Sublime Desire: History and Post-1960 Fiction* (Baltimore: Johns Hopkins University Press, 2001). Some time ago, Linda Hutcheon pointed out that the postmodernist novel was given to the production of what she called "historiographical metafiction," which she characterized as showing "fiction to be historically conditioned and history to be discursively structured," in *A Poetics of Postmodernism: History, Theory, Fiction* (New York: Routledge, 1988), 120.

23. On this "referentialist" conception of "fiction," see Dorrit Cohn, *The Distinction of Fiction* (Baltimore: Johns Hopkins University Press, 1999).

24. Walter Benjamin, *The Arcades Project*, trans. Howard Eiland and Kevin McLaughlin (Cambridge, MA: Harvard University Press, 1999), 476.

25. The genre of the *ekphrasis* (description) is typically used by art historians to extract the symbolic meaning from the literal description of the visual elements of a work of art.

26. I wrote to Friedländer asking him about the omission of the photograph from his book, and he responded that he had not made a conscious decision not to publish it, but that his description of the photograph would have been the same even if he had published it. From a textological point of view, it is the fact that the photograph was not published and that a verbal description of it is put in its place that makes it a trope (*ekphrasis*).

27. Friedländer, *Years of Extermination*, xxiv.

28. Friedländer, xiv.

29. In his Introduction to *Years of Persecution*, 5, Friedländer speaks of "shifts" in his "narration" required by his desire to "juxtapose entirely different levels of reality . . . with the aim of creating a sense of estrangement counteracting our tendency to 'domesticate' that particular past and blunt its impact by means of seamless explanations and standardized renditions. That sense of estrangement seemed to me to reflect the perception of the hapless victims of the regime . . . of a reality both absurd and ominous, of a world altogether grotesque and chilling under the veneer of an even more chilling normality."

30. Kenneth Burke, *A Grammar of Motives* (Berkeley: University of California Press, 1969), 59–61. [Ed: See also Charles Sanders Peirce, *Peirce on Signs: Writings on Semiotic*, ed. James Hoopes (Chapel Hill: University of North Carolina Press, 1991), chap. 16, "Sign."]

31. Friedländer, *Years of Extermination*, xxvi, my emphasis.

32. Friedländer, 26.

33. Friedländer, 663.

34. Friedländer, xxvi.

35. The epigraph in Friedländer is taken from Moses Flinker, *Young Moshe's Diary: The Spiritual Torment of a Jewish Boy in Nazi Europe*, ed. Shaul Esh and Geoffrey Wigoder (Jerusalem: Yad Vashem, 1971). The original was in Hebrew.

36. Friedländer, *Years of Extermination*, 595.

CHAPTER 13

At the Limits of the Concept [2016]

It is often forgotten that the humanities—which are made up of history, philosophy, literary studies, philology, rhetoric, art history, musicology, and linguistics—are characterized not so much by their objects of study, which can change over time, but by their focus on *reading*, the reading of verbal texts, primarily, but also "reading" in the sense of the decoding and recoding of images, sounds, and movements. The disciplines that comprise the humanities teach different ways or kinds of reading practices. The products of these disciplines for the most part belong to the class of prose and poetic discourses. This is why they may often look similar or even the same, especially when they are cast in the same mode: narrative, argumentative, descriptive, or expressive, as the case may be.

In the late eighteenth century, philology was presented as a necessary component of philosophical discourse, the argument being that a proper reading could not proceed without a preliminary construction of a text. How could one analyze a Platonic dialogue without a text purged of errors of transcription, translation, and/or material completeness? In the nineteenth century, with the advent of "realism" and the new genre of the novel, it was thought necessary to distinguish rigorously between "factual" and "fictional" no less than between "literal" and "figurative" or "grammatical" and "rhetorical" meanings in texts that typically mixed the pairs indiscriminately. In the twentieth century, with the invention of the science of linguistics, the "language" of texts was separated out from other elements of text for special consideration as key to the cognitive functions of mind. So nowadays when one chooses a discipline in the humanities, one is not only choosing a particular kind of reading practice; one is also rejecting or being licensed to ignore a host of other kinds of reading. So, it is fair to ask: What is being lost or given up in the choice of a particular kind of philosophy over another (or of an alternative view of what "philosophy" is)—one, say, that relates to its shared origin in discourse with literature?

To be sure, there is considerable overlap between literary studies and philosophical studies in the contemporary American university: philosophical works are regularly taught in literature departments (Kierkegaard, Nietzsche, Kafka, Sartre, Simone de Beauvoir, Judith Butler, etc.), and literary works are analyzed in philosophy classes (Sophocles, Ovid, Shakespeare, Milton, Racine, Goethe, Valéry, Mann, Camus, and so on). Once, years ago, following a suggestion of Fredric Jameson's, I taught Kant's *Critique of Judgment* as a modernist novel. My philosopher colleagues were not amused.

Looked at from the perspective of form, philosophical discourse would appear to be a species of literary prose, in which grammar and syntax have as much interest for philosophical as for literary scholars. But grammar and syntax are differently studied in the two disciplines: philosophers have long tried to reduce grammar and syntax to logic; literary scholars, on the other hand, treat grammar and syntax as a baseline of literalness from which analysis departs in search of transgrammatical structures of meaning.

As a form of prose discourse, philosophy in general differs from literary discourse in general by its use of a metalanguage—more or less formalized—to describe texts. The use of a metalanguage—whether it be logic, calculus, or some other technical language—produces paraphrases of discourse and "literalist" translations of figurative expressions that suppress or ignore connotative significance. The result is "clarity," defined by the late Bernard Williams as philosophy's highest aim, but—I would add—at the cost of poeticity.

A fundamental difference between literary and philosophical discourse is the dominance of the poetic function in the former. Plato's exclusion of poets from his ideal city and the philosophical distinction between idea (*eidos*) and representation (*mimesis*) herald a millennial tradition of distrust for poetic utterance and indeed any kind of figurative expression. Because philosophy is indentured to the logic of identity and noncontradiction as its organon and standard of meaningfulness, it cannot entertain the idea that figurative language could be expressive of a form of thought that, although not "rational," is nonetheless cognitively creative. Kant thought that figurative (or image) thinking could be the basis of the "understanding" but not of "reason," by virtue of its non-conceptual, non-scientific nature; and the analytical tradition from Locke through Bertrand Russell to Gilbert Ryle has condemned metaphor as a "category mistake."

So, the choice of philosophy, whether of the "analytic" or "continental" kind, entails a rejection or at least demotion of poetic speech as productive of ambiguity or vagueness of expression. This suspicion of poetic utterance extends to a number of other practices disdained by philosophy as threatening to rational discourse: rhetoric, myth, narrative, ideology, and mysticism.

At the level of cultural valorization, literary studies and philosophy constitute themselves as academic disciplines by what they *exclude* in the way of conventional practices, procedures, and beliefs about the nature of their objects of study. Unlike hermeneutical philosophy, predominant in continental Europe, analytical philosophy, prevalent in Great Britain and the United States, is based on a clearly stated and practicable theory of error. The latter favors a correspondence theory of truth, consisting of: (1) unambiguous propositions to be measured against observable and measurable phenomena; and (2) protocols of combination of elements of propositions governed by a logic of identity and noncontradiction. Knowledge is presumed to grow by aggregation of finite elements tested for consistency with received bodies of lore considered to have been secured or securable by means of scientific experiment. In this version of the matter, knowledge is reduced to the products of the physical sciences, and wisdom is hardly differentiable from technique. But as the sociology of science (Bruno Latour *et alia*) has shown, this is an idealized version of science and any philosophy manifestly committed to it as an ideal of knowledge.

To explain why a given population of students or scholars might choose to study one academic discipline and shun another (within the same ambit of kinds of disciplines—in this case, the humanities), we might begin by asking: What are the current "imaginaries" (kinds of possible objects of intellectual-emotional cathexis) of the fields being compared? The determination of these imaginaries would be necessary even if our ultimate aim were to be a survey of the population for versions of their own answers to the question of "Why philosophy (instead of some other discipline)?" For we are speaking about *choice* and *decision*, however well- or ill-informed, however determined by outside forces (such as parental or peer pressure), and however serious or frivolous at the moment of choice. However considered, however conscious and rational and well-thought-out, every choice involves desire as much as utility and therefore involves the attribution of intrinsic value to the object chosen. Thus, we must inquire into the different "masks" of philosophy, the public disguises intended to make it a possible object of desire.

On a practical level, philosophy can be defined by what it produces, deals in, utilizes as its organon, and aim or purpose. Here, *concepts* and conceptualization are at issue. Even though it is generally conceded that the concept of the concept is vague or ambiguous, conceptual clarity and purity of rational thinking are the principal aims of modern philosophical discourse. But because of this vagueness or ambiguity of the concept, the substance of philosophy cannot be stated as easily as that of the modes of thought and expression it means to exclude from its own practice, even while it may invoke these as examples of that substance. And what it has excluded since Plato has been that with which Plato, too, began: "myth" and the organon of myth; figures of speech and thought (versus concepts), on the one hand, and poetic tropes (versus logical schematisms), on the other. From its beginning, "philosophy" in the West has viewed with suspicion, if not expelled from its purview, fabulation, sophistry, poetry, fiction, drama, rhetoric, figurative language in general, and play. Starting in the modern era, this list has expanded to include any transcendental orientation of feeling and thought. Thus, although philosophy purports to be primarily motivated by a love of knowledge and truth, it sees itself as embodying the attributes of knowledge and truth: clarity, identity (selfsameness), logical consistency, and metaconceptual coherence.

One can then ask: What is the instrument for measuring the conceptuality of any given concept or set of concepts? The answer, of course, is the logic of identity and noncontradiction. To be sure, post-Kantian philosophy knows that Aristotelian, syllogistic logic is not the only kind of logic, that there exist different logics conformable to different possible worlds beyond the one that we (more or less) inhabit. But for that mode of analytic philosophy descended from Aristotle, logic is still the gold standard for the assessment of the validity of sets of propositions as well as for the determination of the legitimacy of the elements comprising a single proposition. A thing cannot both be and not be any more than a thing can be both old and young, both hot and cold, both round and square (without of course specifying the matrix or frame within which the measurement of size, speed, or aspect is being made). Dismissing the claims of "dialectical" thinking on the activity of the mind, neo-Aristotelian analytic philosophy thus holds out the promise of a model of what a coherent world would consist of. It is a world based on a game model in which the rules of performance are laid down in advance, are completely consistent with one another, in which winners and losers are identifiable, and in which rewards and penalties are known in advance of the outcome of any series of plays. Such philosophy holds out the vision of a world in which all problems are translatable into puzzles, in which anomalies and ambiguities are seen as products of mistaken perception or conceptual confusion, and in which crisis and catastrophe are functions of human perception rather than of some defect in the world. How could a real catastrophe occur in a game?

Needless to say, "literature" or literary discourse proffers a worldview much messier and radically less reassuring and consequently less attractive as an object of desire than what I have characterized as the *doxa* of modern philosophy, the goal of positively identifiable outcomes shared by explicitly "historicist" or "fact-based" studies of literature that examine the particular world represented rather than the discourse within which it is produced. The thwarting of such positivist outcomes is especially pronounced in modern Western literature and its most recent incarnation, modernist literary writing. More important, modernist literature, in both its Western and its postcolonial incarnations, has largely abandoned the mimetic model that has provided its orientation towards realism since antiquity. At the same time, Western literature and its extraterritorial extensions in the non-Western world have remained true to their origins in belief in the *figure* (Latin: *figura*; Greek: *schema*) as the organon of a specifically literary (as against generally linguistic) mode of invention. Whereas philosophical invention consists of the creation of new concepts adequate to the conceptualization of an ever-changing reality, literary invention consists more of pushing the limits of discourse beyond the hierarchy of genres inherited from earlier or exotic writing traditions and of creating of new figures incarnating the anomalies and ambiguities of emergent social forms and cultural processes driven by technologies capable of destroying the life world they themselves have created.

"Literature," conceived as play, entertainment, moral instruction, or simply "reading," is quite a different thing from "literary writing," conceived as transcending the limits of ordinary, literalist language use. Whereas in an earlier time, literature was defined by its "set" (*Einstellung*) toward the message, poetic diction, and communicativeness (eloquence), modernist literary writing displaces the weight of meaning onto the code function of discourse (metalanguage) and the deconceptualization of "content" (reference). The conceptualist ideals of clarity and consistency at the heart of modern analytic philosophizing presuppose that the elements of every proposition can be endowed with a specific meaning or range of meanings. The composition of true propositions involves not only clear perception but the correct choice of words to name the elements of any given referent. And while this works perfectly well for the description and naming of material things—tone in music, hue in color, and number in arithmetic—it is anything but adequate for the description of emotional states or affects; of concern for obligations and responsibilities; and of how kinds of decisions called for in critical situations are made. Literary writing—especially non-mimetic writing—also valorizes clarity, concreteness, and coherence but less of the logical than of a poetic kind.

Literature or literary writing can utilize concepts for its production (in the same way that conceptualist art does) because modernist literature rules out nothing, not even "graphics," "diagrams," and "tables," as means of production. But above all and quite specifically, modernist writing is inclined to problematize two mainstays of analytic metalanguage: genre propriety and the logic of identity and noncontradiction.

Indeed, in comparison with literary studies, all orientations of philosophy aim towards the creation of a universal metalanguage by which to assess the truthfulness and value of every species of (nonpoetic) language use: from "ordinary language" all the way over to the metalanguage of the physical sciences, mathematics. This is why philosophy can be defined by what, since Plato, has been consistently held to be its contrary, *rhetoric*, considered as a willful *mis*use of language—writing and speech—for purposes more or less nefarious. If any of the conventional disciplines is held to be philosophy's "other," it is rhetoric, which enters the field of philosophy costumed as sophistry, eristic, and (sometimes) even "dialectic." But *rhetoric* is a catchall term for anything departing from fixation on the concept and the logic of identity and noncontradiction in prose discourse: that which puts metalinguistic analytic philosophy at odds, not only with literature in general and poetic utterance in particular, but with "ordinary language," as well.

There is, of course, a tradition of deviance from the analytic philosophy orthodoxy (in the Anglophone world). It is called "continental philosophy," which resumes a tradition of philosophizing begun during the Hellenistic period, beginning with the Stoics, Epicureans, Cynics, Skeptics, and so on. In modernity, this tradition reemerges with post-Kantianism and can include philosophers as different as Hegel, Schelling, Marx, Nietzsche, Wilhelm Dilthey, Hans Vaihinger, Benedetto Croce, Henri Bergson, Martin Heidegger, Alfred North Whitehead, Charles Sanders Peirce, Jean-Paul Sartre, John Dewey, Hans Blumenberg, and a number of phenomenologists (Husserl, Ricoeur), pragmatists, and existentialists, not to mention certain "anti-philosophers" such as Kierkegaard, Novalis, Schleiermacher, Schopenhauer, Coleridge, Carlyle, Kafka, Theodor Adorno, Martin Buber, Gilles Deleuze, and so on. The important point about this tradition is that it continues, in one way or another, to criticize the Enlightenment ideal of *clarté* and tends to move towards alliances, if not unions, with other disciplines and/or arts as providing "contents" more in line with the "great questions" of the "meaning-of-life" kind featured by premodernist philosophy. In my experience, this deviant strain of philosophy attracts the kind of student formerly drawn to literature, religious studies, and art.

The strength of the deviant strain lies in its recognition of the limitations of a philosophy centered on the concept and committed to logic as the only organon of a properly philosophical thought. While the analytical tradition tends to identify "understanding" as a kind of "thinking in images" rather than in concepts, the continental tradition valorizes image thinking as the basis of the kind of "common understanding" informing an ethics of care and an aesthetic of invention and creativity. The continental tradition tends to be much more sympathetic to rhetoric, which it understands less as an "art of persuasion" than as a theory of the relation between literal-conceptual thought, on the one hand, and figurative-tropological consciousness, on the other. It is more sympathetic to a narrativistic mode of expression than to a syllogistic mode of argumentation. Indeed, it even recognizes that "fiction" may be less the contrary of "fact" than a different mode of mediating between sense and imagination. It even allows that the inherent variation and differentiation of poetic speech, as in Wallace Stevens, Yves Bonnefoy, Ann Carson, W. H. Auden, T. S. Eliot, and Paul Celan, might produce affects and insights to which other modes of expression remain blind.

Note

[Ed: This text was published in the March 2016 issue of the journal *PMLA* as a contribution to a forum on "Why Philosophy?"; hence its brevity and lack of scholarly notes.]

CHAPTER 14

Krzysztof Pomian's Modernist Theory of Culture [2016]

In the 1960s and 1970s, Michel Foucault sought to reform the study of "history of ideas" by what he called the study of discourses. Instead of tracing ideas through their dispersal and development over time, Foucault focused on the conditions under which various areas of society were brought under the control of institutions whose authority depended on discursive practices that made their practices appear to be perfectly "natural" and "in the order of things," rather than invented for the advantage of social groups interested in maintaining their hegemony. Thus, he wrote works on the discourse of madness, of clinical medicine, and of modern criminality and the institutions these discourses authorized for the disciplining of groups deemed too disorderly, irrational, or dangerous for inclusion in "normal" society. The relation between "words" and "things" in human societies was thus revealed as fundamental to the understanding of all other social relationships: familial, sexual, economic, political, religious, and so on.[1] And the history of discourses was taken to be illuminative of the science of history itself. Historiography, one of the oldest of ancient sciences still practiced today,[2] proved to be, in one sense, a paradigm of the power (and dangers) of discursivity. Physicians treat maladies (such as madness) that exist only in discourse, rather than in their patients; prisons treat "criminals" for states of mind, will, or conscience that are wholly imaginary; the churches have a history of persecuting individuals for "sins." Historians over the centuries have treated these institutions and their ideologies as custodians of what is normal and natural for social beings. Historians even today are expert at finding the reasons, sufficient if not necessary, for the contemporary status quo, for "things as they are." Small wonder that Jean-François Lyotard indicted the whole history profession as contributing to a mythical "grand narrative" that undercut every radical program of reform as "unrealistic," unnatural, and ultimately untimely.[3]

Some years ago, at precisely the time of Foucault's entry on to the intellectual scene, Krzysztof Pomian wrote: "la différence essentielle entre la science et l'histoire [c'est que] la première possède des théories, tandis que la seconde n'en a pas" (the essential difference between science and history [is that] the first has theories, while the second does not).[4] The idea that history, or more precisely historiography, operates without a theory (of its own operations) has been a commonplace of discussions regarding the epistemic status of historical knowledge ever since the mid-nineteenth century when history became detached from belles lettres and rhetoric and began to lay claim to being a scientific rather than a literary discipline (*Wissenschaft*). Pomian's idea was not meant to suggest that modern historiography did not use theories borrowed from other sciences—theories of the state, of the law, of class struggle, of war, anomie (Durkheim), gross national product, etc.; it was intended to indicate that there was not and could not be a theory *of* history itself—such as the kind advanced by Hegel, Marx, Spengler, and so on.

But if Pomian is right—which is to say, if history is constitutionally non- or anti-theoretical, if there can be no theory of history—as there can be a theory of geology, of psychology, of literature, of geography, of astronomy, etc.—then history is not and can never be a science. It can be a craft, an art, a game, any number of things, but a theory? No. Where there is no theory, there is no (modern) science.

Pomian is quite aware of the efforts of historians to finesse this problem by attempting to theorize different kinds of science, most famously in the cases of Wilhelm Dilthey and Wilhelm Windelband, the distinction between nomothetic (causal law making) and ideographic (discursive) sciences. The ideographic notion of historiography is deemed proper to the *Geisteswissenschaften*, or "sciences of the spirit," whose creative freedom is extended to include a freedom from causal determination. On this view, history is set off from other domains of existence by virtue of the creativity of its human agents, and history is distinguished from other scientific disciplines by its task of investigating and presenting this domain in all its individuality, originality, and meaningfulness. Nature, by contrast, is conceived as a domain ruled by causal laws that, in their regularity, admit of no ascription of freedom or meaningfulness to its members, animal, vegetable, or mineral. Nature as thus envisaged is primarily a resource and a stage on which humanity demonstrates its right of domination, the right of domination of the spirit over the body, of man over both himself and the rest of nature.

Pomian recognized the ideological nature of the notion of ideographic sciences; he recognized that like the *Geisteswissenschaften*, the concept of "ideograph" was a way of saving the idea of spirit and the spiritual to science. But as a materialist and advocate of a history more scientific than "spiritual," he sought a way of saving history to science without having to abandon the notions of human freedom, creativity, and meaningfulness altogether. The arguments for human freedom were to be found not in the strata of long duration of material history, which Fernand Braudel and the Annales group took to be the true "content" of a scientific history, but rather in human culture. For Pomian, human culture did not fall from the sky as a sign of human difference from the rest of nature, nor was it the product of a qualitatively different substance in the human animal. Culture, for Pomian, is a purely human creation, not so much "caused" by human beings as, rather, constituting a sign of the difference between human beings and other animal species. In answer to the question, "is culture derived from nature or from the human spirit," Pomian might have answered: "Neither; it is the sign of the emergence of culture from nature." So Pomian begins like this: there is culture; culture is created by human beings. To what end or purpose? For human self-identification? Identification in what sense? Identification of self as self-creative. Finally: history is the story of this human self-creation.

And to avoid that infinite regress that would begin, "What is the origin of culture?," Pomian forgoes the search for an origin and locates culture in a practice remarkably similar to Foucault's theory of discourse: collection. It is not in any practical or useful activity that Pomian finds the secret of culture: other animals value certain objects for use and even contrive tools for the solution to practical problems. But it is only the human animal, Pomian says, that collects things, preserves them, labels or classifies them, and makes of them objects whose meaning is apprehended as both their *raison d'être* and as invisible. And although history is not conceived by Pomian to consist only of the history of culture—for it has its practical side in the development of tools and knowledges for bodily and material needs—it is nevertheless the story of the creation of things for use by the intellect, will, and senses—cultural things—that reveals what is original of our humanity. And the secret of the creation of other things lies in the activity of collecting, in the making of collections, and in the "impractical" uses to which the collection is put.

Pomian will call every cultural thing a "semiophor," sign-bearer (or carrier) (from *semeion* = sign + *pherein* = to carry, on the analogy of meta + phor = to carry across or under). And since a sign indicates "meaning" (X = cross = "True Cross" = the instrument of Christ's Passion), the question—brought under question radically by Saussure—is how do things become invested with meaning? As I understand him, Pomian believes that things become invested with meaning by being collected. So, what is collecting, and what is a collection that it can transform a thing into a meaning by way of its semioticization?

A walker stops at the curb of a street in Rome, gazes intently at the rubbish—twigs, cigarette butts, a bottle cap, litter of an indeterminate sort, a couple of rocks, pieces of paper—that has haphazardly assembled in a slight declivity, picks out a stone and takes it home for preservation with other stones in a wooden box with a glass cover. A woman of a cave-dwelling family rises from the glow of the fire, picks up some bones from the animal recently devoured, moves to the back of her cave, deposits the bones in a small recess in the cave wall, and sprinkles dust on the remains. A French artist visiting in the United States walks among the detritus of a junkyard, stops before an abandoned urinal, picks it up, takes it home, writes something on it, and then deposits it upside down in an exhibit of avant-garde artists in the Grand Central Palace in New York City.

In the view of Krzysztof Pomian, all three of these people have participated in the game or ritual of cultural production by the simple act of *collecting*, which is to say, picking up some natural object, such as a stone or a flower, or some utilitarian object, such as a urinal, or simply some haphazardly accumulated heap of used-up, abandoned, or discarded detritus and putting it in some space or locale reserved for things with meaning or thought to be worth preserving. As worthy of preserving, such objects can be thought of as possessing *meaning*. In Pomian's view, everything in nature or culture potentially has what Marx famously called "use-value." Such objects do not "mean" anything, which is to say, they do not project meaning or invite hermeneutical inquiry into their possible meaning apart from the uses to which they are intended to be put. By contrast, Pomian would argue, any object removed from the domain of things for use and "collected" is not only endowed with "meaning" but becomes an organon for the endowment of other things with meaning as well.

Looked at from one perspective, Pomian has contributed to the age-old problem of how to make something out of nothing. For things thought worthy of being collected have fallen out of the use-value category and are relieved of having to be useful again. By being collected, however, they are endowed with a new value, the value of being worthy of being looked at, observed, contemplated, mused upon, and consequently of having some value as yet unknown other than utilitarian. Since this other value, the value that makes them worthy of being displayed, observed, contemplated, does not manifest itself in display, it is easy to think of it as having meaning that remains invisible. The condition of having been collected does not presuppose that the items in any given collection belong to a common genus or species, that they share some common attribute or constitute a family with different attributes but the same genetic endowment. The items of a collection need not be related to one another in any way at all. But the possibility that they might, with adequate attention and inspection, show their commonality means that they are potentially meaningful.

In the last instance of the three examples of collecting given above, the French artist (Marcel Duchamp) "made art" out of a piece of rubbish once valued only for its utility, by moving it from one locale to another. The fact that he wrote the word "Fountain" on the urinal and added the name "R. Mutt" gives to the object additional meanings, although, given their manifestly ironic nature, it is difficult to know for sure what this meaning might be. Nor has his deposition of the urinal in the Grand Central Palace changed it in any way whatsoever. And yet the object—since lost, stolen, or abandoned—remains one of the most famous "artworks" of modern times, a "work" so revolutionary that, according to some art historians, it changed the very concept of art inherited from the nineteenth century and virtually destroyed the authority of the concept of "the aesthetic" inherited from the Enlightenment.

But Duchamp did more than that: he effectively redrew the line separating "art" from "non-art" and, moreover, changed the natures of things relegated to these two domains according to the rules governing such depositions in the time and place of his revolutionary act. Beyond that, Duchamp brought under question the conventions, rules, and even laws defining differences between art and other domains reserved for the collection of things deemed inherently inferior to the things collected in the art space, thereby destabilizing the authority of "culture" to assign value to both the things of nature and the things of culture. And insofar as value is equivalent to meaning, Duchamp changed the meaning of meaning itself. Meaning no longer equated with any "substance" of things, their forms or attributes, or the uses to which they could be put. Meaning was now to be equated with "where" things were gathered together as much as with any substance they might commonly share. At least, so it seemed to devotees of the historic avant-garde of modernist art in the twentieth century.

Krzysztof Pomian's work in the last quarter of the last century on the history of historical thought may have had behind it a thought similar to that presupposed by Duchamp's treatment of his urinal. Pomian's own story of historiography tells of modern historiography's changes in both methodology (attainment of "objectivity") and principal content (from political to socioeconomic to "anthropologico-cultural" history) from the early nineteenth to the end of the twentieth century.[5] It is not a matter of one of these kinds (or, as François Hartog would call them, *régimes*)[6] of historical study supplanting the other or nullifying them in any way. These different kinds of historiography are, as it were, stacked on one another—rather like the three strata of temporalities posited by Fernand Braudel as the properly scientific object of a properly scientific science—or overlap in the mode of a Venn diagram such that they all participate differently at any given time in the panorama of a history that is totally manmade.

As the title of the essay placed at the middle of Pomian's *Sur l'histoire* suggests, "Histoire culturelle, histoire des sémiophores," the history of "semiophores" enjoys a special place for the understanding of both the history of science and the history of (modern) history. For Pomian, history's history consists of a story in which historiography progressively divests itself of "traditional" modes of comprehension and rhetorical service to a patron or specific institution, develops *Hilfswissenschaften* (diplomatics, paleography, source criticism, and the like), and gradually detaches itself from all transcendental points of orientation to become a material science in the sense of being immanentist and systematized, on the one hand, and "objective" (absent of sentiment and affect), on the other. In a sense, Pomian can be considered a metahistorian, inasmuch as, for him, "history," both in the sense of "what happened" and in the sense of the writing about what happened, is conceived to participate in a general process of culture production that is progressive (without being teleological) and posthumanist (without being nihilistic).

Much of the validity of history's claim to the status of a science was based on the idea of history's difference from "literature" understood as "romance," imaginative writing, or more generally, fiction. Pomian came to grips with this idea in 1989 in an essay entitled "Histoire et fiction," published in the French periodical Le Débat.[7] This essay examined the idea of fiction in the wake of a poststructuralism (deconstruction) that, in Pomian's view, indicts history as "la mystification par excellence," precisely in its claim to deal with a "real" rather than an "imaginary" world of a past more fictional than scientific. In the collection of essays entitled Sur l'histoire, published by Gallimard in 1999, Pomian not only criticizes the idea that history deals in fictional worlds; he also provides a defense of historical knowledge in his own theory of the "semiophor" and of "the collection" as a paradigm of cultural production of which historiography can be considered an instance.

The debate over the epistemic status of historiography turns in large part on the question of the "fact." The determination of whether a statement (or proposition) is true or false has to do with whether the event or events of which it speaks are real or only imaginary, illusory, made up, invented, fabricated, and so on. The establishment of the truth or falsity of a statement about some event in the past is problematical because past events are neither observable (they are over and done with, past) nor experimentally reproducible (because, as historical, they are by definition singular, individual, or unique). When there is a conflict between two or more equally authoritative treatments of the same set of historical events, there exists no original, raw, or untreated congeries of those events that might serve as the tertium quid by which to measure the relative truthfulness of the various versions of them. In the absence of any "original" set of events by which to measure the value of contending "copies," historians tend to fall back on a kind of consensus criterion. One is speaking here, of course, of molar rather than atomic events, complex events such "the French Revolution," rather than relatively simple events such as the date of the Battle of Waterloo or where a given person had been at a given time and place.

In lieu of scientific procedures for testing hypotheses, modern historiography has developed rules for the constitution and use of evidence, treatment of documents, assessment of testimonies, criteria of irrealism (no miracles), if not of realism itself (according to the doctrine of plausibility). It promotes conventions featuring the moral virtues of the authentic scholar as against the freedom of invention supposedly enjoyed by the creative writer. And it insists not only on its differences from but even its contrariety to "literature."

But in its representational practices, historiography remains—with more or less opposition—committed to the narrative mode of enunciation and to "the story" as the genre preferred for the presentation of historical truth. The historian narrates—this commonplace remains the *doxa* of historiography from Herodotus to Niall Ferguson; even in the fields of history of art and history of science, it is the full and truthful story of their development that is the ultimate aim of research. The scientist does not tell stories about his electrons, genes, or molecules; she seeks the laws that govern them. Fernand Braudel maintained that historical knowledge could never become scientific as long as it remained committed to the story form for the presentation of its findings. Far from being a container or carrier of ideology, narrative (*le récit*), or what we might call the "storification" of real events, was the paradigm of ideologizing discourse. Thus, Pomian writes, it could be asked whether:

> tout récit est une fiction, selon le dogme du relativisme postmoderne ou de la déconstruction qui, à la suite de Jean-François Lyotard, voit dans tout discours historique un "grand récit" mythique par lequel chaque culture se comprend?[8]
> (every narrative is a fiction, according to the dogma of postmodern relativism or of deconstruction that, following Jean-François Lyotard, sees in all historical discourse a mythical "grand narrative" through which each culture understands itself?)

In the current cultural moment, historical thought is conceived to be scientific only in the sense of favoring objectivity over subjectivity and neutrality over partisanship in the treatment of the past. "The facts and nothing but the facts" is its motto, but as long as the facts remain embedded within a story, history's objectivity remains questionable. Is it possible to have an objective account of historical reality, the form of which is a story, and at the same time reject the charge of fictionalization?

Two prominent literary critics, Käte Hamburger and Dorrit Cohn, interested in protecting the privileged position of literature in modern high culture, insist that history differs from literature by virtue of the reality of its referent. The freedom of the artist depends on the irreality of his referents. Thus, literature is to history as fiction is to fact. True, one will encounter many examples of a mixture of fact and fiction in a given work, the historical romance being the prime case in point. But these cases are just that: hybrids, mixtures, violations of "the law of genre" that asserts that everything has a form proper to it and that to present anything in an improper form is tantamount to a violation of the incest taboo. The mixture of fiction with fact may be possible in literature but never in historiography, in which event and fact are virtually synonymous. So that one can be said to look for the facts or find the facts, as if the fact existed along with the event as its "outside" or "manifestation," the phenomenal form of the thing-in-itself that had only to be "discovered" rather than "created." As in: "It is a fact that Columbus discovered America in 1492."

What is overlooked here is the "constructed" nature of fact itself. If, as Arthur Danto argued, a fact is an event or some thing "under a description," then facts cannot be said to exist before the descriptions of the events to which they refer. This is especially the case with historical events or past events that do not, or no longer present themselves to possible observers but have to be posited as having happened even before they are described and their "factuality" established. And if historical events are established as historical facts by description, cannot the same be said for fictional events, events that have no existence at all except as described as such? As for the "documents" and/or monuments invoked to verify the occurrence of events at particular times and places, these too become such by virtue of the operations by which events are turned into facts by description.

Whence the *epistemic* importance of the archive in the lore concerning the invention of history as a mode of knowledge production and of the fact as the operator that permits the distinction between history and fiction. The archive is the *place* where the raw materials exist out of which histories can be made. Prior to their processing as either authentic documents, false documents, or documents irrelevant to history, the materials of the archive can be said to be indeterminate in respect of their meaning, utility, or status as witness to events worthy of historiographical treatment. We can liken the materials of the archive to language prior to the distinction between active and passive voices or to sound prior to the designation of some part of it as music. Until they are processed, the materials of the archive are in a state of suspended animation, unclassified and useless for any particular purpose. We can say that they are close to becoming rubbish, and it is only the fact of their having been gathered where they are that raises them above the standard of things to be thrown away.

Having been gathered in the archive or, what we may call more generally, the archival space, the materials in the archive have taken on, or been endowed with, a special meaning or rather, to put it in Pomian's terms, with "meaningfulness." Whether their meaning has relevance to one department or other of the culture that preserves them, or no meaning at all, depends completely on the ways they are classified (or dispensed with as useless and meaningless) by one or another savant charged with this task.

And this is where Pomian's ideas regarding the semiophor and the collection come into the discussion. A semiophor, in Pomian's theory, is a thing, any object, natural or artifactual, that is treated as having no practical utility for a given group but which, instead of being treated as rubbish and thrown away, is removed from the sphere of daily life, put in a special place for preservation, and is joined by other objects deemed similarly worthy of preservation. Here "worthy" is the crucial term, because just by being preserved, collected objects are at least tacitly deemed to *have* value; so that, it might be argued, in the primitive collection (the heap of bones and feathers deposited in the declivity of a cave wall), the very category of value or the valuable is created.[9]

The value *of* the collection is shown by the fact that its contents are not used for any practical purpose, that it is preserved in a special place reserved for other objects deemed collectible by their collectors (or collected and thereby deemed valuable), that they are displayed for observation, contemplation, and reverence, and that, finally, particular items do not have to be considered to manifest anything like a generic or species similarity to qualify for inclusion in the collection, as in the curio collection. Pomian calls items in a collection "semiophors" because, being treated as objects worthy of being preserved even though they have no discernible "use-value," they qualify as objects whose value lies less in their being than, rather, in their "meaning." Since the "meaning" of a collection of manifestly variable objects is not given (even when it is a matter of a collection of, say, firearms or cooking utensils or sacred relics), it can be assumed that the meaning of the collection "points to" or "indicates" a domain of things distant, hidden, or present but *invisible*.

As thus envisaged, the collection (whether it be of pins, arms, butterflies, state documents, or paintings) is a proper object of both scientific-pragmatic and hermeneutic investigation. Such investigation will clarify, even when it does not explain, the meaning of the collection's contents, its inherent value (as against its use- or exchange-value), and its "invisible" (as against its material) nature. If it is the differences between kinds of invisible value that underwrites Pomian's distinction between history and fiction, we can gain some insight into the relative value of history and literature by considering the ways, aims, and purposes of the collections to which instances of each have been assigned.

Since our interest here is Pomian's contribution to the question of the value of historical knowledge, we will try to explicate how his ideas of the semiophor and the collection illuminate the history-fiction relationship, on the one hand, and the history-science relationship, on the other. Pomian's principal example of the semiophor is the literary text, poem, novel, theater, or discourse, as the case may be.[10] Here the library as the place of the collection is the crucial institution and, indeed, the place that by what it allows inside, defines what will count as "a book" and its kinds for a given cultural group or constituency. The literary text is a semiophor, not so much by its manifest appearance as a "book" (of which there may be many different materializations, editions, typefaces, quality of paper, binding, etc.), as, rather, by its status as a work (*oeuvre*).

Thus, *Madame Bovary* is a book of many different editions, but it is also a work that tells the story of the dangers of reading the wrong kind of book—provincial adultery and bourgeois hypocrisy in a prose style deemed particular to its author. The book (*le livre*) can be examined for its function as a material "support" for the work, for its place in the history of French printing and book marketing, for the nature of the materials used in its production, for the different modes of production used in its manufacture, and so on.

But this "book" (*livre*) is quite a different thing from *Madame Bovary* "the work" (*oeuvre*). The story of "Madame Bovary," her longings, her loves, her addictions, her delusions, and, finally, her end, all this makes up "the work"—a work that, although it exists, exists only in the minds of readers. The work cannot be observed and examined empirically in the ink in which it is printed, the words that comprise it, or the images of the places, characters, and events that appear in it. The work is real but invisible. Invisible, too, are the characters, places, events, and relations inhabiting the *oeuvre*. But it is not this *invisibility* that makes of *Madame Bovary* the work, a fiction. Contrary to the *doxa*, the fictional is not defined by its non-factuality; it is defined by its non-historicality. It is the "common wisdom" of the society that deems *Madame Bovary* properly preserved in the literature section of the library rather than in the history section. It is not because it is physically similar to some other book or set of books that determines where it will be placed for preservation and displayed as an instance of literary exemplarity. By virtue of

Madame Bovary's difference from every other work in the "literature" section of the library, its placement there transforms not only the "meaning" of "literature," but, more importantly, it transforms the very idea of similarity and difference informing the library's practice of classification. It is by such actions as placement, displacement, and replacement that culture produces and reproduces meaningfulness; and it is because of such actions that literature—along with all of the other departments of culture—can be said to have a "history."[11]

Now, turning to history, Pomian's views of this topic conform strikingly to those of Michael Oakeshott, for whom "history" is similarly invisible except in the form in which it appears in books, articles, and essays and the like written by historians and recognized as such by other historians. On Oakeshott's view, the history found in books—where things are called by their right names: "the Interregnum," "World War I," "the Thirty Years War," and the like—is not a set of events that anyone ever lived or witnessed while they were occurring. This history had to be extracted from the chaos of materials in archives and libraries that, taken all together, could not possibly add up to the relatively smooth plotline of the typical history book. In other words, Oakeshott wishes to distinguish between the past and those parts of it that lend themselves to possible representation in the genre of writing known as "histories." On his accounting, the past has none of the coherence or substantive consistency attributed to it by its greatest scholars. Both because of the nature of its evidence (always incomplete and preserved by chance) and its reality (events and things connected only by contiguity rather than by traceable causes), any limited and coherent account of any part of the past is more fiction than fact. The past that people in both the past and the present live by, the past that serves as a source of "knowledge," hope, and even desire, this is the past of memory and experience, with everyone having a different version of what matters to them in this past. Oakeshott thus sets up alongside of "the historical past" something called "the practical past," which is as malleable and manipulable as memory itself, subject to the rule of imagination as much as to reason. Although he himself does not draw the comparison, the practical past is rather like the past of the modernist novel—the novel of Woolf, Proust, Joyce, Stein, and so on—whereas the typical presentation of the historical past resembles more the realist novel of Balzac or Dickens. Oakeshott still keeps the distinction between real and imaginary events; he just questions the utility of the fact-fiction distinction. Here he falls in line with modernist literary writing, whose "modernism" is typically attributed to its rejection of "history" and disdain for tradition. But, to put it in terms acceptable to Oakeshott, it is "the historical past" that modernists reject, the "official" version of the past hailed by the "realists" of prior generations, not "the practical past" on which modernist views of the present and the future are based.

And it is here that the modernism of Pomian's idea of history can be profitably considered. As a historian reflecting on both history and "the history of history," Pomian cannot have been unaware of the irony of his argument about the invention of meaning by collecting. For when he turns to the subject of history and to the question of its value as a kind of knowledge and as a mode of social existence ("to live in history," to be aware of history as a qualitatively different dimension of the past, to designate something as "prehistorical," etc.), he must finally admit that what he is doing is "collecting" bits of lore about the past, putting them on reserve, limiting their use to observation, contemplation, reverence, and finally designation as meaningful over and above whatever they had been used for in *their* past.

If the history book is a semiophor similar to the literature book in the double dimensionality of its "content," if it is at once a *livre* and an *oeuvre*, then we can begin to understand why history must remain a hermeneutic discipline rather than an explanatory science. The subject of the history book, its *oeuvre*, remains invisible in a double sense: first, the events of which it speaks are over and done with, past; and second, its *meaning*—the equivalent of the *story* of *Madame Bovary* in the book with that title—can have none of the consistency and coherency of the plots that render the literary work accessible to the imagination. It is up to the author to convince the reader of the meaning of the events he recounts by the use of a kind of scientific rhetoric productive of confidence in the reader that the author has done all that is required of him by his profession to establish the reality of the events about which he speaks. Whence the importance in the history book of the apparatus: footnotes, citations, quotations from other historical works, arguments against other versions of the events recounted, and so on. Indeed, it is precisely because history does not claim the closure, the consistency, the coherence, and the *anagnorisis* (recognition scene) that can be aspired to by the literary work that its status as nonfiction is rendered plausible.[12]

Thus, Pomian can be said to have worked out an idea of history consonant with the ideas of the past informing literary modernism. This means that he has devised a concept of meaning as a product of human action alone and deprived of any grounding of a transcendental or metaphysical kind. He has exposed the mythological or, if you will, the *literary* character of historical writing, but without derogating the representation of the past real to the status of fiction. Indeed, Pomian has redefined fiction itself, not in terms of the irreality of its referent, but in terms of its classification with other kinds of invisible but nonetheless real things discoverable by the imagination as well as by reason. And thus, he redefines the meaning of historicity.

For Pomian, history can no longer be construed as a set of objects sharing an essence or substantial "historicity." Historical events are simply occurrences that have been "collected" (archived), taken out of the category of the contingent and placed in the "box" of objects whose meaning is "historical." It is precisely because those objects—events, persons, processes, institutions, etc.—were originally contingent that they can be joined to one another in meaningful relationships by historian-taxonomers whose task it is to discover the species of historical meaningfulness in which they are capable of participating. Because the entities collected under the rubric of the historical were originally contingent, they can be encoded or mapped in a variety of ways—sometimes appearing in literary works without thereby becoming fictionalized. This runs counter to Ann Rigney's argument that when a historical event or person appears in a work of fiction, it is thereby fictionalized or rendered only imaginary.[13] But why not argue the reverse: fictional or imaginary events appearing in a historical work might be rendered historical by this inclusion. Actually, Pomian could argue that, not only are mixed genres more the rule than the exception in modernity, but there is nothing prohibiting the idea of a mixed genre of the kind called "historical novel." In fact, Pomian posits exactly this possibility in his musings on history as a science. But, more importantly, Pomian's modernist idea of literature allows for the possibility of the "novelesque history," the kind of historical novel that, like Tolstoy's *War and Peace*,[14] demonstrates how what was once thought of as "fiction" provides the basis for a *critical* historiography more literary than scientific in kind.

Notes

1. [Ed: White is referring to the French title of Foucault's book *Les mots et les choses* (*Words and Things*), 1966, translated by Alan Sheridan as *The Order of Things: An Archaeology of the Human Sciences* (New York: Vintage, 1994).]

2. Along with philosophy and rhetoric. As far as I know, no one regards modern "biology" as a descendant of Aristotle's tract on "animals." But historians as a rule trace the lineage of their discipline back to Herodotus and Thucydides, as philosophers do to Aristotle and Plato, and rhetoricians to

Aristotle, Cicero, and Quintilian. Medicine is an interestingly different case. Modern physicians in a general way trace their profession back to Hippocrates but often still insist on the differences between ancient and modern medicine. This is because they depend on modern science rather than ancient science for their practice. Historians, philosophers, and rhetoricians do not on the whole fetishize modern science as an ideal to which they aspire. This is because they recognize a similarity between their discourses and those of their ancient progenitors that modern scientists do not see with respect to their ancient counterparts.

3. [Ed: See Jean-François Lyotard, *La condition postmoderne: Rapport sur le savoir* (Paris: Éditions de Minuit, 1979); *The Postmodern Condition: A Report on Knowledge*, trans. Geoffrey Bennington and Brian Massumi (Minneapolis: University of Minnesota Press, 1984).]

4. Krzysztof Pomian, "L'histoire de la science et l'histoire de l'histoire," in *Sur l'histoire* (Paris: Gallimard, 1999), 159.

5. Pomian, "L'histoire de la science," 159. See also Krzysztof Pomian, "Histoire culturelle, histoire des sémiophores," in his *Sur l'histoire*.

6. [Ed: See François Hartog, *Régimes d'historicité. Présentisme et expériences du temps* (Paris: Seuil, 2003); *Regimes of Historicity: Presentism and Experiences of Time*, trans. Saskia Brown (New York: Columbia University Press, 2015).]

7. Krzysztof Pomian, "Histoire et fiction," *Le Débat* 54, no. 2 (1989): 114–37.

8. Alexandre Gefen, "Aux frontières de la fiction," *Sciences Humaines* 174 (2006), https://www.scienceshumaines.com/aux-frontieres-de-la-fiction_fr_14421.html.

9. Or perhaps I should say, the value of value has been created. Because the semiophor, according to Pomian, may well have had the value of "use" prior to its "retirement" from daily use and its placement in the reserve—which gives it, as it were, "added value."

10. Pomian, *Sur l'histoire*, 192ff.

11. It will be recalled that Flaubert was prosecuted not because of the salacious "content" of *Madame Bovary*, which was the usual stuff of French novels of the time, but because of what the prosecutor characterized as its matter-of-fact presentation, the objectivity of its style, which refused to feign indignation or moral offense, but rather showed things as they are. In other words, to the prosecutor, *Madame Bovary* read more like what we would call a sociological tract than a literary fiction. See Dominick LaCapra, *Madame Bovary on Trial* (Ithaca, NY: Cornell University Press, 1982).

12. Pomian, *Histoire et fiction*, 39.

13. [Ed: In response to my query about this reference, Ann Rigney wrote the following in an email dated June 18, 2022: "The discussion about whether objects become 'imaginary' or not when included in a work of fiction is neither the language I would use or the point I would make. For me, 'fictionality' is a matter of the reading contract and is not an ontological issue. The places I discussed historical fiction as such are in the second chapter to my *Imperfect Histories: The Elusive Past and the Legacy of Romantic Historicism* (Ithaca, NY: Cornell University Press, 2001) and in an article I wrote on Kurt Vonnegut ("All This Happened, More or Less: What a Novelist Made of the Bombing of Dresden,"

History and Theory 47 [2009]: 5–24). In the abstract to the essay on Vonnegut, Rigney states: "The article uses the case of Vonnegut to advance a more general argument that builds on recent work in cultural memory studies: in order to understand the role that literature plays in shaping our understanding of history, it needs to be analyzed in its own terms and not as a mere derivative of historiography according to a 'one model fits all' approach. Furthermore, we need to shift the emphasis from products to processes by considering both artistic and historiographical practices as agents in the ongoing circulation across different cultural domains of stories about the past."]

14. [Ed: See Hayden White's "Against Historical Realism: A Reading of Leo Tolstoy's *War and Peace*," in volume 1 of *The Ethics of Theory*, chap. 15.]

CHAPTER 15

Constructionism in Historical Writing [2017]

Introduction: Theoretical Background

This essay will examine the topic of constructionism in historical research and writing. The topic is important because of the foundational status that historical phenomena enjoy among the human sciences. Although anything but scientific in the modern positivistic sense of the term, history continues to provide a kind of "raw," "empirical," or "objective" body of "data" that serves as a model of "given" social phenomena prior to their treatment by the techniques of the various human sciences.[1]

And yet, although by definition, past events, persons, and processes are considered to be "over and done with," complete, and incapable of further change, they are *no longer* observable or otherwise perceivable by anyone. Moreover, although there may exist records attesting to the occurrence of particular events, their historicity or historiological significance was not observable even by any contemporary witness and can be provided only by later analysts possessing knowledge of those events' subsequent impact upon their environments or contexts.

Therefore, we must distinguish between an event's occurrence, on the one hand, and its historicity or historical significance, on the other. Oliver Cromwell's election to the English Parliament in 1640 can now be seen as a historically significant event, but its historicity became discernible only some years after its occurrence. It was an event crucial to any responsible comprehension of the English Civil War (1642–1651), but that could not have been known from any study of the context of Cromwell's election at the time of its occurrence. Indeed, it is unclear what temporal and spatial areas constitute the "context" of the English Civil War or, for that matter, what constitutes the context of Cromwell's election to Parliament in 1640. In point of fact, "historical context" has to be considered a conceptual construction undertaken from some point other than—later than and elsewhere from—any given event occurring within its purported confines.

And so, too, for the "fact" that is made out of the event to be endowed with historical significance. For any "historical" event, it is construction all the way down. This may not be the case for any given event *per se*, because not all events are "historical." It is the adjective "historical" that endows the event with a substance or intentionality and allows it to serve as a part or element of a totality gathered together (conceived) under the Proper Name "The Puritan Revolution."

Thus, the primitivity or "rawness," indeed, the very "given-ness" of the historical event is brought under question. The adequacy of any given event's membership in a set of events deemed collectible under a historical Proper Name such as "The Puritan Revolution" depends on the nature of the *description* of that event by which it is transformed into a fact. For if, as Arthur Danto has argued, a fact is "an event under a description," then it is description itself that, in historiographical discourse, *creates* the fact. Change the description, change the factuality of the event.[2]

But there is another consideration regarding history's status as a construction. A scientific discipline is identified as much by what of past intellectual practices it rejects as by the kinds of objects it takes for study. Thus, from its (legendary) beginnings in ancient Greece, "history" has been set over against myth and legend quite as much as it has embraced a particular part or aspect of "the past" as its proper object of study.

And so too—although this exclusion took much longer—history has excluded the techniques of rhetoric and poetic devices from its favored modes of presentation and expression. Although obviously different in form and content from the sets of events they take as their referents, narrativized histories are typically presented as if their accounts of the past were mirror images of what actually happened. What can be added to the "raw data" of the past is whatever can be inferred as being *implicit* in the documentary record of the past. In other words, if there is an element of construct in a historical account of the past, it has to be what can be inferred by logical extension of what has been found in the evidence. This is because of the conviction that the world is organized on logical principles, not on rhetorical tropes or poetic creations.

Yet, the difference between what happened in the past and any given discourse *about* what happened (the difference between "the told" and "the telling" of a historical story)[3] is a result of a founding move from the chronological order of a given set to an order of presentation in which beginnings are made into inaugurations, endings into recognitions, and whatever is considered to come "between" is fashioned into a peripety more dramatic than logical in mode. By *peripety* (Greek: *peripeteia*), I mean the denouement in the plot-type informing the story told about history or parts of it, such plot-types as tragedy, comedy, romance, pastoral, and epic. These plot-types derive from the archetypal myths of a culture, and it is their use in the mapping of the trajectories of a series of events into sequences that endows them with the meaning of understanding as against a meaning of ratio-logical coherence.

Thus, the scientific status of history consists in the extent to which it resists a fall into myth, rejects the use of rhetorical techniques in its presentation of findings, and excludes poetic effects from its diction. By myth, I mean any discourse that takes imaginary entities as its subject matter; by rhetoric, I mean techniques for negotiation of the relation between the literal and the figurative dimensions of a discourse; and by poetic, I mean devices of language use by which to express the emotional charge of an image or object.

The debate over constructionism, in psychology, cultural studies, sociology, and politics, has gone on a long time, with the question of its "advantages and disadvantages for life" (Nietzsche) centering on the politically debilitating effects of a human subject deprived of any stable substance with which to withstand the pressures to conformity emanating from centers of power. Ironically, many of the critics of constructionism also reject deconstruction because it forecloses any effort to ground knowledge in an ontologically certain "center" or substance. Deconstructionism would seem to leave the subject indentured to relativism in ethics and skepticism in epistemology, not less than the various constructionisms it wishes to deconstruct. Yet, there remains in both constructionism and deconstructionism one domain of knowledge production exempted from censure. This one area is—strangely—history.

Historical knowledge escapes the charge of construction even though the study of "history" is recognized as being something less than, or at least "other" than, a modern science.[4] This is because historical knowledge provides a body of information, which, in its putative concreteness, its virtual perceptibility, and its time-and-place particularity, can serve as a bedrock against which any impulse to theoretical and philosophical closure can be measured and found wanting. In other words, even if there is no such thing as a specifically "historical" explanation of anything, "history" offers plenty of "data" to which other kinds of explanation, more or less scientific, can be applied. By virtue of their status as events that have already occurred and are, as it were, over and done with, historical phenomena are presumed to be "given" in a way similar to natural phenomena but with the added advantage that they are or can be supported by "evidence." According to the *doxa*, there is very little of a constructed nature in history.

The idea is that historical events do not have to be constructed, because they are already "there," lurking in the documents awaiting only the historian to clear away whatever has hitherto blocked access to them and then to "show" them in all their obdurate thinginess. Their existence as they are, when and where they were, which is to say, in their particularity, *is* their explanation. This is why, as the late Bernard Williams had it, there could be a historical *method* (source criticism, contextualization, dispelling of falsities), but there could be no such thing as a historical *explanation* of anything whatsoever.

Indeed, Williams held that the extension to the past of the methods used to explain things in the present was what distinguished a "historical" from a mythical idea of the past. Historical knowledge was constituted by the erasure of the distinction between present and past events as kinds of possible objects of knowledge. In his own inquiries into the past, as in *Shame and Necessity*, Williams explicates the archaic (Homeric) conceptions of selfhood, action, and judgment in modernist (Nietzschean) terms, calling his method "genealogical" rather than "historical." "Genealogy" is a manner or mode of explanation that can be applied to the past as well as to the present. It is not a matter of constructing a past *ab ovo* or of *re*constructing a past that was already there.[5]

The past, according to this view, consists of events that happened, when, where, and as they happened. We have evidence more or less full of these happenings, and it is not a matter of telling whatever story we wish to tell about them. Presumably, the facts add up to one and only one story, more or less diversely completable depending on the state of knowledge prevailing in any given present.[6] Nor is it as if new knowledge changes the facts of the past. We can add facts previously unknown to the story and erase errors in earlier accounts of it. But events that have already happened cannot be changed; they are *there*, like a shell or stone buried in a geological stratum below the surface of the earth. It is a matter of discovering them, rather than inventing or reinventing them. It is a matter of locating them, describing them, and transcribing the stories *already present* in their relationships with other things contiguous and contemporary with them.

Thus, in this view, the story told by the historian about sets of events in the past is in no way the product of the historian's own composition. Historical stories or stories told about historical events are not templates superimposed on a preexisting reality. They are more in the nature of transpositions from one mode of existence—the past real—into another, the present mode, image, or concept, as the case may be.

From the standpoint of historical theory, however, there is a problem with this notion of "the past." There is no *original* (set of events) to which any version of the "raw data" of the past can be compared. Any given *version* of the story of the past must demonstrate responsibility to evidence, the documentary-monumental record derived from archives, and earlier versions of the story in question. But this means that any given version of the historical past—or any given version of the past presented as a history—is a kind of copy without an original, a simulacrum, a copy of a theoretical construction set up in such a way as to endow facts with meanings formerly unthought of or redescriptions of previously described events, to provide new meanings for them. When Williams says that there is no such thing as a historical explanation of anything, he is asserting the primitivity of historical reality—it consists of facts, some of which are known and some of which are unknown. Explanation of these facts, why they happened as they did, when, where, how they did, requires no special method or mode of explanation, only the modes of explanation currently available in the culture. Indeed, to think that events of the past require a way of explanation different from those present in the scientific culture of a given time would be a mistake.

Considerations such as the above problematize the very object or referent of historiographical discourse. If, following Arthur Danto, we could agree that a fact is an event under a description, it is obvious that *facts* are themselves constructed out of evidence of past events *by* description. And although older conceptions of discourse set description in opposition to narration—as synchronic to diachronic representation of phenomena—it is now thought that narration consists of successive re-descriptions of posited objects in the interest of endowing a body of facts with meaning and/or value. This process of successive re-description of an object, especially an object treated as if it had undergone changes of a substantive nature, is a thematization, the aim of which is to provide the object so characterized with a proper name. "Is it a rebellion?" the King of France famously asks his minister, La Rochefoucauld-Liancourt, in the midst of a particularly unruly riot in 1789; "No, Sire," the minister even more famously replies, "it is a revolution."

Is or was there such a thing as "the French Revolution"? It all depends on the story that is told about what happened in "France" prior to the destruction of the French Monarchy and certain events following upon that event in the decades after. It all depends on the story told that will, at its end, justify or seem to justify the designation of those events as a "revolution" rather than some other kind of disturbance better called by a different name.[7]

Now, this notion of narration and narrativity would seem to justify viewing historical events as too "plastic"—as lacking in substance—to permit their certain identification. But real events, whatever their scope and however vague they seem to be, differ from fantastic events, which are manifestly oneiric or delusional in kind. Things happen; people and institutions change. Entities are born and die, come and go, and thrive or decline. But the question is: can these comings and goings, promotions and demotions, and births and death be truthfully described *as stories or as elements of stories*? Which is to say, are the stories told of real events or a set of events *out there*, in the events themselves? Or are the stories products of human thought and imagination imposed upon real events, to give them a meaning they would not otherwise possess? If there is no original of "the past" against which to measure the truthfulness or even the relative realism of stories told about real events, then we are left in a situation with respect to the past quite different from that with which we are left in respect of the present.

The historical past as narrativized is a construction different from the narrated present. The difference lies in the nature of the events spoken about. Present events can be experienced in a way that past events cannot. Indeed, present events can be experienced but not narrativized (because they are not yet completed), while past events can be narrativized but not (or at least, no longer) experienced. The past can be known only *as others* experienced it, so that a historical account of the past will have to consist of the invention not only of the *events* of the past but also of the *facts* to be explained. And this double invention will be the product of narrativization. Which will allow me to suggest that what we mean by a *historical* fact is—among other things—an event so described as to be able to serve as an element of a story.[8]

For professional or academic historians, "history" refers to parts of "the past" where human beings have successfully (if only temporarily) created collectivities capable of enterprises sustaining of a human desire for freedom from natural exigency and confirming of the value of a distinctively human mode of action as against merely animal activity. The interaction, conflict, and compromise among these collectivities are the "stuff" of historiological existence, the proper study of which consists of detailed inquiries into "what happened" within a delimited zone of time and space, leading to identification of the plot informing the "story" of how and why things happened as they did.

In this conception, "history" is simply posited, rather than argued for in a systematic "philosophy of history," and is treated as a genealogical precursor of a sequence of temporal "presents," in which actions and their consequences permit ever more certain identification of the substances of the process involved. The grand, speculative "philosophies of history" in the manner of Hegel, Marx, Oswald Spengler, Arnold J. Toynbee, Eric Vogelin, and so on, have been rejected as intellectual chimeras, monstrosities in virtue of their manifestly constructed natures.[9]

Straight, professional, or normative historiography is set forth as a proper alternative to and antidote for such "metahistorical" monstrosities claiming universal validity. Straight, professional historiography is held to be value-neutral in the "objective" and productive sense of versions of the past that, when properly studied, are self-presenting or, to put it another way, present the meaning of what they are studying as nothing more nor less than their "factuality." In other words, professional history has, or ideally should have, nothing of the *constructed* about it. Historical reality is always already what it is, always "over and done with," already "fixed" and never changeable. How could it be? After all, it is only after events have run their course and effected whatever changes they can cause that we can claim to have a knowledge of them that even the agents or actants causing them could not have possessed.

From the standpoint of the professional historian's *doxa*, it is only lacunae in the documentary record, errors, or prevarications that keep the "historical past" from springing forth unaided, against the background of "the past in general." It is in this sense that the proper historian's work consists of exposing error or fraud in the documentary record or the accounts of other historians and witnesses to historical events, rather than in *constructing* accounts of the past out of a combination of rational criticism of sources and imagination. For the anti-relativist, history appears as a consoling testimonial to a fixity of parts of reality to which "current" events can lay no claim. The one thing about "the past" that makes it an ideal object of study for a low-level, commonsensical, or unsystematic inquiry is that it cannot be changed. Indeed, for the anti-constructionist, the past would constitute an ideal mode of a reality that is both natural, in the sense of being grown rather than assembled, and fixed and unchangeable, ready for discovery rather than invention, in the way that the substances of things were once thought to be. The past would be a domain in which things, originally appearing as spirit, always finally reveal their essences as nothing but matter. As Wordsworth (in "A slumber did my spirit seal . . .") said of his own "spirit": "No motion has she now, no force; / she neither hears nor sees; / rolled round in earth's diurnal course, / with rocks, and stones, and trees."

Therefore, ideally nothing would be added to the facts of the past, even in the representation of these facts as outlining a story. This view allows historiography to ground its objectivity, or at least its realism, on the absence of any rhetoric in its presentation. As Arnaldo Momigliano once put it: "Where there is rhetoric, there is no history; and where there is history, there is no rhetoric."[10]

This argument, namely that a proper history can contain no element of rhetoric, rehearses once more the relationship of mutual exclusivity between rhetoric and philosophy that has characterized mainstream Western philosophy since Plato.

But *no* discourse lacks in rhetoricity: indeed, discourse is itself that mode of language use seeking to negotiate the difference between literalness and figurality without which things cannot be seized by thought as possible objects of knowledge. Discourse occurs when an object's concept is indeterminate, incoherent, or ambiguous, when it has to be brought into focus and rendered "concrete" by figuration, which is to say, endowed with iconicity. Thus it is with "the past" and the objects and processes seeming to inhabit it. By narrativization or, as I would put it, storification, different parts of the past are endowed with the aspects of *drama*.[11]

The principal trope utilized in this process of dramatization is *emplotment*, the structuration of events as dramatic processes by which they can be recognized as instantiations of the kinds of meanings called tragic, comic, ironic, and so on. By means of dramatization, real events in the past, endowed with "reality" by factualization, are, as it were, re-mythified by being plausibly re-described as kinds of spectacle. And "plausibly" means translated into terms intelligible to a given community.

I have tried to demonstrate the operation of this process of re-mythification in historiography elsewhere.[12] The general point to be made, however, is that narrative historiography—the presentation of a set of real events as displaying the features of a recognizable story-type—resembles the operation by which astrologers purport to discern figures of myth (Orion, the Ursa major, the Big Dipper, Cassiopeia, and so on), by drawing imaginary lines between stars of different intensities as if they existed on the same plane and figured forth an image that could not only be said to exist but could equally well be said to have *meaning*. Each image is turned into a symbol, a synecdoche of the myth or story in which something is presented as revealing its meaning by what it does or what happens to it over the course of time.

How Does Symbolization Work in Historical Discourse?

The emplotment of fictional events (or the emplotment of events *in fictional modes*) differs from the emplotment of real events. In the latter, events are presumed to be fixed in the time and place in which they occurred and possessed of the meaning with which their status as facts of a particular kind (social, political, economic, etc.) has already endowed them. They cannot be moved around for plot purposes, or their factual status changed (without, of course, the provision of new evidence not taken account of in any prior description of them as facts). The import of real events—as causes or effects, as more or less effective, and so on—can be changed by the enlargement of the scale of the field they occupy or by their relegation to a lower status of effectivity than they had originally been presented as enjoying. What can be added to a set of real events at first seeming to show no pattern at all, or a pattern of one kind ("progress," "decline," "bridge," etc.), is a plot structure that endows the events with a new meaning while leaving their primary factuality (time, place, intensity of occurrence, end, or beginning) unchanged. While the author of a fiction can invent new events, introduce new characters, arbitrarily end the life of a given character, and the like, *ad libitum*, the author of an account of real events in the past can change the plot structure of prior stories told of those events, as when events originally emplotted as, say, a romance are re-emplotted in the mode of a tragedy. What is involved is not the fictionalization of real events, but a change in the mode of relating beginnings and endings of stories. Coleridge thought that the moral of every story was the teleological: "In my beginning is my end."

This principle overrides the force of the changes that occur in a given state of affairs when something utterly new and inconceivable can be shown to have emerged out of a recognizable, old, and different earlier state, condition, or situation. This principle constituted a real enigma for ancient Roman authors such as Tacitus trying to account for the change from the five "good" years of the reign of the Emperor Nero to the disasters of his late period. The bad emperor that Nero subsequently became had to be thought of as always having been the reality, in spite of the evidence to the contrary of the five good years. This was because of the doctrine of being that denied the possibility of a change of substances of things. Thus, the changes in Nero's behavior and comportment had to be put down to changes in attributes or his feigning to be something he was not.

The modern notion of history is formulated in a post-substantialist mode of thinking, so that changes in attributes can be taken as *signs* of changes in substance. But since modernity also presumes a constitutive ambiguity in human states of affairs, changes in the attributes of any situation become multi-interpretable, which, in the present case, means multi-emplottable.

Emplotment is a structure of "turns" that, in general, cannot be predicted by deduction from what is known at any point in the unfolding of a story. This means that the plot of a historical story, or history told as a story, is not, or is not necessarily, a logical structure. One of the attractions of a narrative treatment of a set of real historical events is the fact that the ending is not logically deducible from any point in the process leading up to it. The whole set of events, once narrativized, is retrospectively graspable as a symbolic whole, which is to say, as a synecdoche of parts related to one another and to the whole by tropes such as metaphor, metonymy, symbolization, and irony.[13]

As thus envisaged, every story, whether of real or of imaginary entities and processes, seeks to make wholes out of particulars by the use of devices of literary writing: these could just as well be described (in Freudian terms) as condensation, displacement, sublimation, and secondary elaboration or revision. In this respect, every narrativization resembles the structure of dream as analyzed by Freud in chapter VI of *The Interpretation of Dreams*.[14] Some theorists make much of Foucault's claim, in his early work, to be showing the "discontinuities" between one dominant episteme and another. In fact, "discontinuity" is a kind of continuity, which would have been obvious if Foucault, like Freud, had used the concept of "displacement" instead of "discontinuity."[15]

It is the tropological structure of narrativizations that renders them comparable to myth. This is why I have argued that every storification of any part of history is a re-mythification. Events happened; they were mythified; then they are "demythified" by factualization, which creates a chronicle of events arranged along a timeline. Then, they are—or can be—re-mythified by turning facts into the elements of stories.

Is the story *already* embedded in some way in the array of facts arranged on a timeline as a chronicle? Well, yes and no. Since, prior to being treated as facts, the events display the coherences of a number of different, possible plot structures, there is no original to which any given story version of the facts can be compared. Ultimately, it comes down to a question of whether a given emplotment seems plausible to a significantly large group of putatively "competent" readers. But here, "competence" has to be defined in such a way as to include a capacity for reading figuratively as well as conceptually. For without the former kind of competence, what Roman Jakobson called the "poetic function," not to mention the "metalinguistic" one, of any discourse will be imperceivable—or perceived only as error, mistake, or flaw, in an effort to be nothing but "literal."

Therefore, my conclusion is that the element of construct in a historical narrative consists at a minimum of its mode of emplotment. Past events do not *arrange themselves* as stories or even as elements of stories. Indeed, in their raw or unstudied state, they do not even separate themselves into "historical" versus other kinds of events. A given individual might so arrange as much of her life as she controls to give the appearance of a story lived rather than only told about, in the manner of a character from a story by Oscar Wilde, and seek to live her life "as a work of art." But such a person would be fictionalizing herself, in the manner of "Don Quixote" or "Madame Bovary." And her *real* story would be an account of this attempt at self-aestheticization—and its failure, as in Wilde's *The Picture of Dorian Gray*.

We must distinguish between the set of events making up a life course, the chronicle of events that can be made out of this set, and the story that can be made out of this chronicle by narrativization—by the literary devices, techniques, tropes, and figures used to turn a chronicle into a history. The history will be a construction made out of events, persons, and processes more or less adequately documented as to their existence and natures. But the plot-structure or structures used to endow the chronicle with story-meaning have to be borrowed from a cultural endowment that provides many different ways of transforming what would otherwise be only a congeries of events into stories. And our final question must be: what is the epistemic status of these plot-structures?

Freud's analysis of what he calls "defense mechanisms" for the understanding of how dreams work is useful for approaching this question. For Freud, dreams engage complex mechanisms of consciousness by which to endow things, processes, and events with different affectual charges (in response to the imperatives of what he calls Censorship [*Zensur*] working in response to phantasms, on the one side, and social imperatives, on the other).[16] Thus, by displacement, the dreamer transfers an affect associated with the memory of event A to another event, to allow retention of the first memory without the unpleasurable feelings originally associated with it. Or the affect could be held in place, and an image of some other, more neutrally charged event could be substituted for the memory of the original event. So, too, an event that looms large in a subject's scenario of his own life could be condensed, that is, reduced in size and significance, and de-signified in importance in the process. And finally, as with a symbol like a cross, it can appear in a dream so as to cast a glow of sanctity over all its elements or, according to the *kind* of cross, endow the dream with a particular kind of religiosity or, indeed, even a particular kind of threat or anxiety to the dreamer.

All such tropical moves work to endow events with meaning.[17] Whether such moves are common to all myths, fictions, and other kinds of literary writing and dramatic performances is a matter for further study. But narrativization, or the endowment of a series of events, whether fictional or real, with story-meaning, is impossible without them. Thus, if a given set of historical events are presented as "tragic" or whatever, this means that the reader of such an account is being invited to recognize that the set of events recounted does *in fact* bear the meaning associated by convention, custom, or habit with the term "tragic." Needless to say, if a reader of a historical account of events emplotted in the mode of tragedy belongs to a culture in which the notion of "tragedy" or "the tragic" is lacking or unknown, the account itself would have no meaning at all.

Now, this account of the element of construct in accounts of the historical past cast in the mode of a narrative might be taken to suggest only that narrative histories bear a great deal of rhetorical baggage—even that where there is no narrative, there is no history, as Benedetto

Croce argued more than a century ago. But I would like to suggest another implication, namely, that historical accounts of the past not only bring with them a lot of constructed material but that this material is necessary for any kind of specifically historiological explanation. In other words, contrary to Bernard Williams's contention that there is no such thing as a specifically *historical* explanation, my argument would be that there is a specifically historiological mode of explanation, and this mode is narratological.

This means that history is not a science in the modern, physical sciences sense of the term, that it does not explain by the discovery and application of causal laws to bodies of empirical "data," but that history explains by applying techniques of literary writing to real events of the past, to endow them with culturally specific meanings, meanings derived from group experiences encoded in terms of the values and ways of world-making peculiar to specific groups. This would mean that historical accounts cast in the form of stories with identifiable plot-structures would meet tests of confirmability and disconfirmability in communities wherein a cultural canon or *doxa* had been formed. Such canons are no doubt constructions rather than natural growths sprouting from the soil of specific regions of the earth. But the modes of emplotment used in a given culture to endow sets of events with a significance specifically historical must be granted an epistemic status equal to that of any science devoted to the pursuit of the concept and explanation by causal laws. For, would anyone want to argue that the notion of "tragedy" is *not* a distillate of reflection on real experiences? Or that the apt application of the notion of the tragic to a given kind of social-cultural events is necessarily a mistake, an error, or is fictionalizing of its referents?

There will probably never be a consensus on such issues. The opposition between "history" and "literature" is built into the cultural politics of Western academic learning. It sustains the illusion of history's affinity with philosophy and the kind of science on which philosophy depends for its conception of truth. So, to argue that history's truth is constructed is not to say that it is constructed in whatever way scientific truth is constructed. It is merely to point out that history's truthfulness is limited and in fact invites speculative supplementation in a way that the truths of science do not. It is in this respect that historians' rejection of any attempt at "grand narrative" or philosophy of history is mistaken. By its nature as truth of the past appertaining to the present in some way, history invites speculative extension into the domain of meaning. The possible meanings of an event such as "World War I ended on

November 11, 1918" are not exhausted by citation of another fact that may have followed upon it. And this is because the *meaning* of "World War I ended on November 11, 1918" can be changed with every new event occurring in its wake. The constructedness of a historical event is what makes it retrospectively changeable in the light of any new event. And this changeability of the past by the present is what assures us that history names a domain of freedom not enjoyed by natural events. Thus, whether the Enlightenment was an apex of human life in the West or the beginning of the West's self-destruction remains so far an open question. It all depends on how the Enlightenment is re-made in the present and future.

Notes

[The following abstract by White appeared at the head of the text: "Even though it is not a science in the modernist sense of the term, history remains foundational—a necessary presupposition—of modern social sciences. History serves as a paradigm referent for contrast with both abstract natural sciences and literary or artistic fictions. Indeed, history serves as the very antonym of fiction in discussions of the nature of a fact. And yet, history considered as a domain of events that are 'real' rather than 'imaginary,' can be shown on analysis to be as much 'constructed' as 'found' in the data it considers to be evidence of the reality of its referent (the past). Construction in historiography begins with the initial description of its referent as a historical phenomenon, moves on through the establishment of the 'factuality' of this phenomenon and ends in the composition of a series of historical facts as a story. Stories are not pictures of reality or even representations thereof; they are presentations in fictional modes of an unobservable past treated as reality."]

1. So, "history" is the ontological site of "events" or occurrences and "conjunctures" that, when established as "facts," promises to unlock the secret of life in the condition of "society." Hence the sense of Foucault's idea of history (in *The Order of Things*).

2. Arthur C. Danto, *Narration and Knowledge* (including the integral text of *Analytical Philosophy of History*) (New York: Columbia University Press, 1985), chap. 8. The whole question of the relation between a fact and an event in modern analytical philosophy stems, I believe, from the idea that a description of an event constitutes, or can constitute, an "explanation" of that event. Danto substitutes "fact" for "explanation" in his discussion of historical events, suggesting that a proper or correct description of an event turns it into a "fact," thereby making "factualization" itself into an "explanation." In historiography, then, we will have explained an event by describing it as a fact, that is, by simply establishing that it happened when and where and how it did. Cf. Louis O. Mink, *Historical Understanding* (Ithaca, NY: Cornell University Press, 1987), 201.

3. Nelson Goodman, *Of Mind and Other Matters* (Cambridge, MA: Harvard University Press, 1984).

4. Derrida and Foucault agreed on this point. Cf. Jacques Derrida, "Structure, Sign, and Play in the Discourse of the Human Sciences," in *The Languages of Criticism and the Sciences of Man*, ed. Richard Macksey and Eugenio Donato (Baltimore: Johns Hopkins University Press, 1970), 262–63; and Foucault, *The Order of Things: An Archaeology of the Human Sciences*, trans. Alan Sheridan (New York: Vintage, 1994), 219.

5. Williams calls his method "genealogical," but in Nietzsche's rather than Foucault's sense. See Bernard Williams, *Truth and Truthfulness: An Essay in Genealogy* (Princeton, NJ: Princeton University Press, 2002).

6. This idea, that a strictly factual and complete account of events in the past would yield one and only one story of "what happened," constitutes the basis of many historians' argument against "relativism." A "strictly factual and complete" account of any set of events in the past remains the theoretical possibility that sustains historians in their resistance to the other *bête noire* of the profession, skepticism.

7. The use of current knowledges to explain past occurrences is sometimes rejected as "anachronism." Whence the common objections to the use of psychoanalytical terms to explain deviant behavior in ancient times. The rejection is based on the idea that past events should be explained "in their own terms," those consonant with the cultural codes and practices of the time and place of their occurrences. But for them to pass for *explanations*, such terms would themselves have to be explicated in more general—and current—commonsensical terms.

8. Mink, *Historical Understanding*, 201.

9. The phrase "philosophy of history" is regarded by many philosophers as an oxymoron, because, as Croce argued, philosophy is about concepts, and history is about particular things, persons, places, and so on. See Benedetto Croce, *La storia come pensiero e come azione*, 1938, translated by Sylvia Sprigge as *History as the Story of Liberty* (London: George Allen & Unwin, 1941). While it is true that mainstream philosophy since Plato in the West has been about concepts and history about things, these notions of the two disciplines' proper objects of interests are purely conventional. For example, there can be a history of concepts (cf. Koselleck) and a philosophy of things (cf. Latour). See Reinhart Koselleck, *The Practice of Conceptual History: Timing History, Spacing Concepts* (Stanford, CA: Stanford University Press, 2002); and Bruno Latour, *We Have Never Been Modern*, trans. Catherine Porter (Cambridge, MA: Harvard University Press, 1993), and Latour, *Reassembling the Social: An Introduction to Actor-Network-Theory* (Oxford: Oxford University Press, 2007). I propose that history is a legitimate subject of philosophical thinking but that it would have to be undertaken in the manner of "history's philosophy," that is, by the study of historians' philosophical presuppositions rather than by the study of philosophers' notions about history.

10. Arnaldo Momigliano, "The History of Rhetoric and the Rhetoric of History," in *Comparative Criticism: A Yearbook*, ed. E. E. Sheffer (Cambridge: Cambridge University Press, 1981). A number of historians, for example, Anthony

Grafton, have cited this essay as the definitive destruction of my views on historiography as set forth in *Metahistory: The Historical Imagination in Nineteenth-Century Europe* (Baltimore: Johns Hopkins University Press, 1973 / 40th Anniversary Edition, 2014). Momigliano's idea that "Where there is rhetoric, there is no history, and where there is history there is no rhetoric" is itself a rhetorical figure: chiasmus. So, too, in his title, "The History of Rhetoric and the Rhetoric of History," Momigliano uses this same rhetorical figure. By his own account, then, his essay cannot be a "history" of either rhetoric or history, since its rhetorical nature is signaled in his title. Moreover, the thrust of his account is rhetorical all the way; there is no logical argument in it. His principal argument against my views is that I do not deal with the research dimension of historiography. I am sure Momigliano was aware of the irony of his essay, because he was not only a witty intellectual whose work is full of rhetorical tropes and figures, but a theoretician who believed that an "antiquarian" viewpoint was more appropriate for the study of the past than "history." See Arnaldo Momigliano, "The Rules of the Game in the Study of Ancient History," trans. Kenneth W. Yu, *History and Theory* 55, no. 1 (2016): 39–45.

11. On dramatism as a branch of criticism, see Kenneth Burke, "Introduction: The Five Key Terms of Dramatism," in *A Grammar of Motives* (Berkeley: University of California Press 1969), xvff.

12. See White, *Metahistory*.

13. These are Freud's conceptualizations of the principal types of figuration identified in classical rhetoric as the tropes of metaphor, metonymy, symbolization, and irony. Cf. Burke, *Grammar of Motives*, Appendix D: Four Master Tropes, 503–17; Donald Rice and Peter Schofer, *Rhetorical Poetics: Theory and Practice of Figural and Symbolic Reading in Modern French Literature* (Madison: University of Wisconsin Press, 1983), 19–34.

14. [Ed: See Hayden White, "Freud's Tropology of Dreaming," in *Figural Realism: Studies in the Mimesis Effect* (Baltimore: Johns Hopkins University Press, 1999), chap. 6.]

15. [Ed: See Michel Foucault, "History, Discourse and Discontinuity," trans. Anthony M. Nazzaro, *Salmagundi* 20 (1972): 225–48.]

16. [Ed: See chapter 5 of this volume for a discussion of Freud's *Zensur*.]

17. Instructive in this regard is the recent fashion of rewriting the history of European music with special attention to the place of homoeroticism in its development. The redefinition of grand opera as a gay-camp, *travesti* genre, and the import this had for the understanding of nineteenth-century cultural history, have been revolutionary. Cf. George Rousseau, "No Sex Please, We're Americans: Erotophobia, Liberation, and Cultural History," in *Cultural History after Foucault*, ed. John Neubauer (Berlin: Walter de Gruyter, 1999), 30–34.

CHAPTER 16

Primitivism and Modernism [2017]

The cultural historian Vita Fortunati has argued for an important relationship between primitivism and modernism, namely, that they often make their appearance together and that when one of them appears, the other is usually to be found nearby, waiting to spring into being. She writes: "L'ipotesi di fondo della [mia] ricerca è che il primitivismo riemerga ciclicamente nella storia dell'occidente, in quanto la riappropriazione del primitivo costituisce una proiezione retroattiva generata dalla presa di coscienza della crisi socio-culturale di un 'epoca.'" (The basic hypothesis of [my] research is that primitivism cyclically reemerges in Western history when the reappropriation of the primitive constitutes a retroactive projection generated by the awareness of the sociocultural crisis of an "era"). In this paper, I want to examine, however summarily and sketchily, the relationship between that mode of "epochal" self-consciousness called "modernism" and the particular impulse within modernism to return to the kind of origins called "primitive."

Modernism is by no means only a "modern" phenomenon. It is as old as Saint Paul's effort to "modernize" Christianite Judaism by extending its compass to the entire gentile world. Indeed, not only is "modernism" a distinctly Christian phenomenon, as old as and named as such in the fourth century AD; it is a recurrent phenomenon, canonized in Western historiography as a series of "renascences" of which "the Renaissance" of fifteenth-century Italy is only the most famous. Within every modernism that has appeared in the West, there has been an impulse to return to the origins, to the moment of foundation supposedly "pure" of the corruption and doctrinal heterodoxy seemingly rampant in every present age. It is my thesis that modernism and primitivism are two elements in a structure of temporality in which the former appears as the "fulfillment" (actualization, realization, sublation) of the latter. Indeed, primitivism, in its most pertinent sense of "firstness" or "primality," is the utopian alternative to the modernizing impulse that informs every effort at "renaissance" in the West, from the fourth century AD down to our own "postmodernist" moment of "globalization."

The relationship between primitivism and modernism is complex, multifaceted, and in many ways paradoxical. The primitivistic idealization of African and other kinds of "exotic" artifacts by the historical avant-garde in the early twentieth century, from Picasso through Surrealism, is familiar enough and the reasons for the avant-garde's fascination with what they considered to be primitivism easily enough understood. Apparently, their interest in what they took to be primitive artifacts—African masks, idols, fetishes, and so on—turned upon their search for new forms adequate to their aesthetic interests; they had little curiosity about the "contents" (the "meaning" or function in the cultures that produced them) of these forms themselves.

However, the relationship between primitivism and literary modernism, as represented by, say, T. S. Eliot and Ezra Pound, James Joyce and Virginia Woolf, Proust, Kafka, Thomas Mann, Giuseppe Ungharetti, Eugenio Montale, and Italo Svevo, is quite another matter. In contrast to the avant-garde, this wing of the modernist movement, at least in its first generation, from, say, 1910 to about 1935, had a real aversion to what the avant-garde took to be "primitiveness." At the same time, there was built into modernism a relationship to another kind of primitivism that it needed to give content to its own sense of epochal originality and to its project of re-making "the tradition," which had fallen into decay. The avant-garde "primitive" had been found in the worlds opened up to Western capitalist exploitation by nineteenth-century imperialism. Here the primitive had appeared as an enigmatic and fascinating "other." This very difference from anything Western was the source of the primitives' appeal to the avant-garde artists and writers of the 1920s.

The literary modernists, by contrast, feared this kind of primitivity as another manifestation of a terrible force that threatened civilization both from without (as native "savagery") and from within (as libidinal force dammed up by Victorian repression, rage against reason, and what Freud called "the death instinct"). Whereas the avant-garde tended— even in its efforts to destroy established artistic conventions to free art for revolutionary experimentation—to be optimistic, inventive, and future oriented (in other words, "modernistic" in the modern sense of the word), literary modernism saw in "modernization" itself a new kind of barbarism more dangerous to culture and art than the "savage" variety still thriving in the heart of "darkest Africa." Thus, if we distinguish between the process of modernization, on the one hand, and the mindset of self-styled modernists of the early decades of the twentieth century, on the other, we can see that the notion of the primitive has quite a different function in literary modernism from what it has in the avantgarde. In the first it is a threat, in the second, a resource.

It must be stressed, however, that "modernization" is a very old and recurrent movement, erupting periodically in different guises from early Christian times down to the present moment of "postmodernist" globalization. It will seem strange to those who identify modernism with the Enlightenment, but the Western impulse to modernize (which is to say, to bring things "up to date" in response to present exigencies) is Christian through and through and, *pace* Theodor Adorno, was utterly unknown to Greek and Roman culture. Modernism derives from the conviction consistently maintained by the Church since the time of Saint Paul that Christianity marks the advent of a qualitatively new temporality, a radically new age, not only *different from* but *opposed* in its essence *to* everything that had come before. From Saint Paul to Saint Augustine and beyond, the Church insists that the life and death of Christ effectively cancels out, eradicates, or simply relativizes and thereby abases the achievements of both Rome and Jerusalem. From the first "modernization" of Christianity, Saint Paul's revision of Hebrew messianism, the Hebrew and classical pagan pasts can be seen as only precursors or anticipations of what will be fully realized or, more accurately, "fulfilled," in the Christian dispensation.

In Christianity, it is held by the modernists of the Church, the whole of history up to the Incarnation is "sublated" or, as Hegel will say, *aufgehoben*, which is to say, at once canceled, gathered up, incorporated, elevated, and transcended in Christianity. This notion of a present time that fulfills all pasts, including that of the Fall of Adam, endows the (Christian) present with the right to judge the past, to decide what within it is worthy of being valorized and what should be condemned

and repudiated. Moreover, this notion of the present time as a fulfillment of what had been "promised" in the past, but only partially or in-
completely delivered previously, gives to the present a particular warrant
to envision actions taken now as themselves promises to be fulfilled, in
their turn, in some divinely determined future.

The eschatological nature of Christianity is well recognized, and its
orientation towards a promised "end of days," when the Messiah will
return and deliver the blessed from the snares and delusions of a merely
earthly existence, gives it a decidedly "futuristic" cast of mind. Less
well recognized is the extent to which Christianity—unlike its Classical
predecessors—valorizes the present as a "now" full of possibilities, not
only for redeeming that part of the past worthy of being embraced as a
legacy, but also, by that act of redemption, preparing for a future life of
blessedness "beyond history." Thus, "modernism," in its original, medieval sense is an element in a specifically Christian view of history, is
inherently presentist in its orientation, and is inherently critical of "the
past" considered as a sequence of errors or misunderstandings of human nature, the human condition, and the possibilities of deliverance
from this condition into a state of blessedness in the future. It is this
"modernism"—rather than a belief in the linear nature of time—that
makes the Christian idea of history "progressive" and inclines any secular ideology derived from it to be radical in nature and revolutionary in
practice. The dominant Western idea of history operates a complex dialectic of present-future-past of the kind cited by Marx in *The Eighteenth
Brumaire of Louis Napoleon* as inspiring the Revolutionaries of 1789 to go
back to the past (to the Roman Republic) for the images necessary to
counter those of the Old Regime and prepare the way for the passage of
the bourgeoisie to power.

The term *modern* is attested as early as the fourth century AD as (the
Latin) *modernus*, meaning "just now," "right now," at the present moment, etc. It derives from *modo*, the ablative case of *modus*, which, in the
dative, *modo*, of Classical Latin meant something like "à la mode" or "in
the manner of." As mentioned earlier, it appears to have been coined to
express a sense that the time inaugurated by the Incarnation is qualitatively different from all other times, that it offers new and unique possibilities of action and thought, and that it possesses a possibility of a
"fulfillment" of a promise given in an earlier time, a promise that, in
being fulfilled, provides a basis for a *vita nuova*. It is this notion of "modernity" and the sense of a new beginning that the term conveys that
inform the sequence of "modernisms"—called "renascences" by later

historians—that have marked the course of Western history from the Carolingian Renaissance, through that of the twelfth century, on down to the Italian Rinascimento, the German Reformation, the Enlightenment, the various "revolutions" (bourgeois and anti-bourgeois) of the nineteenth and twentieth centuries, and beyond these, to the moment of our present "modernity" in which "modernism" itself is finally (supposedly) *aufgehoben* in the advent of a global "postmodernism." Western "renascences" are not antiquarian movements but, rather, products of efforts to reform current practices conceived to be corrupt, by return to the "sources," to the "pure" practices, beliefs, and letters of the original foundation. It is by returning to the source that one leaps over the present into a future made new by grace (or art).

But there is more to the idea of the modern, modernity, and modernism than this. Or at least there is more to it that concerns us in our investigation of "the primitive" in its millennial reappearance as the lost origin and goal of each of the modernisms mentioned above. For just as Christ is conventionally portrayed as making possible a whole new order of historical being and existence by his sacrifice, he is also portrayed in Christian legend as "the New Adam," who, in restoring us, restores also the prelapsarian Adam lost in the Fall.

This is complex, but recall that we are in the domain of myth and legend, rather than of philosophy and science, and that we are concerned with the ways in which the "origin" and "end" of human history are encoded in the figurative language of the "modern" (the "now"), on the one side, and the "primitive" (the "then"), on the other. By decoding this myth-history as a story of pain and suffering (caused by Adam's original sin), we can begin to grasp the ways in which the modernisms of post-Enlightenment times differ from those still elaborated under the sign of Christian religiosity. The "primitive" sought for in the earlier, still Christian "modernisms" (of the twelfth and of the fifteenth century renascences, for example) was the time of the *archē*, the time of the foundation, of both institutions and letters, whether of the Christian Church or of such institutions as the law, philosophy, architecture, etc. Here it is "firstness"—the moment or place of inauguration, still unsullied by any experience—that is being sought to separate out what remains of this purity in the present from the dross of mere convention or practice that has grown up around, clouded, and obscured it. Such modernisms split the community in the way that any "Querelle des anciens et des modernes" is bound to do. The "moderns" claim access to a time before corruption has poisoned the springs of creativity and false traditions, a time that is not so much "ancient" as, rather, eternal—the condition of Adam before the Fall.

And this is true of that modernist moment in Western cultural history when the historical avant-garde in the arts shared with their counterparts in literary writing a conviction of their own temporal exceptionalism (their modernity) but in which the notion of the primitive was differently understood, so that what might have been viewed by the one as a positive thing was viewed by the other as a negative. For the historical avant-garde, the primitive is primarily a contemporary, though spatially remote source of new forms and themes; for the literary modernists, the primitive is both what "we moderns" have derived from and what our civilization is threatened by. The literary modernists of the early twentieth century are beset by a sense of their own untimeliness, of their own belatedness, and of their own time as depleted, passed by, stillborn, lost. The "now" retains its singularity, but it is marked not as a time of opportunity for return to the sources and renewal but as a time of depletion, desiccation, and death.

The tone was set in T. S. Eliot's signature poem of literary modernism, *The Waste Land* (1922), with its images of a culture shattered into fragments, its shards scattered among the rocks and barren sands of a cultural desert, in a world in which every spring raises only false hopes, vapid desires. It is generally thought that the poem's tone was a product of Eliot's disillusionment with the Great War (World War I). But this tone had already been set in Conrad's *Heart of Darkness* (1899), with its vision of a civilization that, on the surface, was all duty, honor, and propriety, but that, at its "heart" was as "dark" and loathsome as its "savage" victims. It turns out that Kurtz, the carrier of European values into darkest Africa, reverts to a savage nature more destructive for being armed with the instruments of capitalism, industry, and science. What was to have been a "civilizing" mission on behalf of a "superior" culture and society turns out to be a journey into the interior of civilization itself, where a vile lust and anger are revealed to preside. The "now" of the historical moment lived by these moderns is infused with a sense of loss and betrayal. Everything is too late, too little, or not at all. . . . The "grand tradition" is depleted, the origins long lost, the fathers dead, dying, or senescent.

This melancholic mood is conventionally put down to the ravages of the Great War, the decimation of the youth of a whole generation, the incapacity of the liberal institutions so enthusiastically established in the revolutions of the mid-nineteenth century to stem the tide of waste and destruction caused by imperialism and industrial capitalism. The avant-garde calls for a movement forward and, with the Futurists, commitment to materialism, technology, and nihilism. The literary modernists turn inward in an effort to map the dark side of human consciousness, taking refuge in myth and associative thinking, cultivating their sense of loss and lamenting their abandonment by the fathers. The modernists are often criticized, especially by the Left, for their "flight from history," by which is meant their failure to recognize that it was society itself that was the cause of their "discontents." But they were also criticized by the Right for their abandonment of history understood as tradition and respect for the past from which they had descended.

And it is true that the modernists regarded history à la Joyce as a "nightmare" or à la Paul Valery as a fraudulent knowledge that substituted fact for meaning and taught any lesson demanded by the State and the Church. Eliot gave voice to this hostility to history and the duplicitous knowledge it provided in "Gerontion" (1920), a poem he had originally intended as a preface to *The Waste Land*.

The poem opens with an epigraph describing death taken from Shakespeare's *Measure for Measure*:

> Thou hast nor youth nor age
> But as it were an after dinner sleep
> Dreaming of both.

And begins, "Here I am, an old man, in a dry month" and continues on to speak of life as a sequence of missed adventures, disillusionments ("Signs are taken for wonders. 'We would see a sign!'"), and disappointments ("In depraved May, dogwood and chestnut, flowering judas"). And then there is a dazzling turn into a discourse about the "cunning" (a play on Hegel's "the cunning of reason") of "history."

> After such knowledge, what forgiveness? Think now
> History has many cunning passages, contrived corridors
> And issues, deceives with whispering ambitions,
> Guides us by vanities. Think now
> She gives when our attention is distracted
> And what she gives, gives with such supple confusions

That the giving famishes the craving. Gives too late
What's not believed in, or if still believed,
In memory only, reconsidered passion. Gives too soon
Into weak hands, what's thought can be dispensed with
Till the refusal propagates a fear. Think
Neither fear nor courage saves us. Unnatural vices
Are fathered by our heroism. Virtues
Are forced upon us by our impudent crimes.
These tears are shaken from the wrath-bearing tree.

I do not have time to gloss this stanza as fully as I might to read it
as a document of modernist historical consciousness. The point is
that, like all modernisms, this one, represented here by Eliot's poem,
presupposes a moment of crisis and conflict, a moment in which
judgment and action are called for, and in which tradition must be
interrogated critically for guidance. But unlike other modernisms, all
the modernisms I listed above, this modernism has no confidence in
the capacity of history to instruct, mentor, or guide. Indeed, a knowledge of history is seen as a major ingredient of the problem. Notice
that here "history" is personified: it "deceives" us, "guides us by vanities," "gives too late," "gives too soon," and finally gives not at all
("She gives when our attention is distracted . . . And what she gives,
gives with such supple confusions / That the giving famishes the craving.") For this modernism, unlike, say, its fifteenth-century Italian
prototype, history offers no resources for renewal, no models or paradigms to revive and succor. There is no point searching for origins or
roots, for they are dead or moribund or dried up. If this modernism
possesses an imaginary "primitive," a "then" to set up as a contrary
of an unbearable "now," it is the Biblical Adam who has already been
corrupted by the Fall, not the primal Adam sprung whole from the
hand of God. Eliot notoriously defined his modernism as committed
to what he called "the mythical method."[1] It was a way of escaping
history and its "many cunning passages" and of finding refuge in the
play of pure forms and images that, however melancholic, at least
deferred despair.

It is interesting, then, to think about Eliot's modernism as being itself
a kind of "primitivism" in the sense that he rejects the search of the past
for some paradigm on the basis of which to effect a renewal of culture.
In his notion of the total bankruptcy of the great traditions of the West,
Eliot returns us to a zero-degree of cultural possibility. "Gerontion" does

feature a prophetic voice, to be sure, but this voice does not come from an origin prior in time. Gerontion is an old man, and whatever wisdom he professes is that of the senile and aged.

There is another instance of this kind of timeless primitivity in Virginia Woolf's *Mrs. Dalloway*. Very near the beginning of the novel, Peter Walsh, Clarissa's friend, leaves her house in a fit of frustration at Clarissa's flirtatiousness, sits brooding for a while in Regent's Park, and then arises to leave, when suddenly:

> A *sound interrupted him*; a frail quivering sound, a *voice* bubbling up without direction, vigour, beginning or end, running weakly and shrilly and *with an absence of all human meaning* into
> ee um fah um so
> foo swee too eem oo—
> the *voice* of no age or sex, *the voice of an ancient spring spouting from the earth*; which issued, just opposite Regent's Park Tube station from a tall quivering shape, like a funnel, like a rusty pump, like a wind-beaten tree for ever barren of leaves which lets the wind run up and down its branches *singing*
> ee um fah um so
> foo swee too eem
> and rocks and creaks and moans in the eternal breeze. (Emphasis added)

Woolf figures the crone as little more than voice, which is the conventional figure of prophecy and divination, but this is a voice that comes from primordial times, as the next passage makes clear:

> *Through all ages*—when the pavement was grass, when it was swamp, through the age of tusk and mammoth, through the age of silent sunrise, *the battered woman*—for she wore a skirt—with her right hand exposed, her left clutching at her side, stood *singing of love*—love which has lasted a million years, she sang, love which prevails. . . . As the ancient *song* bubbled up opposite Regent's Park Tube station still the earth seemed green and flowery; still, though *it issued from so rude a mouth, a mere hole in the earth, muddy too, matted with root fibres and tangled grasses, still the old bubbling burbling song, soaking through the knotted roots of infinite ages, and skeletons and treasure, streamed away in rivulets over the pavement and all along the Marylebone Road, and down towards Euston, fertilising, leaving a damp stain.* (Emphasis added)

There is nothing "modern" about this voice; modernity provides the context of its articulation, but it comes from primeval times and primal memory:

> Still remembering how once in some primeval May she had walked with her lover, this rusty pump, this battered old woman with one hand exposed for coppers the other clutching her side, would still be there in ten million years, remembering how once she had walked in May, where the sea flows now, with whom it did not matter—he was a man, oh yes, a man who had loved her. But the passage of ages had blurred the clarity of that ancient May day; the bright petalled flowers were hoar and silver frosted; and she no longer saw, when she implored him (as she did now quite clearly) "look in my eyes with thy sweet eyes intently," she no longer saw brown eyes, black whiskers or sunburnt face but only a looming shape, a shadow shape, to which, *with the bird-like freshness of the very aged* she still twittered "give me your hand and let me press it gently" (Peter Walsh couldn't help giving the poor creature a coin as he stepped into his taxi), "and if some one should see, what matter they?" she demanded; and her fist clutched at her side, and she smiled, pocketing her shilling, and all peering inquisitive eyes seemed blotted out, and the passing generations—the pavement was crowded with bustling middle-class people—vanished, like leaves, to be trodden under, to be soaked and steeped and made mould of by that eternal spring—
> ee um fah um so
> foo swee too eem oo. (emphasis added)

A similar figure of ancient prophecy or divination is used by Eliot as an epigraph of *The Waste Land*, which features a passage from the *Satyricon* of Petronius in which is reported a visit to the cave of the Sybil of Cumae. The passage is quoted in Latin with the exchange between the Sybil and her acolytes in Greek. The acolytes find the Sybil withered with age hanging in a glass bottle, and when they ask her what she desires, she replies: "I want to die." The image of the Sybil recalls Ovid's account of the young nymph who refused Apollo's love even after he had given her the gift of immortality. Enraged, the god withheld eternal youth. The Sybil lives for a thousand years, shrinking ever more until little more than a voice, a prophetic voice, remains. It is this voice, the voice of song, poetry, and oracle, that remains to the moderns of what was once original and primal. This celebration of voice does not, however, augur a return to sources for those who hear them. They are voices rusty with age and time. They are remnants, not accesses to the origin.

In her summary of her project, Vita Fortunati stresses the "ambiguous" nature of both the notion of the primitive and of the efforts on the part of various modernists to expropriate the primitive for purposes of cultural and artistic renewal. Thus, she already anticipates a part of my argument, namely, that "the primitive" can be used as a *concept* (expressing the notion of "firstness" or "primariness") but also can be concretized in any number of *figures*, from that of "Adam, the first man," to "the savage," "the barbarian," the "native," the *autokhthon*, and the innocent, all the way over to the rustic, the countryman, the farmer, the peasant, the proletarian, and the fool, to suggest its distance from the present and its deterioration with age. In other words, the primitive is a trope that can be imported into and employed in a number of discourses, of which those of the twentieth-century avant-garde and twentieth-century literary modernism are only two of a number of relatively recent ones.

Primitivism, or more precisely, the idea of the human primitive, derives, in the West at least, from the story of Adam, the first man, sprung whole, innocent, and naïve from the hand of God. Of course, the real and only "primitive" entity in the Judeo-Christian tradition is the God who created Adam and the rest of the universe. Which means that, far from being ontologically "first," Adam is already secondary, derived rather than original, product rather than producer. This may be the reason why, according to the myth, there are effectively "primitive" Adams: the Adam who existed before the Fall, before both need and desire; and the Adam who existed after the Fall, the one whose humanity is defined by his capacity to sin, the creature who is not only subject to the ravages of time but who must live in the awareness of his imminent death. The postlapsarian Adam is primitive only in the secondary sense of the term, in the sense of being uncivilized, rough, simple, and basic, rather than innocent, pure, and undefiled.

So, the idea of the primitive is inherently "antithetical," possessing both negative and positive senses, in the way that Freud thought typical of all "primary" words. "Primitive" is "primary" in the sense that "firstness" will usually indicate or suggest some kind of "authenticity," the authenticity, for example, of the "original" as against any copy. But "primitive," even in the sense of "original," does not necessarily and always carry a positive connotation. Thus, the prelapsarian Adam is primitive in the sense of being first of his kind and a paradigm of perfect humanity, whereas the postlapsarian Adam is primitive in the sense of being the first of *his* kind in his imperfection, his subjection to time and desire, and his inclination to sin. But the first Adam is not a model of what we should aspire to be, because the first Adam is not fully human. The fallen Adam is a template of what we are and what we must suffer as the price of our humanity, but neither is he a possible model of a redeemed humanity. Not even the ancient Hebrews accorded either of these Adams such an honor. Which may account for the fact that there is no image of primitivity in the Hebrew Bible. No, the new Adam, the real Adam, the truly "primal" Adam is, as the Epistle to the Galatians tells us, Christ himself. The West uses this new Adam to justify its belief in history as the Story of human salvation; so that in Christian times, a return to the origins is a return to the time of Christ, as in the *imitatio Christi*. A history descended from the old Adams goes nowhere. This is what Saint Paul teaches: the Hebrew past must be sublated—at once canceled, saved, elevated, and gone beyond—in a word, fulfilled.

So, it seems that the primitive as paradigm of the human enables the myth of a history that goes nowhere, a history that consists of an eternal return of the Same, insofar as it tells of countless human attempts to transcend the condition caused by the Fall and the inevitable failure of these attempts (in the absence of divine aid in the form of Revelation and Providentialism). In the Christian (as against the Hebrew) version of this history, both Revelation and Providence are manifested paradigmatically in the Incarnation, Death, and Resurrection of Christ, who effectively provides the means by which the condition of the Second Adam can be transcended and attainment to the condition of the First Adam be achieved. In this sense, Christ re-primitivizes or provides the conditions for the re-primitivization of humanity by inaugurating a qualitatively different time or era within which Adam's descendants can seek their redemption, not only from sin, but also from time itself. In order to indicate the qualitative difference between the history that occurred between the Fall and the Incarnation, on the one side, and that which occurs and can occur ever afterward (until the Second Coming), Christian theologians by the end of the fourth century AD coin a new term with which to designate a new idea—the idea of "modern." It is the idea of the "modern" that will come to serve as the antitype of all of those other terms that, like "primitive," seek to grasp the nature of humanity's "beginning." For the modern is to the primitive as the end or terminus is to the beginning. It would not be too far wrong to say that modernism—the modernism of the literary modernists—is the "fulfillment" of primitivism, the cultural moment in which primitivity is canceled, gathered up, elevated, and transcended in a vision of civilization that has not only come to nothing, but lacks any resources to rebuild itself.

Notes

[Ed: This unpublished manuscript, dated February 7, 2017, was apparently given as a lecture for an event in Italy organized by Vita Fortunati, a longtime friend of White's.]

1. [Ed: See chapter 11 of this volume for a discussion of Eliot's "mythical method."]

CHAPTER 17

Is My Life a Story? [2017]

Mr. Baird suggested my topic for this talk: "Is My Life a Story?"[1] He and I have been thinking together about history for many years and trying to determine the function of storytelling in historiography (history writing) for just as long. "Is history a story?" might seem like a rather banal question, since history and story have been linked as content and form since ancient times.

But the content-form relationship between history and story has become muddied lately as the very concept of story has become complicated and historians have become concerned to purge their accounts of the past of any elements of fiction. Story and fiction go together like the legendary "horse and carriage," and the question arising from this conjunction is: Does the casting of a report on real events in the form of a story effectively "fictionalize" those events? If the difference between fact and fiction turns on the difference between real events and imaginary events, then would not the casting of real events in the form of a story "imaginate" them, endow them with the aspect of imaginary events? And if real events are so endowed, what becomes of their claim to truthfulness? Does not the very idea of a "true story" become compromised?

Or, *per contra*, does the idea of a "true" story tell us something about a kind of truthfulness to be found in certain kinds of fiction, like the novel, drama, epic poetry, dance, grand opera, and other kinds of narrative expression such as biography and autobiography? I ask: in casting a life in the form of a story, am I not fictionalizing it? And does such fictionalization of the real deprive it of truth or, in the hands of an artist, enhance its truthfulness?

With every major change of phase in one's life course, one is increasingly beset by the need to connect the events in one's life in such a way as to be able to identify this self, ego, or person who remains constant throughout all of these changes. One way of doing this is to view one's life as a story or (what stories are increasingly called these days in the media) a *narrative*. This is a difficult, not to say dangerous, enterprise for a number of reasons. First, unlike the effort to write someone else's life story, one has a subjective and purely personal interest in one's own life that may make objectivity or simple truth-telling particularly difficult. Second, insofar as memory is concerned, this faculty is peculiarly prone to error and failure. Third, the documentation required to give one's autobiography a sense of historical validity is often lacking; and, moreover, the kinds of documentation available in public records offices seldom lend access to the personal and private events for which one is most often anxious to account. Fourth, storytelling is very difficult, even when it is a matter of public institutions, where documentation is ample, much less for an individual whose record-keeping habits may be quite casual, not to say nonexistent. Finally, when it comes to trying to produce a plausible story of one's life course, there is the matter of what *kind* of truth you want to come up with: literal truth and nothing but the truth (what we might call "truth about") or viable truth (what we might call "truth to," as in "true to life" or "true enough").[2] All of this is difficult. The danger lies in having to face the truth about oneself and especially the truth that every story is a fiction, so that the notion of a true story seems to be a contradiction in terms.

The idea of a *true* story contains problems both ontological and epistemological. As Hegel reminds us, any merely truthful account of the life course of anything presents the aspect of a chaos, not so much for want of documents to verify accounts as, rather, due to the fact that the number of merely truthful statements about any life course is infinite, and they do not spontaneously take on the form of a well-made story. Any given set of data requires the help of an author or some authority telling us what is important and what is not in any body of fact and giving us rules for putting things together to provide meaning as well as information. *Stories are a way of distilling meaning out of fact.*

The history of literature provides us with a number of warnings against trying to live one's life as a story of a particular sort: *Don Quixote*, *Madame Bovary*, and *Lord Jim* being only the most notable paradigms of that kind. We are inclined to idealize our own life story or at least to justify the parts we played in it. Which is why, I suppose, that the genre of the *confession* is the archetype of every autobiography. It is alright to romanticize one's account of someone else's life, but as Don Quixote, Emma Bovary, and Lord Jim teach us, nothing good can come of romanticizing one's own life. Fictionalization is a way of escaping from the harsher aspects of real life. If you want to know the truth about yourself, you have to tell the truth about yourself. And the question I want to raise with you here this evening is whether anyone whosoever can ever tell the truth about anything whatsoever using the form of a story.

And it is here that we have to face a difficult problem, namely, the difference between fact and fiction or, more generally, that between history and literature or literary writing.

Discussions of these differences usually ignore the problem of story's relationship to historical reality by simply distinguishing between two kinds of stories, stories whose referents are imaginary and those whose referents existed in real life. Or stories made up of imaginary events and stories made up of real events. In other words, in autobiography we have to begin by separating out events that really happened as against those that we may have only imagined to have happened. But this presupposes access to past events of the kind that we have to present events, a capacity to *reexamine* or *reinspect* them to determine which were real and which were only imagined. But we do not have such direct access. It is not as if we can go and see whether we acted in good faith or in bad faith in a given situation.

Moreover, when it comes to history or to biography and autobiography, we have to conjure with the fact that real events, whether of the present or the past, do not present themselves in the form of or as *stories*. Indeed, historical processes, of which the life process of any given individual is an example, have to be worked up—changed from the linear mode in which the events that comprise them occurred—and presented in a different order, if they are to assume the form of stories (and be endowed with story-meaning, such as "the best-laid schemes of mice and men" or "they lived happily ever after"). In a word, the author who would tell a *true* story about some person, thing, or event that actually existed will find herself caught like an astronomer gazing at the night sky and having to make of that plethora of stars, planets, meteors, and the like, something like a mapped territory or a set of figures (Orion, Cassiopeia, Seven Sisters, etc.) that can serve as entities connectible by virtue of their similarity to mythical figures, whose meaning is that they can be constellated: grasped as forming a cluster or group, changes in which can be emplotted or reemplotted over the course of time. The teller of true stories, our historian or autobiographer, must—like our imaginary astronomer or astrologer—presume that the objects and events that make up the life course of his subject actually existed and actually did or did not do the things he or she is purported to have done.

But even when one has established the factuality of those events and arranged them on a chronological line of their original occurrence, our autobiographer still does not have a story. And he does not have a story because the story of which the events of a life are a manifestation is not there in the events in the way that their time, place, and provenance may be. When the detective or the prosecuting attorney of our typical film noir says, "The facts as we know them do not add up, do not aggregate and figure forth the kind of meaning that stories are supposed to do," he seems to be waiting for some vagrant piece of evidence or some fact that has so far eluded investigators. What he is waiting for, however, is not another fact or even a piece of evidence such as a *corpus delicti*; what he is waiting for is someone—usually a senior investigator, who has "been around" and brings to the investigation a lot of "experience"—who is expert at emplotting the facts so that they can function as elements of a story. This means that the facts must be hierarchized in terms of their relative importance to the structure of a plot, sequentiated so that their significance as "hinge" events (events that hand us over, as it were, to other events on the basis of resemblance, contiguity, or symbolism) can be discerned, and synecdochized ("taken up," *aufgehoben*, grasped together, symbolized). In storytelling, the facts have to be laid out on a timeline, redescribed so as to function as story elements, and then gradually reaggregated so as to demonstrate that that subject who has undergone his or her *agon* (test, or passion) and who, as a result, has undergone manifest changes of attributes and even character, is the same subject as the persona who aroused our interest at the beginning of our inquiry. The story must have plot coherence, which it is to say that its parts must conform to those schemata of meaning that constitute the substance of archetypal genres of thought and imagination in a given cultural endowment.

Novelists, short-story writers, narrative poets, cinematographers, screenwriters, directors of MTV, rappers and hip hop artists (like KRS-One), and preachers: all of these know this, and the most creative ones (standup comics and rappers) build into their narratives signs of the difficulties of narrativization, as in certain kinds of modernist stories: Sartre's *Les mots*, *The Education of Henry Adams*, a play like Harold Pinter's *No Man's Land*—or a novel like Toni Morrison's *Beloved*.[3]

But storytelling in itself is not so easy, especially when it is a matter of forging one's own story, the story of one's own life course and the value it can claim for itself as we reach what Paul Harvey used to call "the rest [the end] of the story." Indeed, far from being natural or easy, storytelling is, as anyone who is addicted to standup comedy knows, very difficult and for most of us, who may have tried to write a novel or even keep a diary, actually impossible. Where do you begin? Where do you end? How do you choose the most significant events of your life, especially those that mark significant turning points in the development of the real "me"? And what, or rather where, is the "real" me? What is that substance that remains the same while undergoing not only the aging process but those events that have determined the attributes of an essential self? What kind of evidence can I credit for the construction of a chronology of turning points in my life that have made me what I know myself to be today—in spite of all the stories told about me by others—parents, spouses, lovers, siblings, friends, teachers, enemies, my health care provider, my parole officer, the US Navy, my examiners in all walks of life and jobs that I have been involved with, etc., etc.? When I ask students to provide me with an account of the first five years of their lives, they find that they cannot do it. Sartre, in his autobiography, *Les mots* (*The Words*), limited his life story to the period between ages four and eleven. In his *The Education of Henry Adams*, Adams left out twenty years of his life without comment. The assembly of the evidence for and the selection of events and actions by which to make of a life a story are more difficult than the task of writing a history of a whole epoch in the past. In the writing of a history, there are rules for the treatment of evidence, and the discovery that there is no evidence for certain events can be as valuable as the discovery of exactly the evidence you need to make your account of the historical past plausible, if not established as fact. There are even rules for determining what is and what is not "fact" in or about the historical past. But none of these rules apply unambiguously when it is a matter of finding out the story of one's own life.

Many of you here this evening may be too young to have seen the scene in the old movies about journalism and journalists, such as *His Girl*

Friday or *The Front Page*, in which at one point in the drama the City Editor shouts to the veteran (or apprentice) reporter: "Go out and get that story." The daily press could hardly function without the idea or myth that reality, or at least that part of reality of interest to readers of daily newspapers, is made up of a congeries of lived stories (or life stories) just waiting to be discovered and "told" by some diligent reporter. It is a myth of modern American culture that "everybody has a story" and of modern "reality television" that everybody's story is worth the telling and can even be turned to profit (*Real Housewives of Atlanta* [$750,000 per episode] or *Here Comes Honey Boo Boo* [$50,000 per episode] or *Keeping Up with the Kardashians* [$500,000 per episode]), if properly presented in the right media.

Of course, there are sets of events in both public and personal life that appear to have the kind of coherence that certain kinds of stories (fables, satires, pastorals) appear to have. But the idea that every story is a fiction can be confirmed by a cursory examination of the narratives that natural history museums and zoos used to post on exhibitions in the mode of "Mr. and Mrs. Snake and their kids enjoy life in the Florida Everglades." The attribution to animals of the kinds of life stories presumed to be lived by human beings is called anthropomorphism and is commonly recognized as a kind of mythification.

But what about the attribution to human beings or human institutions of life courses that bear the form of stories? Is this not also a kind of anthropomorphism too?

It is less a kind of anthropomorphism than a kind of theo-logism or aristo-logism, since for most of humankind's history it was thought that only gods or aristocrats—presumed to have descended from the gods—were considered worthy of having stories told about them. The only character subjected to ridicule in the *Iliad* is Thersites, who speaks for the commoners and asks the devastating question of the heroes: what is the point of this endless war against Troy? (Thersites has no patronym and is therefore presumed to not be noble himself.) Modern literary realism is supposed to be distinguished by the treatment of ordinary folks or commoners as if their lives were worthy of having stories told about them. And Catherine Gallagher has made her reputation in showing how—in her book *Nobody's Story*—the modern novel in the West depends upon the elevation of women to the status of "heroines" worthy of having their stories told.[4]

The important point is that the story is the *substance of the form* of expression of narrative discourse, as against the substance of the content of such discourse, which is: first, the doings of the gods; second, the acts of heroes or aristocrats; and finally, the "condition" of commoners or the lowest classes of society—Zola, Theodore Dreiser, etc., but also "history from below." To which should be added the idea that this substance of the form of expression belongs to the domain of the "imaginary" and is a way of making "the real" conform to the requirements of the "symbolic" system of a society, rather than a form of a way of life existing in reality. Here the story is to be understood in the modern sense of "myth," or an imaginary form that can be imposed upon the life of an individual, a society, or its institutions, real or fictional, as the case may be, to endow it with the kind of meaning(s) found in the archetypal *logoi* or plot-types of a given cultural endowment. It is one way of giving form to what otherwise can be grasped only as a chaos of happenings without meaning ("signifying nothing") or an algorithm that subsumes the singular event, person, thing to the (animal) type to which it belongs.

Now, modern science denies to storytelling any significant cognitive content, among other reasons because stories presuppose *qualitative* differences among the drives motivating their protagonists to action. Stories exist in consciousness or language, but not in things. If applied to real things as instruments of representation, stories have to be invented; they are not found. Their effectiveness—as putative truths *about* real things, or as instruments of self-identification (of individuals or collectivities)—depends upon the skill of the storyteller in adapting the culturally provided plot-type to the raw (chaotic) materials of a given subject's life course. So, "is my life a story?" Well, it may be, if you (or someone else, your biographer) is a good storyteller. But "is my life a *true* story?" Well, as President Bill Clinton might have said about his relationship with Monica Lewinsky, it all depends on what you mean by "true." True *to* the facts or true *as* fact. Is the story a reflection, as in a mirror image, of what actually happened in your life course from birth to death, or is it a filter helping one to select out those facts in a life course that can function as elements (agent, patient, scene, motif, theme, etc.) of a recognizable story-type, such as epic, romance, tragedy, comedy, farce, etc.? This filtering process I have called "emplotment," which I take to be the process of *combination* of story elements in a way that relates an ending of a process to its beginning—to reveal continuity-in-change or the reverse, according to rules of *peripeteia* or substitution by successive redescription of the subject of the story, as it changes or is changed by the events described as story elements in the original inspection of the subject's life course.[5]

The emplotment of a set of real events (as in history) is more difficult than it is for a set of imaginary events (as in a fable or other fiction) because, obviously, the fiction writer can invent events that might be needed to give to her protagonist the kinds of situations required for a proper execution of a given genre. The history writer or life writer will find herself in the situation of the astronomer who turns a telescope on an area of night sky filled with stars of different intensities and distances from one another—out of which she may wish to discern recognizable constellations and changes within them over time. The astronomer can hypothesize the existence of stars imperceptible to the eye on the basis of relations discerned among those stars that she can see (or record electronically). But if the aim is to perceive and record changes in any given constellation, the constellation in question has to have been constituted by the combination in a structure of stars that do not inhabit the same plane. The constellation is of course a structure caught, as it were, at a given time and changes in which are a result of different observers' symbolizations rather than by actual changes in time. But the constellation is a good, or at least a serviceable, analogue of the chaotic sets of events inhabiting the memory of an individual or constituting the archive of the historian's field of perception. In this respect, the constellations of modern astronomy (eighty-eight currently recognized) are related to the constellations of the ancients (forty-eight for Ptolemy) as a modern map is related to an ancient one: whereas the modern map deals primarily with quantitative features of a territory, the ancient one is filled with symbolical figures, with proper names and symbolic associations connected with the treasury of myths of the given culture. The individual life, or a historical period, changes more rapidly than a constellation, but the number of events waiting for emplotment is just as large and just as chaotic to perception.

What is a story? Or rather, when it is a matter of construing or imagining my own life *as* a story, what should I be looking for in the evidence relevant to my life and my memories and those of friends, etc., that might serve as elements of a story, *my* story? I distinguish between *a* story and *my* story because when it comes to my story, just any old story will not do. Joe Biden was forced to withdraw from his 1988 presidential primary campaign because he contrived his own life story by plagiarizing large parts of the life story of Neil Kinnock, the Labour Party opponent of Margaret Thatcher, in the 1987 general elections in the UK. Biden did not realize, or did not know, that there is a difference between a story and the plot of a story. The plot is a general algorithm of a particular kind or genre of sequences of events, such as the plot of any *Bildungsroman* (novel of education, coming-of-age story) into which one can insert any number of concrete events to endow them with a culturally recognizable meaning. Every real-life story that is authentic is unique, if for no other reason than because of the name and identity of the protagonist, and a story can be copyrighted, owned as a property or commodity. Biden had copied the story, when he should have been content to have copied the plot, the story of ascent from rags to riches by virtue of talent rather than favor or patronage, which is a plot-type that can legitimately be told of oneself by anyone.

A story develops or is elaborated on two axes, conventionally called a vertical axis, in which agents, agencies, and scenes are successively *re-*described to endow them with motific meaning (such as "beginning" or "battle" or "power"), and a horizontal (or linear) axis, in which the motifs aggregate into themes that foreshadow and backshadow events, so as to progressively reveal their shared substances as elements of the same story at different times and places in the diegesis. Certain plots or plot-structures are called "archetypal" because they are thought to derive from foundational myths revered as revealing of "the meaning of life" (or a life world): tragedy, comedy, romance, satire, pastoral, farce, novel, and so on, are examples. Stories tell of beginnings and endings, entrances and exits, births and deaths, unifications and dissolutions of things, etc. Plot-structures help us identify such subjects as elements of the story or stories we wish to tell ourselves about ourselves or have recognized by others as a true story about oneself.

Now, as mentioned above, when it comes to fiction, the writer is free to invent the characteristics of the agents and agencies, scenes, and events of the story she wishes to tell, to build up or to maintain the interest of the reader or auditor. It is another matter when it comes to the effort to tell a true story about a real life, as Joe Biden wished to do when he stole Neil Kinnock's story and told it as his own. Here the danger is that, in telling Kinnock's story as if it had been his own, Joe Biden told an untrue, false, or lying story.

Or was it only a fiction?

It is well known that there is a school of psychotherapy that deals with neurosis by what might be called psycho-narrativization, the aim of which is to get the patient (analysand) to "contrive" a life story with which the patient can live and substitute it for the disabling life story that was imposed on the patient by others and that forecloses the patient's ability to cope with the real world in which she must operate. In other words, in the ordinary process of socialization in the family, school, work environments, the patient may have been provided with (and internalized) a life story in which some real or imagined offense to self-esteem has become experienced as an ineluctable element that can neither be ingested fully nor effectively discarded as a structuring principle of one's "true life." Psycho-narrativization does not try to deny or disavow the crippling incident, bury and cover it over, but rather displace or move it to a place in the life account where it can be provided with a new and less crippling "affect." A place where it is no longer a structuring principle but is merely a secondary or relatively minor element in the life story.[6]

The modern novel and its modernist counterpart have been interested in history for the same reasons that speculative philosophy of history has been interested in it: for practical reasons. I argued in *Metahistory* that every work of historiography presupposes a whole philosophy of history. And so, too, for every modern or modernist autobiography. If autobiography it is to make sense, if it is to figure forth a "substance of its content," then it must presuppose a philosophy of life, an ideal view of life or a view of an ideal life. Which means it must be informed by a kind of Quixotic illusion: a wager on the possibility that commitment to an ideal life is in the end both more realistic and more authentic than any simple or complex choice to affirm "things as they are."

Notes

1. [Ed: This lecture was given in March 2017 in Springfield, Missouri, at the invitation of Andrew Baird.]

2. [Ed: White indicates that there should be a note here: "Note: distinction between correspondence and coherence models of truth."]

3. [Ed: See Hayden White, *The Practical Past* (Evanston, IL: Northwestern University Press, 2013), 21–24, for a discussion of Toni Morrison's *Beloved*. White had pasted in these paragraphs to this lecture. I removed them, since the passages were taken verbatim from his book.]

4. [Ed: Catherine Gallagher, *Nobody's Story: The Vanishing Acts of Women Writers in the Marketplace, 1670–1920* (Berkeley: University of California Press, 1994).]

5. In navigation, "to plot" a course on a map presupposes the locales or sites over which one must pass en route to one's destination; these sites are presumed to preexist the plotting of the course through them. When it comes to contriving the main line of the story of a life, I speak of "emplotment" to indicate that the events of a life are not identifiable, locatable, and as endowed with significance (as points "along the way") in the way that elements of a

geographical area or zone might be. The points along the way of a life course not only have to be located; they have to be presented as manifesting the elements of a story as well. They have to be symbolized: assigned a substance.

6. [Ed: In addition to the paragraphs on Toni Morrison's *Beloved* mentioned above, several paragraphs on Otto Dov Kulka's *Landscapes of the Metropolis of Death: Reflections on Memory and Imagination*, have also been removed. These can be found in chapter 8 of this volume.]

INDEX

abject, the (abjection), 57, 99
Abstract Expressionism, 25
Adam (Biblical figure), 45, 233–38, 241–42
Adams, Henry: *The Education of Henry Adams*, 248
Adler, H. G., 190n22
Adorno, Theodor, ix, xii–xiii, 104, 124, 126, 138n4, 164, 198, 233
aestheticization, xxxiv, 79–80, 111–12, 119, 122, 143, 145–46, 164, 169; self-aestheticization, 225
aesthetics, xxxi, xxxiii, 13, 26, 121, 175, 198, 203, 232; aesthetic nihilism, 4–5; autonomy of, 152; Eliot's conception of, 167n18; and the Enlightenment; 134–35, 203; Greenberg's conception of, 153; Hamann's conception of, 131; and Holocaust representation, 108, 111–12, 175; Kermode's conception of, 44–45, 86n5; and modernism, 152–53, 165n10; of narrative form, xxxiv, 119; versus art, 48–50, 148; versus literature, 119–21; Winckelmann's conception of, 135–36
agon, 54, 129, 170, 247
alienation, 9, 161
allegory, 171, 175
Althusser, Louis, 104, 152; and concept of interpellation, 62–64, 68
American Revolution (of 1776), 102
Améry, Jean, 146
anagnorisis (recognition), 170, 211
analytic philosophy, 195–97
Ancien Régime (Old Regime), 234
Anderson, Laurie, 50
Anderson, Perry, xxxviii n29
Ankersmit, F. R., 54, 69n4
Annales school, xxvi, 17, 79, 201
anthropology, ix, xxxiii, 143
anthropomorphism, 249

apocalypse (myths of), 4, 67, 70, 73, 76, 80
archetypes (*mythoi*), 7, 16, 107n15, 246
Arendt, Hannah, 53, 80
argument, mode of, 15, 192, 198
aristocracy, 134, 249–50
Aristotle, 17, 54, 63, 79, 92, 212n2; distinction between history and poetry, 142, 149, 150n5, 195
Aron, Raymond, 28
artifact, xxiv, 208; cultural, 232; historical, 136, 181
Attenborough, Richard: *Ghandi*, 26
Auden, W. H., 198
Auerbach, Erich, xxiii, xxxix n45, 19, 73; "*Figura*," xxxv; *Mimesis*, 21, 29, 86n6
Augustine, Saint, 33, 69n7, 125, 233
Auschwitz (concentration camp), xii, 80, 110–18, 146. *See also* Holocaust, the
autonomy, 124, 130; of the aesthetic, 152
avant-garde, the, 23, 25, 40, 48–50, 153, 165n4, 202, 204, 232–37, 241

baby boom (United States, 1946–1964), 100
Bachelard, Gaston, 52, 69n2
bad faith (*la mauvaise foi*), xxxiii, xxxv, xxxvi, 246
Bakhtin, Mikhail, 76, 149, 150n6
Bal, Mieke, xxxv, 48, 51n8, 86n4, 165n7
Ball, Karyn, xxxviii n31, 122n1
Balzac, Honoré de, xxx, xxxvii n9, 29, 145, 156, 162, 210
Banville, John: *The Untouchable*, 26
Barthes, Roland, xxiii, xxxvii n14, 149; "The Discourse of History," 23, 24n4, 79, 87n17
Bataille, Georges, xxiii
Bateson, Gregory, 92
Baudelaire, Charles, 21, 49, 153, 164n4, 165n6

Printed in the USA
CPSIA information can be obtained
at www.ICGtesting.com
LVHW041552151123
763622LV00026B/7